Deep Water Passage

Deep Water Passage

A SPIRITUAL JOURNEY AT MIDLIFE

Ann Linnea

Little, Brown and Company

BOSTON • NEW YORK • TORONTO • LONDON

First Edition

Library of Congress Cataloging-in-Publication Data

Linnea, Ann.
    Deep water passage : a spiritual journey at midlife / Ann Linnea. — 1st ed.
        p.   cm.
    ISBN 0-316-52683-5
    1. Women outdoor life — Literary collection.   2. Spiritual life.   3. Sea kayaking —
Superior, Lake.   4. Explorers — Women.   5. Linnea, Ann.   I. Title.
GV788.5   94-48635

10   9   8   7   6   5   4   3   2   1

HAD

*Published simultaneously in Canada
by Little, Brown & Company (Canada) Limited*

Printed in the United States of America

To Hart

Contents

Prologue

March 31, 1993

THE FLAG ABOVE ME is flying straight out. Starched. How can a cloth flag do that? Fly with no ripples.

The wind tears at the hood of my rain parka. Tries to rip open my shell of protection. Tries to congeal everything in its path. I cannot gaze into the gale without shielding my eyes. Tiny bullets, pellets of ice, bombard me. Moments earlier they were spray from raging surf, now they are piercing shrapnel.

I turn my head to protect my face from the wind, from the vision of the big lake. I gaze down the expanse of sand beach littered with ice from the long winter. The lake's twelve-foot surf pulverizes the ice; it is eager to destroy the last vestiges of frozen bondage.

A gust of wind blows me backward several feet. I remember the summer past. Gusts of wind that tried to knock the paddle from my hands, tried to blow my kayak over. The many times Lake Superior engaged this kind of fury and I was not standing safely on shore.

I drop to both knees, bow my head into my body for protection. In the cocoon of my thoughts I can hear the tiny pellets hitting my jacket, can hear the deep, steady pounding of the surf. Pik, pik, pik, pik, pik, Boom. Pik, pik, pik, pik, pik, Boom.

This is the symphony of She-Who-Is-The-Biggest. The symphony of She-Who-Changed-My-Life. I bow before her. Humble. Respectful. Grateful to be alive.

Lake Superior

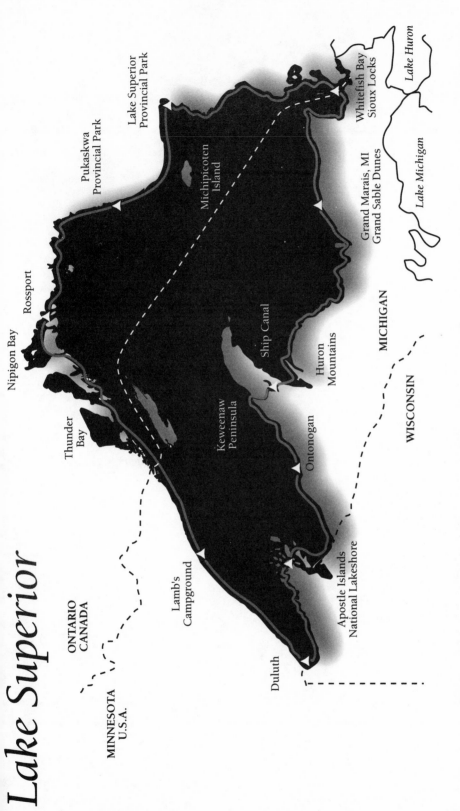

- Largest lake in the world by surface area • Average annual water temperature: 40° Fahrenheit • Highest recorded waves: over 40 feet
- Greatest depth: 1,333 feet • Distance around shoreline: 1,826 miles / same as driving distance from Duluth to Miami

Map labels

MINNESOTA
U.S.A.

ONTARIO
CANADA

Rossport

Nipigon Bay

Thunder
Bay

Lamb's
Campground

Duluth

Apostle Islands
National Lakeshore

WISCONSIN

Ontonogan

Keweenaw
Peninsula

Ship Canal

Huron
Mountains

MICHIGAN

Michipicoten
Island

Pukaskwa
Provincial Park

Lake Superior
Provincial Park

Grand Marais, MI
Grand Sable Dunes

Whitefish Bay
Sioux Locks

Lake Huron

Lake Michigan

Deep Water Passage

1

First Day

When we deliberately leave the safety of the shore of our lives,
we surrender to a mystery beyond our intent.

O N JUNE 14, 1992, the day of my forty-third birthday, one day
before I was to leave on my kayaking trip around Lake Superior, I
rose with the dawn, slipped on sweatpants, sweater, and windbreaker, and walked to a nearby park in my home city of Duluth.

I passed no other walkers, and the neighborhood dogs, accustomed to my early exercise routines, didn't bother to bark. Down the
long block of faculty homes on the hill behind the university
campus where my husband taught, I made my way with quiet confidence through familiar scenes of my comfortable life. Lilacs in the
neighborhood, late blooming in this latitude, were beginning to
fade, and here and there I noticed peonies emerging in people's
yards. Friends and family would phone in birthday wishes from
warmer climes, but I was used to bundling up, and enjoyed the
coolness and changeability of lake-edge weather.

Near the end of the street I entered the park, and a whole parade
of chest-high blue and pink lupines saluted me. I love the season of
my birthday in the north. It is a time of beauty and fullness for the
plants, which must endure so much to claim a space in this harsh
land. In the ravines and pathways of Chester Park, it took me twenty
minutes to follow the narrow, rocky trail over the creek, up one of
the highest hills in Duluth, past the ski jumps, to my special place.

My habitual sitting, or standing, spot is a small outcrop of exposed volcanic rock five feet by six feet — large enough to make myself a sense of place — a rock to stand on. Local guides claim it is some of the oldest exposed bedrock anywhere on the planet, about one billion years old. The claim makes it sound famous. It looks ordinary — a gray-black, pockmarked slab of Canadian shield. It feels extraordinary — steady, calming, reassuring. I call it my listening place.

From this spot I can survey the southwest finger-pointing tip of Lake Superior, much of the city, and the complexities of my personal life. I make the trek to my special place every week of the year. For at least five months that means trudging through snow. But that June day, the rich green knee-high grasses surrounding me waved and pulsated in the wind, and my eyes were drawn upward and outward by the spectacle of blue sea dotted with whitecaps stretching into the horizon before me.

Lake Superior is well named. No other body of water on the continent even approaches the size of this inland sea. The lake is about the same size as the entire state of Maine. To paddle around it is the equivalent of hiking three-quarters of California's Pacific Crest Trail from the California/Oregon border to just north of Los Angeles. Because it is more than a thousand feet deep in some of its trenches, Superior contains more water than the other four Great Lakes combined. Lake Baikal in Russia contains more freshwater by volume, because it's deeper, but in terms of sheer size Lake Superior is the biggest lake on the planet.

The choosing of names is an important, symbolic act. We cannot know what name the earliest human residents chose for the lake. They were a nomadic group, hunting the mastodon on the edge of the receding glacier. Evidence left by the Old Copper Culture of seven thousand years ago on the south shore, even with its more permanent civilization, includes no remnant of written language or way to know the words they spoke for this lake. It was not until the first white explorers arrived in the 1600s and reported that the Ojibway people called the lake Gitchee Gumee, "Great Lake," that a name was first recorded. One of these explorers, Étienne Brûlé,

added his own name: "Northern Sweetwater Sea." And shortly there-
after the French began referring to it on fur-trading maps as Lac
Supérieur.

At 7:30 A.M. the next day I planned to set out in my seventeen-
foot sea kayak and paddle around this lake. My paddling partner
and close friend, Paul, and I had worked hard these past several
weeks, packing and repacking food, gear, and clothing. We had
been preparing for five years — paddling the lake in all its conditions and seasons — to gain the skills we needed. For both of us this
represented a lifelong dream to do one extended, challenging wilderness trip.

I have always been a seeker of wild places. As a lanky, blond ten-
year-old, I rode my blue, single-speed Raleigh to the edge of Austin,
Minnesota, to Turtle Creek to catch crayfish and wade in the shallows and climb trees along the banks. As a junior in high school, I
was the camp counselor leading nine- and ten-year-olds on canoe
trips in northern Minnesota. As a U.S. Forest Service naturalist, I
wrote hiking and skiing guides to the northern Utah mountains.
With Paul and two other colleagues, I wrote a book about environmental education and taught Sense of Wonder workshops to
teachers, parents, and children. All my life, I have sought wild places
for adventure, for my livelihood, and for good counsel.

When my son and daughter were tiny and newly adopted from
Korea, and I was adjusting to my much-longed-for motherhood, I
drove with them into the wilderness to create the foundations of our
family life. In the spring of 1985, Brian, Sally, and I wandered
through the desert southwest for three months, letting the gentle
warmth develop and seal the bonds between us. A few years later,
when they became school age, we packed up again and took books
and papers to sandy arroyos and shady, moist canyons in search of
answers beyond school walls. My deepest adult friendships have
always bubbled up from the spring of shared enthusiasm over
mountains climbed, sunsets watched, or lakes paddled. The lessons
of the wilderness have not always been easy, but they have been
profound.

I remember the first time Paul and I sat in a kayak. It was 1987. A camp in Wisconsin. A warm August day. The instructor cautioned us about the boat's tippiness and delicate balance, but my slim, canoe-wise body slid easily into the narrow hold. The small, river kayak, its hull shaped like a horizontal cigar, was like pulling on my favorite pair of pants. Comfortable. Snug. Close to the water. My hands moved back and forth along the shaft of the double-bladed paddle. Smooth, long, and lean, the paddle curved to fit the cup between my curled fingers and palm. I found my arms and shoulders rotating automatically to the dance rhythm of paddling. Forward with the right blade. Pull the paddle while pushing on the right foot peg for leverage. Forward with the left blade. Pull the paddle while pushing on the left foot peg for leverage. I was delighted by how quickly the boat slid across the smooth skin of water.

For me, who had grown up in Minnesota and swum and boated since I was a toddler, this was the watercraft of my dreams. I had always paddled canoes, but a kayak is different from a canoe. You get into a canoe. You wear a kayak. In a kayak you are only a step above swimming. You become a creature with license to explore beyond the realms of ordinary, earthbound existence. A creature capable of moving in inches of water or handling immense seas.

On this gusty June morning, I sat on the hilltop for half an hour, feeling the steady, strong wind and worrying about our proposed morning takeoff. Then I knew it was time to return home and cook Sunday breakfast for my family. I left a small pebble I had collected from the shore of the lake — an offering, a request that I be watched over on my journey by the steady presence that I always seemed to find on this rock. This morning I was deeply aware that my leave-taking from Duluth meant letting go of more than just special people. I was a woman raised within solid, Protestant, midwestern values. They had served me and limited me. I knew, vaguely, that I was approaching the end of some kind of life cycle, and I was hoping the trip would teach me what that was and where I might be going.

My friend Christina and I had recently started combining teaching skills to create circles of self-empowerment for women. We were excited by what was beginning to happen in these settings, and hesitant about our abilities to "lead" because we felt ourselves in as much upheaval as the women who came into the circles we were teaching.

A week earlier, on the drive back from Wisconsin to drop her off in Minneapolis, Christina had said to me, "Ann, you must be willing to let this voyage change everything — to prepare yourself for the second half of your life."

"I know," I'd answered, "but I don't know what that means. Do you?"

"No. I support you and I'm afraid for you and I'm confident in you. You are just going to have to trust the journey, day by day by day."

I sighed deeply, remembering these words, and turned my face toward home, making my way downhill back into the neighborhood and the comfortable embraces and exchanges of the life I knew. Birth. Day.

Nine-year-old Sally admonished me the minute I walked in to the house. "Mom, why did you get up? Brian and me are serving you breakfast in bed for your birthday."

"Well, how would it be if I just sat right down on the porch and you brought me breakfast in the sunshine?"

She wrinkled up her little Korean nose, put her hands on her tiny waist, and said, "Oh, all right."

Fifteen minutes later twelve-year-old Brian carried the scrambled eggs, toast, and coffee out on a tray. Sally carefully laid out the silverware, napkins, and plate. Both of them joined me on the porch steps. Their father, Dave, having supervised the entire affair, remained inside reading the paper.

"Where were you, Mom?" asked Brian.

"Saying good-bye to my listening place."

"Well, you're not going forever," retorted Sally.

"No, but it is for a long time. I left a present for listening place just like I've left presents for you. I'm thinking a lot this morning about what I'll miss being gone."

The next morning I rose at 5 A.M. and went into my upstairs office. Fierce lake winds were pounding rain against the skylight. I was sure Paul and I would choose to delay our start. Still, it was important to me to begin every day between now and the end of the trip with a ceremony. I put some ground sage in a small pottery bowl, lit a candle, ignited the sage, wafted the smoke around me to clear my heart and mind. Then I prayed for safety and dialed Paul's number.

"Doesn't sound too great, Ann," Paul said. "My weather-band radio says northeast winds of twenty to thirty knots, waves are four to seven feet, and small craft should stay off the lake." We agreed it was not a day to start out, called friends to let them know we weren't launching, and then drove down to look at the lake together.

We stood on the beach, studying the surf. One white-water mountain after another rolled in and smashed itself against the sand, an image repeated again and again. Rows and rows of white mountains as far as our eyes could see. Relentless. Persistent. Loud.

"You know," said Paul, shouting over the roar of the wind. "We could make it out. We've done surf like this before."

"Yeah, but why give our families the message that we're going to take chances? Let's wait a day and see what happens. We've been telling everyone that we are going to be cautious."

A sea kayaker looks at raging water differently from anyone else. Paul and I did not stand there simply mesmerized by rolling surf. We were calculating how many sets of big waves separated the small waves. Looking to see how far out the breaking waves or the surf line actually extended. Measuring our skills against the incoming challenge.

"You're right, Paul. We've been out in worse. But I still want to wait. This is forecasted to continue for a couple of days. We might get out okay and even make it to Stony Point, but we'll be exhausted, and then what about tomorrow? It isn't efficient to go today." He nodded. It was our first summit about the weather. We were neophytes in conference. In the next sixty-five days, every day that we weren't on solo we would meet many times a day, and always, topic One would be the weather.

My journal entry from 4 p.m. that same day reflected the challenge of waiting when I was so ready to go:

Ah, the disappointment of remaining put when one is ready to leave
. . . a lesson I will undoubtedly learn more than once from the lake
this summer. It has been a quiet day of getting our broken disposal
replaced and taking kids to the show. On the way home from *Sister
Act* at Cinema 8, I drove down to the lake. The kids said, "Mom,
where are we going?"

"To the lake. My body wants to be on the lake."

"Oh, Mom!" But they got out of the car with me near the Aerial
Lift Bridge, which marks the beginning of Park Point. Watched the
surf pounding in against the rock breakwater. Stood next to me,
admiring the waves.

Brian said, "Isn't it amazing that something invisible like the
wind can make something like these waves?"

I reached over and put my right arm around him, my left arm
around Sally. I felt grounded and safe nestled between these
shoulder-high pillars. Thought about what it would be like to be
apart from them for nine weeks. Thought about how different the
summer would be for them.

Yet, even in that moment, the call of the lake was so strong that
it erased the tether of doubt and concern I felt. Yes, the summer will
be different for them and for Dave, but they will be safe and, I hope,
well in their adventure together.

By Tuesday afternoon the marine forecast was calling for a wind shift. I drove down to Paul's with the kids. His children and mine began to play games on the living-room floor. Friends since birth, home-schooled together for kindergarten and first grade, these four children were more like brothers and sisters than friends.

Paul and I sat on stools in the kitchen, drinking coffee. "Well, what do you think, kiddo?" I asked of my curly-haired friend with the impish blue eyes.

"I think we should go. We need a shakedown paddle on big seas." The truth of his statement stirred a queasiness in my stomach. I remained silent for a moment.

"Yeah, you're right. The storm is supposed to end Thursday. Let's go for it." Paul reached over to shake my hand. I matched the strength of his grip.

This time we had shaken on the contract. Five years earlier we had spoken about our desire to paddle around the lake. Last summer after our weeklong sea kayaking trip on the lake's south shore, we had sat down and figured out an itinerary for our circumnavigation of the lake and drafted a letter to friends and family inviting them to join us on shore or to paddle alongside for parts of the trip. First we spoke of intent. Then we wrote the commitment. Now we shook hands. Each sanction of the dream had pushed us further along the river of preparation leading to the lake. Around rocks, over ledges. Now we were prepared to drop over the waterfall onto the surface of the great lake. Irreversible. One never goes back on a handshake, never goes back up a waterfall.

Wednesday, June 17, 10 A.M. Park Point beach in Duluth. Low clouds and fog. Strong winds. Four- to seven-foot surf still breaking on the sand beach. I knelt by my boat, making last minute adjustments to its load. Nervous reorganizing. Little rituals designed to convince me of my own readiness.

Dave had helped me carry the boat and all the waterproof gear bags the fifty yards from the car to the edge of the pounding surf. Paul's wife, Mary, was helping him. Our children were busy playing tag with the cold, relentless waves. A few friends with cameras or last minute gifts of food were mingling between Paul's blue boat and my yellow one.

At last all the gear was safely stored in the waterproof hatches. "Are you ready, Mom?" asked Brian. He was eager to perform his official launching duties, had been pleased when I asked him if he'd mind getting wet feet and pushing me off.

"Just a minute, bud. I've got to say my good-byes." Each friend bestowed a special thought, a warm hug. Some of them would rendezvous with us at different points along the way. Each of them would forward gifts or cards. Having gotten wet, Sally and Eva, Paul's daughter, were curled up in a blanket together.

I knelt on the sand to kiss Eva, then walked around to the other side and lay down next to Sally. I carefully took her into my arms and said, "It'll be okay, sweetie. We'll miss each other, but you're coming to visit me twice on the lake. And I promise to be careful." She said nothing, just clung tightly to me.

I stood up, brushed the sand off my wet suit, bent my body into the wind, and headed toward Dave, who along with Brian and Galen, Paul's son, was making sure the boats remained safely out of the grasp of the surf. For twenty-one years, nearly half my life, I had called "home" the place at this good man's side. I reached out with all of my five feet nine inches and held his tense body in an embrace that was longer than his shy nature was comfortable with. "I love you. Be well," I said.

"You, too," he replied.

I slipped into my boat.

One woman. One kayak. One spray skirt. One paddle. One spare. One rescue float. One pump. One compass.

One woman dressed in long underwear, wet suit, paddling jacket, life jacket, rain hat, neoprene mittens.

One woman equipped with tent, first aid kit, cooking gear, dried food, water purifier, sleeping bag and pad, one change of clothes, one journal, one camera, one pair of binoculars, one collection of maps, one waterproof pouch with treasures.

One woman with longing for some vague dream of knowledge and transformation.

One lake with unbelievable power.

With Brian and Galen's help I stretched the elastic edges of the neoprene spray skirt around the edges of the cockpit, creating a waterproof seal between my lower and upper torso.

I reached up and hugged Brian, gave Galen a high five, picked up my paddle, and nodded. The boys grabbed the back of my boat and slowly slid me forward on the sand into the shallow water.

"Hold on tightly so my bow stays steady," I yelled over the wind. "It's really important that I take off straight into the waves." Knee-deep, then thigh-deep, the boys waded into the thirty-six-degree water, slowly pushing the bow within reach of the surf. Three large waves crashed in, one behind the other. The boys struggled to hold the boat straight. Three small waves. Three large waves. The boys still held me steady. The pattern was holding; the next wave would be small.

"Okay, let go!" I yelled.

"Be careful. . . ." I heard Brian's voice in my ear. My son. Letting go of me. Trusting me to return. With one strong stroke of the paddle I was in the lake's power, beyond the help of anyone on land.

The first wave crashed innocuously on my bow. I wasn't yet out to the big ones. This was the window of calm I needed, and the boat was hardly moving. Stroke, Ann. Pull. Get out of here before that next big set of waves comes in. My boat felt like a barge, would hardly move forward. Oh, of course, it was fully loaded! I leaned into each stroke of the paddle. Pulled the 65-pound boat and its 80 pounds of gear with every muscle in my 125-pound body. None of me could rest or hold back. I needed every muscle fiber, every cell working at top efficiency.

The next wave broke over my spray skirt. The next hit me in the face, a cold, shocking slap. No time to recover. Just keep paddling forward. Moving to get beyond the breaking surf. Can't look back to see how far out I am. Just keep stroking. Yes, I'm getting there. One more big one to get through.

WHAM. A wall of cold water hit me, engulfed me in stunned blackness. Terror. But as quickly as it hit, it was gone and there was light . . . and another wave coming. Paddle. Quickly up the slope of the wave. Don't let it break over your head. Yes, yes, I'm going to make it. WHAM. My boat slammed down the back side of the wave with a loud noise. But that was it! No more breaking surf. I was free!

I had made it out into the rolling clutches of the open lake. "YAHOO!" I shouted.

Carefully I turned my boat to face the beach, making sure to remain perpendicular to the waves, so I could watch Paul paddle out through the surf. I backpaddled steadily to keep from being pulled in.

Shore was so far away. When I rode a wave down into the trough, I could not see land. Up on the crest of a wave I could see dark little stick figures on the beach and Paul's boat resting on the edge of the surf. Brian's pink sweatshirt stood out next to the blue of Paul's boat. Then Paul was stroking. Stroking. Struggling against the surf as I had.

It seemed forever before he got out to me. During that forever, I kept paddling and maneuvering my boat out of the reach of errant side-waves that kept taunting me, trying to tip me over. But I wasn't going to tip. There was only one thing on my mind. I was waiting for my friend, my companion. I did not want to be alone out here.

Paul got to within earshot and let out a war whoop. I yelled back and we turned our boats in tandem toward the north shore of the lake. We held our boats in a position called "quartering." Not a simple position to hold; it's a bit like trying to walk along a steep, precipitous mountain ridge when the wind is blowing forty miles an hour from the side, constantly threatening to blow you off balance. But I felt calm, skilled.

Gone. We were gone into our new lives. The sun emerged and lit up the city of Duluth. I was warm inside my wet-suit cocoon. The Aerial Lift Bridge, which went up and down to allow oceangoing freighters in and out of the harbor, was not more than a quarter mile due west. Ahead were the silhouettes of the downtown buildings. With a population of eighty-eight thousand Duluth doesn't have skyscrapers, but the thirteen-story Radisson Hotel, Duluth First Bank, and other businesses create an impressive enough skyline. I took a quick glance above the buildings to find the top of the ridge the city was settled along. I was looking for the ski jump that marks my listening place, but it was too hazy to see more than blurred images of houses that seemed to be stacked atop one another.

Mostly I could see Paul, because we were paddling about twenty feet apart, but once in a while a big wave would come between us and he would disappear from view.

Paul yelled something, but I wasn't sure what. Then he motioned off to the east with his head. A thousand-foot-long ship loomed above the waves like some giant monster born of this storm. My God! We had passed by the ship canal barely in time. Twenty minutes later and that ship would have been on top of us. We were no more than two floating toothpicks to that hulk. It would never have seen us, never picked us up on radar, never even known it had ground us to bits.

Three hours later the clouds descended and a cold, driving rain began to fall. At first, I liked it. Felt smug about the teal, broad-brimmed, Gore-Tex rain hat I had bought, about how it acted like an umbrella and sent the rivulets down the back of my waterproof jacket instead of down my neck. Liked feeling as impervious to the weather as the loons we occasionally passed. Liked waving to a couple of friends whose cars were following our progress along the rocky shore of Scenic Highway 61 just outside Duluth.

But then I began to feel tired. We were five hours into the paddle. Longer than any of my training paddles. The longest paddle since last summer's lake trip. And it seemed to me that it was getting colder. My hands inside their black neoprene mitts were barely warm. My ears hurt from the cold. These warning signs were just distant messages, tallies on a neon scoreboard on someone else's playing field. Lake 10, Ann 2.

"How you doing? Want to stop and eat something?" asked Paul.

Stop? Change the routine? Introduce some new discomfort like trying to land in the surf? Paul's words picked me up by the nape of the neck, removed me from the rut of resignation, and placed me back into the mainstream of survival. "I don't want to stop, but would you help me snap on my rain hood?" I asked. He pulled over next to me and held on to my boat, providing the double-hulled safety position called "rafting up." I pulled back my spray skirt and searched for the hood to my paddling jacket.

"We don't have far to go to Stony Point," he said, to reassure himself and me. We both peered ahead into the gray, menacing clouds. Our visibility was about a quarter-mile. The point of land ahead of us couldn't yet be Stony Point, which we had set as our goal for the first day, but I wanted it to be. I wanted to be done with my sore muscles, my cold body, my fear.

Paul fastened the Velcro of my hood onto the back of my jacket and handed me a Jolly Rancher candy for sustenance. I pulled the hood over my rain hat and tied it, liking the feeling of shutting out a little more of the cold, wet world.

We kept paddling on through the driving rain. The rain had beaten the waves down to a three- to four-foot level, making paddling more manageable, but now moisture was seeping into my wet suit. There was not one dry place on my body.

Each point ahead looked prominent enough to be Stony Point. I tried to read the plastic-encased map held in place on my deck with bungee cords, but the truth was I had no idea where we were. I simply trusted that I'd recognize Stony Point because I'd been there so often, hoped the fog ceiling wouldn't lower any more, hoped no lightning would come from the ever-blackening skies.

Paul and I didn't talk much. We couldn't converse above the sound of the wind and waves and rain. We just kept paddling forward, keeping land on our left side and each other in sight.

"Paul, look! There's a white car up ahead and some people getting out. I think it's your mom." He slowed down so I could repeat what I'd yelled. As we got closer, we realized we were approaching Stony Point, seventeen miles from our start.

"Wait a minute," said Paul.

I didn't want to wait. I wanted to get on shore, get my tent up, and get out of these wet clothes. My mind had shifted from its locked position called "paddle" to a position called "quit paddling," and it couldn't deal with anything else.

"Why?" I asked crossly. He didn't answer, just pulled back his spray skirt and lifted a large plastic bag out of his boat.

"We need to make an offering to the lake," he said, pulling a bit of tobacco out of the bag. "We have a lot to be grateful for today."

I was stunned, humbled, ashamed. Paul handed me the tobacco as he said, "For the privilege of this day." A simple ceremony taught to us by friends. A short pause. A precedent.

Paul's mother was waiting on shore with a thermos of hot chocolate. "I rented a cabin for the night. You will join me, won't you?"

Without taking my neoprene mittens off, I reached for the cup she offered. Drops of cold rain fell into the hot, sweet beverage. I peered into it, let the steam warm my face. Lifted the chalice to my lips with two hands. "Bless you, Nancy. Bless you."

2

First Solo

Solitude offers the greatest opportunity
for the fine-tuning of our souls.

As I LAY in my sleeping bag on the floor of the one-room cabin
Paul's mother had rented, all I could think about was the pain in my
arms, shoulders, and lower back. It hurt to roll over on my side to
change position. It even hurt to pull the sleeping bag up over my
shoulders, to ward off the chill along the cabin floorboards. This
pain from physical exertion was not new to me. I have been running
or skiing marathon distances of twenty-five and thirty miles every
year since 1974. To train for those races, to train for this marathon
journey, I had worked out for hours daily, learned to move beyond
the pain into stamina and fortitude.

I expected the first week to be about pushing through pain,
about adjusting our bodies to the rigors of exercising eight to ten
hours a day. And so, I dismissed the pain, pushing my mind to other
thoughts. I opened my soft-bound journal to the first entry of this
month, June 7.

> Last night I dreamed about Betty. In the dream I was at a picnic with
> Dave's folks, my folks, Dave, Brian, and Sally. We were seated on
> two sides of the park picnic table. I was busy making sandwiches
> for Brian and Sally when I overheard Dave's mother say, "Why, Betty,
> you look as I remember you!" I did not dare look up, kept making
> the sandwiches. Then a similar comment was made by my mother.

This time I looked up and saw Betty's face gazing at me. Nobody at the table seemed the least bit upset or surprised by her presence. She looked as I remembered her from before her cancer, but her skin was opalescent. Angelic in quality. A tremendous calm came over me. She asked if I would go for a walk. We walked away from the table arm in arm. She turned and said to me, "I want you to know that being your guardian angel is my full-time job." I was completely stunned by this information, and in that instant she disappeared.

Betty died in 1990. She had been the closest friend I ever made. At five feet three inches, she was a dynamo, an internationally known biochemist, a fearless mountaineer, the namesake of my daughter, Sally Elizabeth. She and I had taken numerous wilderness trips together during the twelve years of our friendship. The journal entry reminded me of the last time I'd been here at Stony Point: March, more than two years ago, one month after her death. Paul and I had come to scatter her ashes, as she had requested. I laid down my journal, closed my eyes, and remembered that afternoon.

I was scared, but it was the day we had set aside to do this. There was still ice scattered along the shore. Temperatures were in the twenties. The wind was blowing twenty miles per hour, creating a below-zero windchill. Paul and I paddled out beyond the protection of this rocky spit of land into three- to five-foot waves. We paddled beyond the light-green water where it was shallow, into the deep-blue lake far enough out so the ashes would remain at sea.

All I could think about was the waves and getting the ashes into the water. I was not cognizant of Paul's whereabouts when I stopped paddling, slipped the spray skirt cover back, and pulled out the blue denim bag I had sewn. The bag and its contents terrified me. I wanted them out of my boat, out of my hands. I ripped off my neoprene mittens, unceremoniously opened the bag, and turned it upside down at the side of my boat.

The wind blew most of the ashes back over the top of my boat and spray skirt, little cream-colored bits of bone and dust. My friend, dead just one month, rested on my lap.

"Ann, hold on a minute," said a voice from the lake. It was the same

voice I could now hear on the other side of the cabin. I had known it was Paul talking to me, but I couldn't speak. He slid his boat in next to mine and rafted up for stability. I did not want to look into his face. I was ashamed about having the ashes land on my boat instead of in the lake.

"Ann, we need a toast." He pulled out his small silver thermos, unscrewed the top, and poured a steaming cup of coffee. "To our lady of the lake!" he said as he offered me the first sip.

Warmth and ceremony massaged my throat back to life. Fear retreated, opening the door for Mystery to come forward. I looked at the bows of our boats bobbing up and down in perfect synchronicity in the waves. The waves didn't seem so high now. I looked at Paul, smiled, and offered the next toast: "To a woman who lived life to its fullest." Paul took a sip and began reminiscing about the sea kayaking trip Betty had taken with us.

"Do you remember the time we were paddling across Black Bay and you and Betty had to go to the bathroom so bad?" I nodded and smiled. "The whole trip Betty had been hanging back, having a hard time keeping up. All of a sudden you and she went paddling by me like your boats were motorized. You didn't even say anything. You just zipped by, hit shore, hopped out of your boats, and pulled your wet suits down right there next to your boats."

We both laughed. Paul picked up a bone chip from my spray skirt, dropped it into the cup of coffee, and then dumped the contents of the cup into the lake. "This one is for Betty," he said. He helped me wash the bone pieces off my deck and spray skirt, and suggested that I might like to keep the denim bag and what remained inside it.

I opened my eyes. Paul and his mother were still talking, oblivious to my wakefulness. I stared at the open log beams of the ceiling. Where were Betty's ashes now? On the bottom wedged between dark boulders? If she was my guardian angel as the dream suggested, what did that mean? Would I be able to know when her spirit was present? I had tried, unsuccessfully, these last two years to find ways to be reassured that she was still present in my life.

Days two and three took us past the most spectacular cliffs along the Minnesota North Shore: Palisade Head, Split Rock Lighthouse,

Tettegouche State Park. Standing atop these 150-foot cliffs, one is compelled to take a step backward, lie prone, and then inch to the edge for a safer look. Gulls are mere specks floating on the water below. Trees and ferns perched on tiny ledges are entire ecosystems unto themselves, islands suspended off the cliffs — hanging half in sky.

Paddling below these cliffs on these overcast, foggy, windy days, I looked up at some of those tiny ledge islands and wished for as much stability as even they had. I remember wondering, but not daring to look up for fear of being capsized by the waves, if we were the object of any tourists' conversation when we paddled under the Split Rock Lighthouse. I imagined a tourist standing atop the cliff behind the wire mesh fence, curiously pointing to our toothpick-size blue and yellow boats below him. Perhaps he made a comment to friend or family about people being crazy to paddle in weather like this, then returned to his heated car.

On day three, June 19, my journal read, "My body feels awful." The handwriting was more telling than the words themselves. The scrawling looked like that of a third-grader who had not yet learned to hold a pen properly for cursive writing. I was writing in my tent with wool gloves on. The temperature at the time was thirty-six degrees.

Other events I catalogued on that day also reflected my discouragement:

> We did a "hand test" today. I put my bare hand in the water next to my boat while Paul timed me. Nine seconds was the longest I could hold it underwater before the burning sensation was so severe I had to pull it out. Paul's hand lasted twelve seconds in the water. Very sobering. If one of us went over, our wet suits would preserve our torsos for a while, but we would very quickly lose the dexterity in our hands needed to perform a rescue.
>
> No matter how hard we paddled, we were barely warm. When we pulled our boats up on the cobble beach of Split Rock Lighthouse for lunch, we went into the picnic shelter. Folks from the

Duluth Gospel Tabernacle were having an indoor picnic. There was a fire in the woodstove, hot coffee brewing. I didn't want to leave. Felt only fear as we paddled off. Fear at the coldness in my hands. Fear of tipping in the bitterly cold, confused water ricocheting off the cliffs. Tettegouche State Park's tall rock faces were dark and foreboding, not beautiful and spectacular, as I remembered them. It seemed they were guarded by evil spirits. I just wanted to paddle around them as fast as I could to find a camp for the night.

The weather was kinder the fourth day. The sun actually shone. Temperatures climbed into the low fifties. There was only a two- to three-foot chop on the water. I went from being the exhausted kayaker who could only focus on how many miles it was between breaks, to the curious kayaker who wanted to explore little coves and inlets.

Early in the day we were paddling in tandem, quiet, respecting each other's need for solitude. When we came around one set of cliffs, we simultaneously gasped. There was a waterfall, a twenty-foot-long wall of root beer–colored water pouring hundreds of thousands of gallons over a ledge thirty feet into the lake. The roar was audible even over the light surf hitting the cliffs next to us. And the cliffs! Their pink-gray faces were adorned with gorgeous orange, green, and yellow lichens. Precariously clinging to their ledges were a host of cedar trees — sentinels, guarding this place. On this first day of summer we sat side by side in silent respect.

Two hours later we stopped at Lamb's Campground in Schroeder for a scheduled two-day layover to rendezvous with friends. Paul's mother, Nancy, and our crone friend Fran greeted us with a delicious whitefish dinner. We regaled them with stories of cold and wet and waves, but we both were optimistic that we had endured the worst of the weather.

Frost was the morning's answer to our prediction that the weather would improve. As we sipped hot chocolate around the campfire that seventy-four-year-old Fran had risen early to build, we joked about picking the wrong summer to make this trip. By midmorning several friends had made the ninety-minute drive from Duluth to bring care packages and to hear stories. One of them complimented me on my "beautiful purple sweater and pants." I was drawn out of the doubt and fear of the last four days and back into the confidence of the month before my trip, the confidence that the newly sprouted, lime-green leaves of May bring to the brown, drab world of a northern Minnesota spring.

The first of that month my teaching partner, Christina, and I had been returning from a weeklong women's workshop in Ontario. En route home in the car she had said, "There's a present for you in the back seat. An early birthday gift. I want you to open it." I carefully removed the flowered paper, lifted the lid, and exclaimed, "Oh, it's exquisite."

"You said you needed a wool sweater for the trip."

"La Abeja. Made in Uruguay. 100% Virgin Wool," said the label. I ran my fingers over the simple design of turquoise, green, and light purple that was knitted into the front of the sweater. I had always taken an old brown wool sweater on camping trips. My suggestion to Christina had been for a new, warmer one. Never had I imagined wearing something so magnificent.

"Is it okay?" she asked.

"Yes, of course. I just don't know about taking something so gorgeous on this trip."

"Annie, you're not just going camping. You must mantle yourself for the journey."

Christina is a city woman with an adventurer's heart. She had made it clear from the beginning of our friendship that if she was going to get wet, cold, or dirty, she'd feel a lot better about it wearing purple, teal, or pink. At first I had internally dismissed as frivolous and indulgent the idea of outer fashion. But over time I was beginning to see a different side of myself surface as I dressed to enhance my own femininity. And the truth of the matter was that donning the purple sweater after a long, often brutal day of paddling did more for my self-esteem than anything else available to me in the spartan conditions of our camp.

In the middle of that same afternoon at Lamb's, I was having a conversation with my artist friend Annie. She and I were sitting on an immense boulder of the same bedrock that graces my listening place back in Duluth. This smooth black rock was marked with glacial scratches made by rocks caught in gigantic fields of moving ice tens of thousands of years earlier. Annie was arranging a handful of smooth, half-dollar-size blue pebbles she had collected into lines that paralleled the striations.

"So, if the weather has been so bad, why keep going?" she asked, as she admired her handiwork.

I looked at the rows of lines — ancient lines, modern lines — and thought of my own life as movement that refused to follow a straight line. "I keep going because I am trying to find the rest of my life. I have children, a husband, a home, work; and yet, I know there is more."

"Sometimes we keep doing things over until we learn them," she said, stroking the grooves of the glacial scratches with her fingers.

"What do you mean?" I asked.

"Well, wilderness trips and hard physical challenge have always been important to you. Something tells me this trip is going to enable you to break through that old model of always pushing through the pain. You are going to find other ways to grasp deeper knowing." She lifted her clear blue eyes to meet my gaze. They were kind, inviting.

Our eyes held steady for a while, then I looked out over the lake. I could not see across it; at this point it had widened into an unknown sea. In that moment I surrendered further to Mystery, forgot the fear and discomfort of the last few days, knew my commitment to transformation was as ancient a calling as the grooves on the rock before me.

After the two-night stay at Lamb's Campground, Paul and I parted company for a few days. He had to return to the university for a work obligation. We were to meet five days later near the Canadian border. I was alone to navigate the waves and fog and cold. Alone for the first time on this trip, to test my skills on the lake.

Solo wilderness trips have been important to me for the last dozen years. I started timidly — in my back yard. I was scared that first night. But my deep conviction that spiritual wisdom comes only from extended solitude propelled me through my fear into a self-imposed regimen of solo skill-building: afternoon walks and paddles, overnights in campgrounds, winter camping in the Boundary Waters Canoe Area of northern Minnesota. Two years earlier I had taken my first sea kayaking trip alone on Lake Superior.

It was in late April, when spring in northern Minnesota and Wisconsin is still mostly wishful thinking. My own life then felt as frozen as the inland lakes. Betty had been dead two months. I had gone for long walks in the woods, sat for hours by the lake. Wildness was the only embrace that comforted me in my grief. It was the only embrace that was large enough. I was searching for reassurance that my friend was somehow all right. That I was all right. That the path in my own life went somewhere beyond dead end.

On April 30, 1990, the day Betty would have turned forty-nine, I put my kayak into the waters of the Apostle Island National Lakeshore in search of a way to honor her birthday.

After several hours, I stopped paddling, removed my spray skirt, and pulled the blue denim bag with the rest of Betty's ashes out of the cockpit of my boat. I was glad they hadn't all fallen out when Paul and I scattered them a month earlier, taking it as a sign that something was yet unfinished. I reached into the bag and dropped a pinch of the dust into the lake. Down, down into the green, infinite depths trailed this fine line of white powder.

"Where are you, my friend? Where are you, my friend?" I choked out the question, watching the various-sized pieces of dust stretch out before me like a gesture. Was that bone chip once her leg? A sturdy leg that would have helped me lead the children on our long-planned trip to Alaska this summer. Legs that were supposed to join mine in leading treks for women when Betty took early retirement, so we could start our own business.

Only a passing gull answered, but in watching its flight I caught sight of a magnificent white swan floating not seventy-five yards from me. Angel white. Perfectly still. The swan stared intently at me. Through me.

Past the wall of my grief. Into the center. Tears formed at the corners of my eyes, rolled down my cheeks. My heart beat hopefully in its protected cage. Neither the swan nor I moved.

After a long time, my mouth formed the words, "You're here, aren't you? I feel you in my body. You're here." The swan lowered her head, turned, and swam away. She disappeared out of sight behind Hermit Island. I looked down into the green depths. The trail of white dust was gone. Gone, but not gone. Betty was not gone. Her presence in my body felt like the faint stirring of spring wind. Barely detectable. A whisper.

My first solo day started quietly. Fran, Nancy, and Paul watched me launch my boat in one- to two-foot waves and light fog. Temperatures in the low forties. I found myself stopping to rest every few hours, whenever I could find a beach where storms had reduced the ancient volcanic bedrock to smooth, hand-sized cobbles, kind in their treatment of the bottom of my boat. But mostly this stretch of shoreline had very few safe places to land.

About 1 P.M. I took a cup of pea soup from my thermos that I had prepared that morning. I was now on a cobble beach no bigger than my family car, just below Highway 61 near Cascade Lodge, about twenty miles from where I had pushed off that morning. I could hear cars passing by on the embankment above me. The fog had been descending all day. The wind had built waves to the three- to four-foot level. I was tired, aware that I had already put in a long day. I was ready to stop, but this small space was too close to the water's edge and too close to the highway and the lifestyle I had abandoned. So I pushed on, the wilderness explorer on the lake that was only partly wilderness. The woman in search of a new life, still working on that old model of pushing through the pain, never even considering the option of spending the night in the comfort of Cascade Lodge.

After an hour of steady stroking, I realized I still had not warmed up. I balanced my paddle across my lap and pulled a wool stocking cap and my neoprene mittens from the waterproof bag I always kept between my legs. The wool under my rain hat and the mittens over my icy fingers felt good, boosting my confidence. I picked up the double-bladed paddle and resumed stroking. In and out of the water. First, reach forward on the left side, insert the blade, pull it down parallel to the boat. Lift. Then, into the water with the right blade and pull. In and out of the water. Sometimes reaching way out to the side of the boat to execute a sweeping stroke to correct for the side-pushing action of the waves.

In my kayak I was sitting right on the water. Only one inch of Tupperware-style plastic separated me from Lake Superior's thirty-six-degree cold. Cold water below me, cold water falling from the sky. Cold water seeping through my paddling jacket, through the neo-prene wet suit, where my body is barely capable of warming it. Slowly, steadily, the reservoir of warmth inside my body is depleted.

Two P.M. Nine hours into my paddling day. No safe place to land. An hour beyond what I had ever paddled before and way beyond my endurance. Ahead, in the fog, a light! A house but no dock, just big, black, jagged rocks guarding the shore. Sorcerers in fearsome robes and jeweled swords. My mind cut itself adrift in ancient memory. I was afraid of what I saw beyond my eyes.

"God help me," I said aloud. Three words. Nothing more. It was enough to shock me back into the present. Push on. Push on. More houses without docks or lights. Mirages of safety. Destroyers of hope.

My mind turned my arms into iron pistons, shunted all physical sensations into a file named "denial." I paddled the yellow kayak on through the fog, rain, and waves. I felt like the only living creature in existence.

When I could steady myself, I looked at the plastic-encased map on my kayak deck. What good is a map when every fog-enshrouded cove looks the same, when there are no cities or big cliffs or other landmarks? Where was I? All I knew was that I was somewhere between Cascade Lodge and the city of Grand Marais. Questions ate at my mind's rigid control, but it would not bend, kept ordering, "Push on. Push on."

Then I started bargaining with God. "If you'll just give me three feet of sand to land on . . . If I only have to paddle for thirty more

minutes . . . If I could have a safe place to land before it gets dark . . ."
The bargains got less demanding, less hopeful, as I paddled further
and further into my fate.

I just wanted relief. Somewhere. Somehow. Relief from this pilot
named "Grit." Relief from the ache in my arms, the stitch in my side
from all the sweeping strokes. Never had I felt this exhausted — not
stumbling the last two blocks to cross the finish line of my first
marathon, not skiing back to camp with frozen toes after falling
through the ice, not in the first week of Sally's arrival, when she
wailed all night for the country, for the family she had left behind.
This exhaustion was combined with a shattering of confidence such
as I had never experienced before. There was no finish line, no campfire, no other pair of arms to contain my own longing for the family
I'd left behind. By the road that paralleled the shoreline, I was ninety
miles from home. By the water route, I was lost in time and place.

Then a black sand beach appeared. It was not a mirage. I paddled
closer. The waves were rolling in three to four feet high and crashing
on the beach. One careless move and I would be dumped, pushed
over the razor-thin line that separated me from hypothermia. I
paddled closer to shore, backpaddling while I counted sets of waves.
Four large ones. Three small ones. Five large ones. Two small ones.
Four large ones. GO. Get in on one of the smallest crests.

"Yes!" I shouted to myself. "I did it! Quick, jump out. Pull the boat
up and away from the waves." I needed to speak aloud. To hear
direction. To drown out the sound of relentless, crashing waves,
dripping rain, and howling wind.

"Unpack the tent, Ann. Put it up. Quick, before it gets wet inside.
Good, now put up the tarp so you can get out of these clothes and
cook supper. Damn, my fingers are too cold to tie the four corner
ropes to trees. No, you can do it. Just one more corner to tie. Okay,
now sit down on the stump under the tarp and get out of your wet
clothes."

I wasn't sure if the monologue was keeping me from madness or
was the first sign of madness, but I didn't care. I was moving and I
was not in the lake. I was on land. I was safe.

I bent over to ease myself onto the stump. "My God!" Sudden and engulfing pain pulled me to the earth. The muscle spasm began in my side, spreading to my stomach and thighs with the speed of a lightning bolt. The only other time I had known cramping from fatigue was during swim team practice as a kid. Once, my coach had had to jump in after me because my calf muscle cramped so severely. Now I was again lying curled up and helpless, but there was no one to help me. It hurt to breathe. Hurt worse than anything I'd ever known. Worse than waking up after kidney surgery. I was helpless. Never had my body done this to me before. My mind could no longer control and solve the problem. I needed help.

I looked at the young aspen trees holding up the tarp. Their branches seemed to be reaching down, gesturing. "What should I do?" I said in my mind. "Please help me. What should I do?"

Breathe. Slowly. Just like us.

The first breath was so painful, I dared not try again. But there were the trees. And they were alive. Breathing. One small breath went in. The pain was deep, but I could breathe on the surface above it.

Breathe deeper. Slowly. Down into the layer of pain. Melt it with warm breath.

I am not going to die. I can breathe. But I cannot move. Help me. Now what should I do?

Breathe. Just breathe. Relax and breathe.

With each breath the overtaxed muscles eased their grip on my life. Finally I could straighten out my stomach. I lay on my back and looked directly up at the trees. "Thank you," I whispered.

I lay there in the wet grass with the rain falling on the tarp above me, afraid to sit up for fear the pain would return. But I was calm. I was not utterly alone. I kept looking at the trees, listening, knowing I would be all right if I could just keep listening.

After a time, I sat up, as big an accomplishment as the first time I sat up in bed after the kidney surgery. First I struggled to unzip my life jacket, then I pulled my paddling jacket over my head. I was aware that a sudden movement would send me back into spasms, that the violent shaking of my hands meant I was already hypo-thermic.

Getting my clothes off felt as significant an accomplishment as landing safely on the beach some long, long time ago. Another lifetime, perhaps. All I knew was this moment. I was standing naked in the wind and fog and shaking so violently I could scarcely pull on my dry long underwear.

"Slowly," I said aloud. "Slowly, or you'll go into spasms again." Finally I was dressed and dry.

"Food. I must eat something." It comforted me to keep speaking aloud, to test the clarity of my thoughts. I walked over to the kayak, which rested just beyond the grasp of the lake. I struggled to unclasp the front hatch cover so I could pull out my stove. My hands were shaking too violently.

I saw the thermos sitting on my kayak seat. I reached for it, managed to unscrew the lid. Wonderful warmth! Soothing liquid. Creamy soup and ancient memory of milk. Milk from the breast of She-Who-Is-Always-There.

"Tent. I must get into the tent. Tie the boat and turn it over and get into the tent."

I crawled into the tent, zipped it closed, removed my boots and rain gear, and climbed with my wool socks, long underwear, wind pants, wool sweater, and gray fleece jacket into the womb of my sleeping bag. I lay on my back staring up four feet at the dry roof of this tent that Betty had left me in her will. I reached for the pouch that still held some of her ashes, set it on my chest, listened to the rain and wind beating on the tent. A relentless knocking, a ruthless stalker, a giant beast foiled by its prey. "What if," screamed She-Who-Is-The-Biggest, "that muscle spasm had come while you were paddling?"

I cringed, pulled the sleeping bag over my head, rolled my body onto its side, and tucked my knees up to my chest to protect my soft belly. "Drowned," I whispered. "I would have upset the delicate balance I use to hold the boat upright. And I would have gone over in a totally helpless, cramped position." And then I slept.

3

She-Who-Was-Afraid

There comes a time when we can no longer run from our fears.
We must ask for help and listen carefully.
Wise counsel comes from many sources.

As IT TURNED OUT, my camp spot in the grove of young aspen trees was less than three miles from Grand Marais. The next morning I paddled into the fog-enshrouded, rain-soaked harbor at about 10 A.M. Gone was my discipline about rising early. Gone was my rule about eating before breaking camp. Gone even was my confidence about continuing this trip alone. Walking up the street after pulling my boat safely away from the water's edge, I was an apparition emerging from the dark sea onto the foggy landscape: paddle and small gear bag in hand, neoprene spray skirt dangling from my waist down to my knees, life jacket around my chest, rain hat pulled low over my brow, skinny, wet-suited legs propelling me toward refuge in this town of five thousand.

She-Who-Was-Afraid felt everyone look at her when she opened the double glass doors into the Bluewater Cafe. She carefully maneuvered between tables with the seven-foot paddle in hand as she followed the waiter to a corner booth by a window. He handed her a menu and brought a glass of water. Ice water. She shuddered. She opened the menu, and when she looked up, she noticed everyone quickly gaze down at their plates of pancakes or cinnamon rolls or poached eggs on toast.

The waiter returned. "Coffee, just coffee right now," she managed to say. Coffee was the forbidden drink, because previous kayaking trips had shown her that its effect would be a forced pee stop in one or two hours. But this morning she didn't care, couldn't worry about getting cold because she had to stop her boat and strip to pee in an hour or two. At this exact minute she was warm and comfortable and that's all she knew, all she cared about.

She stared at the wall above her, at the map of Lake Superior painted on it. Shrunk to wall size, five feet by ten feet, the lake looked somehow manageable, understandable. She looked at where she was on the map. Not very far from home. The trip had really just begun, and here she was, in a restaurant getting up enough courage to call her family and . . . and what? That was really the question. What was she going to say to them? That she had nearly drowned yesterday and to please come take her home? Or that she was scared shitless and didn't know if it was wise to continue? Or that the weather was a bit rough, but she was looking forward to seeing them at the Canadian border?

"Excuse me," said a voice from the next table. "Did you just come off the lake?" Even in the stupefying fear, She-Who-Was-Afraid turned her social face to meet the question.

From deep within my hiding place I looked at a balding man, his wife, and two teen-aged children eating their breakfast at the table next to me. All four of them had the same blue eyes and Scandinavian dishwater-blond hair that I did. They were dressed as I might have been if I'd driven here — tailored shirts and pants, polyester rain-resistant jackets. Midwesterners on vacation. I was a midwesterner on vacation from my life. Their journey would take them back home refreshed and ready to get about their daily routines. Where would mine take me? I heard my voice respond, "Yes, I did just come from the lake."

"Not very nice out there, is it?" His voice was inviting me to talk. Perhaps this was what I needed. Someone to witness my story.

"No, it certainly hasn't been," I said.

"How long you been out? Where are you heading?" the father asked.

"I began in Duluth seven days ago and am spending the summer paddling around the lake."

"Alone?" all four of my new acquaintances chorused at once.

"Only some of the time. My paddling partner had to return to Duluth on some business for a few days, but will be rejoining me near the Canadian border. We've basically had a solid week of paddling in forty-degree temperatures, big waves, fog, or rain." I listened to myself speak confidently to these strangers and was reassured by what I heard myself say. After a while, with my story intact, I asked to be excused so that I might call my family. As I walked to the other side of the restaurant to the public phone on the wall, I wondered again what I'd say.

I let the phone ring ten times. No answer. The insecurity and loneliness of thirty minutes earlier returned and settled on my shoulders, draping them under the weight of despair. I needed to talk with someone I knew. "Christina will have something to say," I thought to myself. She answered on the first ring.

"Annie, you caught me in! I'm about to leave for a meeting. Where are you?"

"The Bluewater Cafe in Grand Marais."

A wonderful chuckle came out of the phone's earpiece. "Here I have this idea that you've disappeared into the wilderness and you call me from a café!" It was so good to hear a familiar voice, to be recognized, that I was momentarily speechless. Emotion pushed tears to the surface. I felt them coming, wanted to speak quickly to force them back down, but my mouth would say nothing.

"How are you?" she said now, in a gentler voice. I knew this question was coming. Heard it spoken into the receiver from some 250 miles away. And yet I was still struck dumb when it arrived. The silence returned across the 250 miles and signaled another response. "Sorry, silly question. The weather in Minneapolis has been cold and wet. I can only imagine your level of discomfort."

She-Who-Was-Afraid pushed forward inside me and grabbed the phone. Her voice quivered. "The weather so far, and the hours of paddling, have been more brutal than I ever imagined. I'm only eight days out and already I'm feeling pretty scared." I could hardly finish the sentence, but I had made my quick admission. Tears poured from my eyes. "I think I just need you to talk to me."

Words flowed from her across the phone line. She spoke of the flowers in her yard, jogging with her dog, booking seminars for us in the fall, life in the city. Everything sounded so normal. Usual. Routine. "I feel like I'm just babbling," she said after a while, "and I can tell you're crying. Does any of this help?"

"Yes," I managed to respond. "Please keep talking. . . ." Christina did as I asked, providing what encouragement she could, pushing her goodwill down the phone lines, hoping something she said would offer comfort.

I choked out a thought. "I'm having trouble with confidence. Every day I wake up afraid of what will happen to me on the lake, and my fears are well founded."

"Are you doubting the trip?" she asked.

"Yes. The trip, myself, everything." I turned my back to the restaurant, steadied myself against a doorjamb, crying and hanging on to the phone for dear life.

"Where's Paul?"

"In Duluth on business. He'll paddle to catch up to me later in the week. Right now I'm alone."

What I needed was someone who could see what even I did not see. Someone who could understand my fear and help me cope with it. Someone who would notice the level of my disorientation and help me reorient myself. But She-Who-Was-Afraid was wrapped inside the shell of She-Who-Pushes-On, wrapped inside the shell of She-Who-Gets-By-Without-Complaint, wrapped inside the shell of She-Who-Is-Her-Father's-Daughter, wrapped inside the shell of She-Who-Stands-Strong-Alone, and none of us had our stories straight. I couldn't unravel the accumulated bundle of my needs no matter how long I stood with my back to the noises of the restaurant, no matter how long I delayed my friend from her meeting. I could only hope she'd be able to guess what I needed.

"Remember last November when you went through a time of doubting? What did you do then?"

"I got mad at anyone who tried to talk me out of going. I went out on the lake, paddling in the worst weather, to prove my toughness. I got stubborn."

People had been asking me probing questions about the trip ever since Paul and I made our declaration and sent out invitations for friends to join us at different spots around the lake. My parents had wanted to know how I could leave Sally and Brian. Dave had wanted to know why I had to be gone so long. One friend wanted to know if we'd really considered the dangers, and another pointed out that if no woman had ever gone around the lake, it probably meant no woman could — or should — do it. I had coped with these challenges by attaching myself firmly to my determination. Now the problem was, my determination was lost.

"Now that I'm out here," I said, "the lake is wearing away my stubbornness and I don't know how to help myself."

The clatter of the restaurant behind me was loud. I covered up my left ear with my free hand, pressed the phone farther into my right ear, and prayed Christina would think of something to say.

"Ann, you have to keep remembering that the trip is happening on a number of levels. No one but you even knows what these layers are. On one level, the trip is an awesome — perhaps awful — adventure. On another level it's a spiritual odyssey."

"I'm afraid."

"Of what?"

"Of the lake."

"What about the lake?"

"That she'll beat me down so hard I won't remember the quest part."

A long sympathetic sigh came whistling softly in my ear. "Ahhh, that is exactly what you cannot let her do. You are out there enduring all this hardship because you've chosen this trip as the way to learn some very important things. You have two jobs: to use your training to stay safe every day, and to use your spirit to stay connected to your purpose — even when you don't know what your purpose is."

Though she couldn't see me, I was nodding my head, wiping tears from my eyes, getting ready to turn around and face the curious onlookers again. "I know you have to go. . . . I hear you, and I'm better. . . . Thank you."

"You hang in there. And keep in touch. Let me know what's going on and if I can help."

I hung up the phone with deep gratitude and restored composure. She had become the one I would call, would use as my touchstone to the other life. The calls would be little reality checks. Little "Are you still thinking about me?" checks. Tenuous tethers to the world I'd left behind.

I walked back to my table, ordered a large stack of blueberry pancakes, and resumed talking with the man and his family at the next table. After I devoured the three plate-size pancakes, they insisted on escorting me out into the rain and fog. They had never seen a sea kayak and couldn't imagine how enough things for a whole summer fit into such a small craft. The five of us huddled around my boat in the light mist and fog. I slipped into the familiar mode of being a teaching naturalist, opened the front and back hatch, and pointed out the location of my tent, sleeping bag, extra clothes, cook kit, stove, and food.

"Pretty spartan," said the woman.

"You're not kidding," I said. "No room for blueberry pancakes in here." They laughed.

The mother said, "Be careful. You have a long way to go." I nodded and smiled, stepping quickly into the kayak. Her concern was left hanging in midair between us, something I didn't know how to tuck into my small boat. With one strong stroke of the blue paddle blade, I pushed the yellow boat away from the pebble beach and headed again into the gray world of the harbor and the whitecapping waves beyond.

The conversation with Christina, with the restaurant family, and with the waiter, who insisted on sending me off with a free thermos of hot cider, fueled my optimism for the next two hours. I remembered to take a compass reading as I rounded the mouth of the harbor and set out toward an unseen point of land ahead in the fog. I liked feeling the return of the watchful eye of Skill. I remembered this morning — rising late, throwing down the soaking tent, stuffing it into the kayak, and taking off with no breakfast, after dinner the night before of just pea soup. At the time, I had reasoned that Grand Marais was close enough that I could eat breakfast there. But I hadn't really known if it was one or two hours away, didn't know if seas would build, didn't know how badly discouraged and scared I was. As I settled into the grayness and fog, all my thoughts gathered around me like a cocoon. I was held by them . . . worries about the children, about navigating in the fog, about being away from work for a summer. I was paddling back into the armor my life had constructed around itself, returning to the rigidity of She-Who-Was-Afraid. This time I caught myself. Stopped paddling. Let my boat bob around in the choppy seas. Felt the gentle mist of rain on my face. I lectured myself out loud with words of encouragement: "You had a warm, good meal. You had some good conversations. It is time to stop and give thanks."

I laid the paddle across my lap, listening to the sound of water washing against a shore I could not see. This thought came into my mind: "For the first of what may be many times on this trip, I nearly died. Yet, I survived." I began to sing a blessing to the four directions, then to the earth, which at the moment was invisible to me, and then to the sky, which enveloped me like a benevolent but overbearing mother. When my voice died down, the sound of lapping waves against my boat provided a benediction that filled the infinite gray space. I picked up my paddle and stroked on.

Now that no one else was trying to wear away my resolve to undertake this voyage, I realized I had nothing and no one to push against. I had been strong when the questioning was external. I was unprepared for the onslaught of internal question and doubt. I wandered back through memory looking for the first inkling I had that I might one day break free like this.

In my senior year in college, the beginning of winter quarter, I enrolled in an honors class on current issues taught by a tiny, gray-haired woman named Dorothy Lee. It was my last quarter in college. I was graduating early, having completed more than the required numbers of science and math classes to get a double major in botany and zoology. I had studied hard, gotten nearly straight A's, spent summers working at scientific research field sites, was being groomed for graduate school and my Ph.D.

Dave and I had met in science labs, struck up an awkward friendship that turned into awkward courtship. We spoke of marriage, since we seemed headed down similar academic paths. We were deep in scientific study, and our union seemed to make rational sense rather than call up passionate attachment. My future seemed mapped out: leave college early, travel to Alaska for another field experience, come back in the summer to marry Dave, start the cycle of work and graduate school. I'd already had one undergraduate paper published in a scientific journal. My father would be proud of my academic achievements. My mother would be relieved to see me safely married, setting a good example for my younger sisters. I was twenty-one years old. It was 1971.

Campuses were full of protest. Four students were about to die at Kent State. The war in Vietnam was at its height. The first Earth Day had just been held. Some women in New York were starting a magazine called "Ms." In the shelter of Iowa State University and the denial of my upbringing, I was fairly untouched by all this upheaval until I sat down in Dorothy Lee's living room.

I'd never been out of the classroom before. She offered this course in her apartment two evenings a week. The hours were 7 to 10 P.M., though we often ran overtime. The reading list was immense, but there were no tests. There were no right or wrong answers.

This was a radical departure from my biology and chemistry labs with their rigid procedures and guidelines and multiple choice tests. Instead of coming up against something foreign and having to "master" it, I was asked to immerse myself, to trust my intuition, to bring my feelings forward as well as my opinions. Dorothy Lee held class like council — facilitating discussions, making sure everyone spoke, asking us to think, to listen, to reconsider, to change our minds.

For the first time in my life, my mind was actively connected to my body and my heart. To Dave, a biologist already in search of a Ph.D. and a teaching position, the lecture hall contained truth and meaning. But I glimpsed my difference. My life depended on connecting with people and knowledge the way Dorothy Lee taught us to connect. I made the decision to get out of academia and try something different. I still married Dave, but I started to look within myself for guidance in one part of my life. I decided to get my teaching certificate, to share the wonder of science with a clientele I'd had a lot of experience with — kids.

It was the seed. It had taken a long time to germinate, but I could trace the connection. My mind associated from one memory to the next — paddle stroke by paddle stroke. I watched myself progress up the years to launching this boat eight days ago. I could see no further, but I could see how I got here. And that was enough. In my mind I began to take responsibility for the risks I was taking, for the hopes and expectations I had for the journey. I chanted in time to my paddling — quest, live, quest, live. Quest. Live. I knew I could do both.

An hour later the fog moved in like some ominous, lumbering beast that blocked my safe access to the shore. I no longer trusted navigating with my compass, no longer trusted that there was shore beyond the gray wall. I paddled in until I could make out the faint silhouette of rocks and trees, and resolved to follow the shoreline rather than try to save miles by navigating from point to point. Later in the trip Paul and I would be forced to trust our compasses while making long open-water crossings in dense fog, but not today. I wasn't taking any chances. In the café I had studied my map and determined that it was about twelve miles to a friend's cabin. I knew I had a safe, dry place waiting not more than four or five hours from the restaurant. I remembered the danger of yesterday. All I cared about today was safety.

I stayed close enough to shore to occasionally see cabins tucked behind the trees along the pebble beaches, little lighted cottages peering out from the aspen, birch, and pines. I waved at an older couple sitting at a table in the picture window of one cabin perched right on the shore. They rose and came out on the porch to get a better look before returning my wave. They yelled something, but we were too far apart to hear one another above the splash of the waves rolling onto the pebble beach. A short distance farther on, I spotted a tiny, recently constructed lean-to of cedar boughs. It was sitting three feet from the high water mark on a flat, deserted stretch of red pebble beach. Someone had made a shelter three feet high and six feet long from which to watch the lake. The pebble beach was too steep for me to land safely, so I bobbed up and down about ten feet away, admiring the construction, half expecting someone to crawl out and say hello.

This simple structure was very different in scale from some of the spectacular homes and cabins I had seen on the shore so far. Yesterday, in the earlier part of my paddle, before I got into trouble, I had passed a gazebo suspended twenty feet below a cliff. Access was via an iron circular staircase from the cliff top. The ten-foot-diameter circular viewing deck was completely enclosed in glass. I could see deck furniture inside. That millionaire's gazebo, this simple lean-to, the old folks' cottage, me in my seventeen-foot yellow, floating temple — all of us were answering the call to revere She-Who-Is-The-Biggest.

Several hours after leaving the café, I needed a pee break from all that coffee and was beginning to feel hungry. Unlike most of the rocky shore of the first hundred miles of the trip, the stretch from Grand Marais north seemed to be all steep pebble beach. Not the sharp, unforgiving death boulders and cliffs of the earlier shore, but not particularly easy to land on, either.

The act of landing or taking off from the shore, of making the transition from land to sea or sea to land is the most difficult part of sea kayaking. While it can be challenging to be afloat in high winds and big seas, the danger of capsizing is greatest while landing or taking off. Every day on the trip I was encountering shorelines that presented new challenges. Every day I chose to leave the safety of the shore, never sure how I would return. It was clear that the steep pebble beaches next to me plunged into water that dropped off sharply. I could not execute a bow- or stern-first landing, because the pebbles came down to the shore at a sixty- to seventy-degree angle — the boat's sharply pointed ends would simply bounce off the incline. Stepping out of the boat with bow or stern resting only at the water's edge meant a step into water five or more feet deep. The only way to land, then, was to come in parallel to the shore and put myself in the position of being sideways to the incoming waves.

Having figured that out, I kept thinking about sticking my neoprene booties into thirty-six-degree water, then having wave after wave slosh water into the cockpit while I struggled to pull the sixty-five pounds of boat and eighty pounds of gear up the steep bank. The whole scenario was so discouraging that I kept putting off the stop, hoping for a less steep bank or a shore more sheltered from waves.

Finally my bladder announced its desperation. I committed myself to landing, and ran through the plan in my mind: one, paddle in parallel to shore; two, pull my spray skirt off; three, put the paddle down to brace; four, hop out; five, scramble to the bow; six, pull the boat out of the water.

Steps one, two, and three went fine. What I forgot was how cramped several hours of paddling made my legs, and how uncoordinated those first few steps out of the boat can be. I stepped out of the kayak and nearly sat down in two feet of water. Stumbling forward, I grabbed the bow and pulled with every ounce of my strength to haul the boat up the steep bank while, just as I feared, wave after wave splashed water into the cockpit. By the time I had pulled it safely beyond the reach of the lake, I was desperate to pee, and executed the complex movements of unzipping my life jacket, taking off my hat, slipping my paddling jacket over my head, unzipping my wet suit, dropping the shoulder straps, pulling my wool sweater and long-underwear top over my head in one motion, and pulling down my wet suit and bathing suit with the precision of a sailor hoisting sail in a storm.

Squatting there, I spotted some shale cliffs not far from me. One of them had an overhang that looked like a cave, a place to crawl in out of the mist and wind. I redressed, pulled the gear bag with my lunch and the thermos of hot cider the waiter had given me out of the cockpit, slogged across the red pebbles to the overhang, and unceremoniously sat down. Instantly I felt comforted by this little spot. There was no wind. The pebbles were dry. The rain could not reach inside. I struggled with the black pinch clamp on the water-proof gear bag. My icy fingers were as dysfunctional as my feet had been moments ago. I couldn't unsnap the bag, cursed it, and re-sorted to unscrewing the silver top of the Stanley thermos. Steam poured forth from the mouth of the thermos as I guided the precious amber liquid into the silver cup. Carefully I took a sip and then cautiously stuck my right thumb and forefinger into the liquid to warm. Now warm, they could operate the pinch clamp and open the waterproof lunch bag.

The sack of gorp was at the top of the bag right underneath the waterproof seal. My hand reached for the high-energy mixture of M&M's, peanuts, sesame sticks, almonds, sunflower seeds, and rai-sins as I was saying, "Thank you, God, for warm enough fingers." Nothing in the mixture was easy to chew, so it seemed an eternity before anything solid made its way down into the gnawing hunger of my belly. When at last sustenance began to provide relief, I glanced beyond my little cocoon of focus on survival and caught sight of two hooded mergansers swimming three feet from the wa-ter's edge in front of my little overhang. They stared at me curiously. I was clearly not a creature they were accustomed to seeing. Their presence made me aware of my own loneliness. I waved at them and then felt foolish, laughed at myself, and went back to concentrating on getting fuel into my body. A thought came into my mind: "I like this comfort of no rain, no wind, no movement. It feels good to be out of the weather, off the lake. I would like to quit right now."

Then, as quickly as that thought came, I shuddered. I had been off the water less than ten minutes and already I was bone-chilled. My body was not moving, not creating heat. The damp long underwear, wet suit, wool sweater, paddling jacket, and hat were not enough layering without movement. So I glanced at the map, reasoned that I had at most two more hours to paddle, stuffed one more handful of gorp into my mouth, and headed my lean body becoming leaner down to muscle the boat back onto the water, back into its journey.

I knew how to find my friend's cabin from the land: drive four-teen miles beyond Grand Marais, then turn on the dirt road marked "fire number 8514." But finding places from the water was a whole different story. He had told me to look for the metal-roofed sauna building next to the shore and the new log cabin at the edge of the forest. Dave and I had stayed at this cabin for an anniversary cele-bration several years earlier, so I had some idea of what I was look-ing for. When my watch showed 5 P.M., I began to paddle past some small islands that I knew were near the cabin. I paddled closer to shore looking for the metal roof of the sauna. As it turned out, the roof was easy to spot. What was not easy was pulling the boat up and off the beach. It was a huge, steep, terraced, pebbled obstacle that presented me with a task comparable to pulling a 145-pound, seventeen-foot sled up ten rows of stadium bleacher seats. I mar-veled at the steepness and extent of the terracing and was simul-taneously grateful that the creator of this majestic terracing, the southeast wind, was not blowing today.

I took advantage of the fact that today's northeast wind could not reach around to this shore. I paddled my boat parallel to the water's edge, climbed out, and stood in the calm, cold water. I knew I didn't have the strength to pull the loaded boat up to the grass line. Piece by piece I took each waterproof, color-coded gear bag out of the hatches and tossed them up to the first terrace level. Then I pulled the nearly empty boat up to the first terrace, turned it sideways to rest, moved the gear bags up to the next terrace, moved the boat, and began the process all over again. By the time I had carried all the gear bags and the boat to where the vegetation began, some four terraces up, I was totally exhausted. I looked at the cabin, turned to look at the lake, and simply sat down on the wet pebbles. Grateful to finish another day. Safe.

By 9 P.M. I had the two-room cabin warmed. It was a large, log structure, so I shut the bedroom door and lit both the cook- and the woodstove to heat it up more quickly. The couch, the stuffed rocker, and the easy chairs were like me — cold and greedy gobblers of every bit of heat that was produced. While the fires were blazing, I made myself a spaghetti dinner and took a sponge bath. It appeared that my friends who owned the cabin were not going to join me. The thought saddened me for a while, but then I got excited about the prospect of two nights and a day alone in this comfort. No neighbors, no phone. Just me and the beach and my journal.

When I awoke the next morning, I made a schedule of what I'd get done on my rest day: read a book, write some of the first letters of the trip, haul water from the lake, write in my journal. In short, be productive. Regiment my day as I did at home. Ann, the organized. Ann, the efficient. My plan worked fine for a couple of hours, until I went down to the lake to get water. The sky was steel gray; temperatures were in the high forties; it wasn't raining; there was no wind. Something about the smooth, dark skin of the lake stopped me. Yanked the efficiency training of forty-three years right out from under me and sat me down on the dry pebbles in my beautiful purple pants.

I wanted to stroke the glossy surface of the water, as smooth and soft as my stomach. I reached through the layer of windbreaker, fleece jacket, purple sweater, and long underwear to stroke my own smooth, soft-skinned belly. It felt so exquisite. My body had not felt alive in this way since the start of the trip. It had been strong, resilient, alert, aware, but not tender, sensuous, and aroused. The absolute, total calm of infinite nakedness before me drew me deeper and deeper into my own nakedness. Teach me, O Lake. Teach me how to feel and be alive. To know the pleasure of my own ecstasy as surely as you've taught me the terror of my own fear.

From the moment of my self-arousal on, my day had no schedule. I filled the buckets with water, left them standing on the first terrace of the cobble beach, and went walking, a beachcomber idly searching for smooth rocks, carved pieces of driftwood, the unusual patterns in stones.

When I returned to the cabin, I dumped my beach treasures on the pine picnic table. Slowly I rearranged them, created a natural altar. To the stones and driftwood I added a candle and the contents of my waterproof pouch: a hawk feather, a marble with Earth's continents sketched on it, the bag of Betty's ashes, pictures of Brian and Sally, a small booklet called "Tribes," and some sage. At supper that night I lit the candle.

In this cabin four years earlier, I had sat looking at a candle burning, wondering what Dave was thinking about the three-month-long southwest desert camping trip I had just taken with the kids. Sally and Brian had been in kindergarten and third grade, respectively. I had made arrangements with their teachers to home-school them for the last three months of the school year. The kids and I had loaded our used Volvo wagon with food, camping gear, and schoolbooks. Although we had plans to visit some friends, mostly our itinerary had been to camp and see national parks and museums.

I thought Dave understood why we were taking the trip. At this table, on our seventeenth anniversary celebration, just a month after the kids and I had returned, he had put his hands behind his head and said matter of factly, "I just figured you and the kids were leaving me."

My mind had raged in silence: "How could he think that and say nothing? Not try to talk us out of going? Didn't he understand that the trip was a logical extension of the other home-schooling I'd done?" Neither of us said anything. We rose and did the dishes in silence, climbed into separate mummy bags lying on the wooden floor next to the stove. I lay awake a long time, searching for something to say that would make everything smooth on our anniversary night.

Five years after that anniversary trip, the wooden floor under my sleeping bag still felt hard. I lay with my cheek resting on the gray fleece jacket Betty had made for my birthday six years earlier. "Where else but Duluth could I give someone a warm jacket for their June birthday and know they'd immediately use it?" she had joked. I had replaced the jacket cuff after burning it on that desert trip. Had replaced the zipper last year. It had several holes from flying embers, because it had gone on every camping trip I'd taken since receiving it. Gray and weathered, it was a sharp contrast to the new purple

pants and sweater, but comfortable, useful, and in recent years almost magic in its ability to bring my departed friend's spirit to me.
By accident, rather than design, I'd started using it for a pillow the
first night of this trip. It had comforted me after the memory of
Stony Point and Betty's ashes. And so, a ritual began. A ritual that
grew in strength and importance as the journey's harshness forced
me to find solace and comfort in whatever ways I could.

Sometime in the darkness, I awoke from a confusing dream in
which Betty was with me in my childhood home along with a host of
other women friends who had never visited there. My parents were
upset about having so many people in their tiny southern Minnesota
home. As usual, Betty was being enormously helpful, serving food
with my mother, talking comfortably with my father, who was trying
to assist in the kitchen. Like a lot of dreams I had been having lately,
it combined parts of my present and past.

When I first opened my eyes from the dream, I could see nothing
in the cabin. But after a time my eyes adjusted and began to fill in
silhouettes around the edges of the rocker, the sofa, the windows.
My mind drew a silhouette of me on the floor: a womanly bump in a
sleeping bag. I felt the presence of light next to me. The light made
me aware of my own breathing, my own heartbeat. I could not actually *see* a light — my mind told me it was still dark — but I could
feel a light making me aware of my body. I closed my eyes. The
awareness did not go away. I opened my eyes and was conscious of
straining my ears at the same time. I wanted to hear something if I
couldn't actually see something. My mind wanted confirmation from
one of my senses, but I did not have the courage to pull my arms out
of the sleeping bag and reach over to touch whatever the presence
was.

After a time, after practicing the sentence, I ventured to say
aloud, "You're here, aren't you?" At the sound of my voice, I no
longer needed confirmation. My friend was here, as she had promised in the dream before the trip. I continued, "I need help, you
know. I'm having a pretty rough time. I'm scared and I'm lonesome.
I had no idea how tough this trip was going to be." Tears trickled

down my cheeks. The tears turned into sobs. I had to sit up in my sleeping bag so I could breathe through the mucus and liquid. I reached for my flashlight and walked over to the stash of toilet paper near the cookstove in the kitchen, lifting the metal coffee can that protected it from mice. I blew my nose, threw the tissue into the woodstove, and tossed in a couple of extra logs. The tissue caught fire immediately. I stirred the embers until the logs caught, left the door open, and stared into the flames, remembering the eerie light next to my bag on the floor. Closing the stove doors, I returned to my sleeping bag and lay very still, trying to feel the presence again. I fell asleep trying.

Rays of sunshine on my face woke me in the morning. Familiar, unfearful light. I was grateful for an end to the mysteries that had come out of the darkness, was ready to see my family today. Yesterday had been one of many days on the first half of the trip that were disorienting: a mix of elation and fear, excitement and lethargy, sensitivity and dullness. The adjustment to living in such harsh physical conditions, to letting go of my old life, to searching for a new one, would disorient and depress me for weeks. Weeks where, over and over, I made the choice to keep going. Weeks where, over and over, I kept asking, "From where will help come?"

Until this trip, twenty miles had seemed an impossible distance to paddle in one day. My training paddles had never been more than twelve miles. Previous summer trips never found us paddling more than eighteen miles in a day. Now I was little more than a week into the trip, paddling alone, thinking, "Twenty miles won't be that bad." Seventeen miles the first day in the big seas and cold rain seemed an eternity. Twenty miles on my first solo day in the fog and seas nearly took my life. Twenty miles on this day, after two days of rest, with the promise of sunny skies and a visit with my family, seemed not so difficult.

The day passed quickly. I noted the change in shoreline from pebble beaches back to immense boulders and rocks. I delighted in watching the antics of newly hatched gulls atop some of those boulders. One doesn't see much wildlife on Lake Superior. She-Who-Is-

The-Biggest is so cold that her flora and fauna are relatively sterile. The lake looks and acts like an ocean, but it does not support seals or whales or dolphins or kelp or sea turtles or starfish. Birds are often one's only animal companion on the water. Later on the trip, our heightened awareness would enable us to spot otter, beaver, bear, deer, and even caribou along the shore, but today the only creatures I saw were occasional loons and nesting gulls.

The young gulls were like Paul and me, still fledglings. The little brown fluff balls on stilts hopped precariously around on the house-size gray-brown boulders as I paddled by. The "nesting boulders," as I called them, were always closely clustered and far enough off shore to be considered small islands. Gulls have a certain wisdom about raising their young. The islands provide safety from predatory coyotes and raccoons. A good thing, since gull parents are notoriously sloppy about their nests. The few sticks or tufts of grass or feathers they drop on top of the rocks do not look like they will keep the brown, racquetball-size speckled eggs from rolling into the lake. I decided to stop and photograph one of the nest boulders.

No sooner had I pulled the camera out of the gear bag and begun to fiddle with the telephoto lens than I became a target. Though they may not win prizes for precision in home construction, gulls are fierce protectors of their young. One adult gull after another swooped low over my head. I snapped a few photos, set the camera in my lap, and paddled quickly by before stopping to pack away my equipment securely. It occurred to me, looking back on the nesting boulder through my binoculars, that these young birds had basically the same time frame Paul and I had to reach maturity. They, and we, had just hatched and were in the infancy of our experience on this lake. They had nine weeks to become strong enough to migrate to warmer climates as mature adults. We had nine weeks to become strong enough to migrate back into our lives as mature adults.

I arrived at Hollow Rock Resort about two hours earlier than my family. It gave me a chance to shower, unpack, and wash my clothes. I was sitting on the front porch of the two-bedroom, white frame cabin, reading a book, when I spotted our old Volvo wagon loaded with kids, food, and kayaks. Sally didn't wait for the car to stop. She opened the door, yelled, "Mom! Mom!" and raced toward me. All seventy pounds of her four-foot-nine-inch frame jumped into my arms as I was standing up. The greeting knocked me back into the chair. "Mom, I never knew you'd beat us here!" she said as she laid her head on my shoulder and tightened her grip around my stomach.

Tears tumbled down my cheeks into Sally's black hair. My daughter needed me. She knew little of paddling on dangerous lakes or pursuing challenging dreams. She just needed me. And in the warmth of our embrace, I also needed her.

4

In the Company of Men

To grow beyond the expectations we're raised
with is a radical act necessary to the claiming
of one's full self.

BRIAN STEPPED nonchalantly out of the car with Paul's red-haired son, Galen, right behind him. I marveled at their stature. Just ten days ago these two young men had pushed me in my loaded boat out into the surf to begin this trip. At twelve and thirteen years of age they *were* young men. Although they were not yet taller than I, they weighed more and certainly had more muscle mass. I wondered if all parents of adolescent boys had this "My God, he's not a boy anymore!" awe when seeing their sons after a separation.

"Hi, Mom," said my black-haired, black-eyed, olive-skinned son as he turned and headed for the beach.

"What is this 'hi' stuff?" I asked. "Come here, and give me a hug." Sally, not about to share me with anyone, tightened her grip. Brian bent down and planted a kiss on my cheek and patted me on the shoulder.

"How you doing?" he asked. "You look really good." I thought to myself, "He's even talking to me like a man."

"Thank you. I am doing really well. It's wonderful to see you." He waited patiently for a sign from me that it was okay to join his buddy on the beach. I reached for his hand, gave it a squeeze, and nodded. He smiled, turned, and sauntered in the direction where Galen had disappeared. This boy, this old soul who had come into my life to be my friend, was not to be worried about. I could already see that my summer's absence had signaled a formal launching of his own journey to independence.

The whole time I was talking to Brian, Sally kept her head resting on my shoulder, her arms tightly grasped around my stomach. I resumed stroking her soft black hair. "And how is it for you, my little one?" I thought to myself. I knew she was not ready for her own leave-taking, probably not for mine either. I hoped Dave was able to give her the care she needed.

Dave had already carried one load of gear into the cabin during my exchange with the children. Reassured that Brian was no longer a source of competition, Sally hopped out of my lap and announced, "I'll help you carry stuff, Dad." I walked to the car with her and embraced Dave. He gave me a polite, friendly hug, a "There's a lot of work to do" kind of pause. I honored his mood and began unloading. Within ten minutes we had transferred gear and groceries to the cabin, the boys had returned and unloaded the two additional kayaks, and Paul's mother, daughter, and niece had arrived. Once Sally had peers, she, too, disappeared from our side.

As Dave and I were unpacking the food, he said, "I've brought you some surprises." I was delighted. Dave is not given to indulging in flowers or presents. Gifts from him are strictly for birthdays or holidays and are only pragmatic in nature. He pulled some beer and wine and apricot jam out of one of the grocery bags. "I bought your favorite jam to pack in your food tubes for the trip. And I bought some beer and wine so we could all celebrate tonight." I planted a kiss on his lips and hugged him.

We finished moving food into the refrigerator and then carried our things into one of the small bedrooms. Sally and Eva returned. Eva, Paul's younger, blond-haired daughter, is Sally's best friend. "Mom, me and Eva are sleeping in this bedroom together. Brian and Galen are sleeping on the floor of Paul's mom's cabin. You and Dad can have the other bedroom." I chuckled as the director and her friend carried their duffels and stuffed animals into the tiny room.

All of a sudden I heard Eva exclaim, "My dad is here!" She and Sally dashed out of the cabin.

Dave and I headed down to the beach to welcome Paul, who was talking to the kids. "Hey, hey, buddy! Good to see you again," he said, reaching out to give me a hug. "You're looking great!" The camaraderie of storytelling began. He had paddled from Lamb's Campground in three days with no apparent difficulties, and had even rendezvoused with his mom, daughter, and niece for a steak dinner one night. "How about you, Ann? How was your first solo?"

The kids, Dave, and Paul all turned to look at me. They expected an easy story, one that matched Paul's tone. "Well, I sure didn't have steak." I hesitated. "But let's get your stuff into the cabin and we'll tell stories over dinner."

That night after supper, sitting around the fireplace of the bigger cabin, the storytelling resumed. "Were you scared to be alone?" asked Paul's mother.

"Well, yes and no. I was looking forward to the time, but I did have a scary thing happen." Eva and Sally looked up from their game of Uno on the floor, reminding me that my story was being heard by three generations.

"My first day out after leaving you all at Lamb's Campground was longer and colder than I bargained for. I paddled over nine hours, mostly in dense fog and moderate seas, and was pretty hypothermic by the time I quit."

"What does that mean?" asked Eva.

"It means I got so cold my body was in danger of not being able to warm itself back up. I almost needed medical attention."

Brian, who was playing checkers at the table with Galen, got interested. "Did you get rescued, Mom?"

"Well, sort of," I responded. I took a sip of my wine and continued. "I finally found a beach safe enough to land on in the three- to five-foot waves, pulled my boat up on the shore and was setting up camp when BAM! I got the worst stomach cramp of my life. It was so bad I doubled up and fell to the ground unable to breathe."

"Geez, where was this?" Paul interrupted.

"At the time I only knew I was still some distance from Grand Marais."

"So, how did you get rescued, Mom?" persisted my son, who loves to watch *Rescue 911* on television and has been interested in policemen and firemen since he was tiny.

"Well, I lay there in my wet suit in the rain and looked up at the trees all around me, and I thought, I'm going to die. I can't breathe. But you know what the trees told me?"

"What?" chorused Eva and Sally.

" 'Breathe.' They were alive and they were breathing, so I started breathing as slowly as I could. It hurt really, really bad, but I kept trying, and slowly the cramp went away." So that was my story, watered down, cleaned up, the fear stowed neatly away — not to disturb the children. Not to disturb myself.

"What do you suppose the cramp was about?" asked Dave.

"Overtaxing," I replied. "It was the longest, coldest, wettest day I've ever paddled. My muscles were totally spent. If I had gotten that spasm while I was still paddling, well . . . I don't know what could have happened." It was as much as I could admit to those who counted on me to return, to be at the next rendezvous, to be mother and wife and steady friend.

The room was quiet except for the crackling of the logs in the fireplace. Paul spoke up. "We have to be so careful. This trip is beyond what either of us knew."

"Dad, will it be too dangerous for me to paddle around by shore tomorrow?" asked Eva.

"No. I wouldn't let you paddle if it was," said Paul, reaching out to touch his daughter's head. The conversation drifted to other things. I was grateful not to be in the spotlight anymore. I pushed my back firmly into the embrace of the couch, rested my elbow on the support of its arm, and relaxed in the room's warmth. The story was still so new, so raw for me. I had been terrified to share it for fear of . . . of what? Of being told I couldn't go any farther? Told by whom? I didn't know for sure, just felt the racing of my heart, the flush of my cheeks, the relief at not being the center of attention. If anyone in the room heard my terror, my well-disguised plea for help, they said nothing. And so I remained deeply entrenched in denial of the fear that reigned over me daily on the lake.

After lunch on the second day, Dave and I found ourselves in the cabin alone. He put his arms around my shoulders and pulled me close for a tentative kiss. Then he stood back and searched my face with his brown eyes. "How long do you suppose the kids have disappeared for? I have some plans of my own in mind," he said.

I was pleased that he felt this way about me. His advance cut away the cloak of guilt I'd donned since seeing him again — the guilt that said it was wrong for the wife and mother to go off and leave the husband to take care of the children. The guilt that said I should be home safely cooking, not out risking my life kayaking the lake. The brief moment of tenderness was interrupted immediately by Sally. "Paul is taking all us girls out in kayaks. Would you help me get ready, Mom?" While I helped Sally search for her sweatpants, I considered Dave's kiss. Part of what I felt was gratitude that circumstances prevented us from pursuing his desire. I did not know why I felt this way, but the thought wrapped the cloak of guilt back around my shoulders.

When I awoke early on the morning of our departure, I could hear the lake making noise not fifty yards from the partly open window of our bedroom. My mind held the lingering fragments of a disturbing dream. I rose, dressed quietly, picked up my journal, and walked to a large, smooth boulder to write.

June 28, 5:30 A.M.

And so, we do not know if our start today will be delayed because of a trip up to customs officials at the border. I have just awakened from a dream about my best friend in high school. She and I are walking together. She seems distraught and disoriented. We are walking outdoors in a forest. She is leading. All of a sudden she lies down in the grass by the side of the trail and pulls me close to her. We snuggle for a while and then she abruptly says, "No closer!" She rises quickly and marches us straight to the beauty parlor. I want

nothing to do with makeup or having a perm, and say I have to go
or I'll miss the start of my sea kayaking trip. I leave her there getting
her hair done.

I was surprised to find myself thinking so much about my own
sexuality — this strange dream, my relief at the lack of privacy in
sleeping arrangements in the cabin, my self-arousal on the solo a few
days earlier. I am a middle-aged woman who'd been unable to bear
my own children, who had sex very sporadically with my husband,
and who had recently told a good friend, "I'm just not a very passionate person." Usually in times of strenuous physical exercise my
libido was muted, even totally absent, but the lake aroused something in me. Hours spent rocking on her fluid skin. The sheer raw-
ness of her waves and storms. The wildness in which I was encased.
It aroused something in me that was unsettling back in the normalcy
of my expected role.

My reverie settled nothing, and by 7 A.M. Jon, the only paddler
who accepted our invitation to join us for any significant portion of
the trip, arrived from Duluth. Born and raised on the shore of Lake
Superior, Jon had either sailed, kayaked, canoed, or watched She-
Who-Is-The-Biggest for forty-four years. His adventures on the lake,
including a daylong sail on a wind surfboard from Two Harbors
across the open lake to the Apostle Islands, are legendary among
area adventurers. He is a big, robust man with a ruddy complexion
and a warm heart. After a perfunctory trip with us by car to customs,
he unpacked his gear and unloaded his kayak, and we were ready to
paddle. Our twosome became a threesome and I went from solo
adventure to the company of men.

It was a dreary morning. A day when earth and water and sky
were all the color of old asphalt. A steady, probing wind out of the
southeast kept all of the landbound spectators indoors until our
boats were loaded and ready to go.

The good-bye with Brian was easy. It was clear that he was enjoying the summer of freedom and no mom. But when I reached for
Sally, the tears in me rose when I saw the tears in her eyes. I lifted

her up and whispered, "Be well, honey. Dad will take care of you. I will pray for you. You pray for me, too, okay?" I carefully set her down, then turned to Dave, who had the hood of his well-worn navy blue parka tied tightly under his chin. He was not given to showing emotion in public, nor was he good about expressing what was going on inside him. I reached for his hand and said, "Take care of her, Dave. She especially needs it. And take good care of yourself." Then I stepped forward and gave him a polite kiss on the lips.

"You, too," he said. I climbed into the boat. He helped me attach the spray skirt around the cockpit. Sally gave me one last, hard hug. Brian pushed the boat off the cobble beach, I waved, and with a strong stroke of the paddle headed north to Canada.

I needed reassurance about leaving my family for a thirty-day stretch. Stroke. Stroke. Stroke. "Focus on the trip. Focus on the trip," I chanted to myself. Stroke. Stroke. Stroke. "The kids will be all right. The kids will be all right." Stroke. Stroke. Stroke. "I will come back. I will come back." Within five minutes I was to them a tiny speck on the gray horizon — a woman far from the shore of wife, mother, home.

For several hours the three of us were pushed north by steadily building southeast seas. By the time we passed the shallow mouth of the Grand Portage Harbor, waves were ricocheting off the lake bottom, creating a rebound effect that took incoming waves of four and five feet and doubled them. Each stroke had to count. Every placement of the paddle had to anticipate the angle and size of the trailing waves we could not see. It was a dance with a powerful, invisible partner that was as likely to spin me upside down as push me farther up the shore. I had never paddled in waves this big, yet I was so busy paying attention to the rhythm, to the right moves, that my mind did not have time to register fear. There is an ecstasy that comes from such intense athletic concentration. I had felt it before in the last miles of skiing a marathon — a careful, purposeful placement of skis and poles on steep, curvy terrain. I knew how to let my mind and body operate in perfect synchronicity. It is an internal survival mechanism that delivered me from danger to safety. I felt confident and exhilarated.

As we approached the Susie Islands, I knew what to do. All three of us simultaneously, steadily, steered our boats toward the largest island, skirting the west side so we could duck in on the lee side of the waves behind the island. Once out of the roar of the wind, Paul shouted, "Ann and I camped here a couple years ago. We know a good spot."

The three of us paddled on flat, calm water into a little cove with a cobble beach. Just above the cobbles there was a small opening in the tangled birch and fir forest with enough cleared area to pitch three tents.

"I think we should set up camp and sit this out the rest of the day," announced Jon. "It's not going to subside until late. We'll make no progress and just endanger ourselves." I was surprised. I had figured we would rest for a while and then continue to make our way across the Canadian border. How could we quit at 11 A.M. after paddling only nine miles? As the only woman in the party, I was determined to keep up with these two men, was not going to be the one who held anyone back. If my father had taught me anything, it was that you pulled your weight; you kept up; you never quit. But I said nothing, kept quiet in the way my mother had taught me. Rarely did she question an opinion or edict that Dad handed down to her, or to any of their four daughters. "Don't challenge the authority of a man unless you have good reason," was a cornerstone of my upbringing.

It was quiet in the forest. The roar of wind and whitecapping waves was a different world far away on the other side of the island. We pitched our tents and changed out of wet suits, and I found a comfortable rock to prop myself on to read a book. Paul and Jon started a driftwood fire on the cobble beach below me, put some water on to boil, pulled out maps and the weather-band radio, and began conferring. After finishing another chapter, I closed my book and joined them. Paul made me a cup of tea.

"So, what are you guys thinking about?" I asked.

"Well, the weather band says the winds are going to settle down after all," Jon replied. "We're wondering about watching waves and taking off in a few hours if they drop. What do you think?"

What did I think? I had already been persuaded to stop and stay. Here was my authority figure changing his mind *and* asking for my opinion. Now that they'd encouraged me to settle, I did not want to leave, was comfortable and happy. The thought of taking down the tent, packing up the clothes, putting wet things back on, hurrying through dinner, was abominable to me. This time I spoke up. "For what?" I asked. "Nine more miles?"

They were already in the correct expedition mind-set: Go when the going is good, keep analyzing the situation. I, on the other hand, was in a quester's mind-set: Go when you must, but part of the task is to be still. In this moment of discussing the pros and cons of leaving versus staying, the unspoken question of "purpose" swirled around the three of us like the smoke from our campfire. In the end, we decided to stay, and to embark at 5 A.M. the next morning to get in a full day.

After two more full days of paddling, including crossing the dangerous Thunder Bay shipping lane, we arrived at Middlebruin Island on the last day of June. Like so many of the Canadian islands of Lake Superior, Middlebruin is covered with a carpet of dense lichens and mosses and a tangle of scrubby spruce, aspen, birch, and cedar trees. This rich diversity is held in place by a scant layer of topsoil in a climate where summer is less than two months long. Finding flat, cleared spots for pitching tents on these humps of billion-year-old lava flow is not easy, nor is trying to find a safe place to land a boat. The shoreline of this and most of the islands is jagged black lava that seems not so much eroded by the lake as blasted apart by its action. But Middlebruin Island held an element of the familiar. In the summer of 1988, Paul and I had camped here with Betty.

I spoke up as soon as Jon, Paul, and I landed on the beach at 5 P.M. "I would really appreciate having the smaller tent site set back in the woods," I said. "It's where I slept four years ago." Paul knew, but Jon did not, the significance of my setting up Betty's tent on that spot, without Betty in it. He disappeared to set up his tent a good distance away. Jon followed Paul's lead. First I unloaded my boat and carried all the different-colored waterproof gear bags to the tent site. Then I opened the yellow bag, pulled out the pouch containing all my sacred objects, and put it around my neck. Christina had given me this waterproof pouch. A few days earlier, alone in the cabin, I had emptied its contents to create a small, personal altar. Tonight I wanted to wear the altar right over my heart, but first I took out some sage to lay on the ten-foot-square tent site. I sprinkled a dime-size pile on a tuft of moss, lit it, and bowed my head and tried to remember the night four years ago when Betty and I had camped here. I could recollect some images and details, but couldn't feel any emotion. It started to rain lightly. I needed to hurry to set up the tent and get into dry clothes. That's what Betty would have done: focus on the physical details, take care of the emotions later. In thirty minutes I had my tent up, the eight-foot-by-ten-foot nylon tarp rigged between two cedar trees, and a fire burning.

Our dried Indian-curry-and-rice dinner put together from ingredients purchased at the Duluth food co-op was a rushed affair as the rain intensified. All three of us retired to our respective tents by 8 P.M. We had listened to our weather-band radios and agreed that we'd sleep in and at most try to accomplish the eight-mile crossing of Black Bay the next afternoon. I lay inside Betty's tent, amazed that the two of us used to sleep in it together. There wasn't more than a foot and a half on either side of my foam pad. My sleeping bag touched the far end of the tent where the ceiling was only a foot and a half high. Up by my head the ceiling was four feet high. It was a little nylon cave — cozy or claustrophobic, depending on my frame of mind. It really was a one-person tent, which two very compatible people could use if they needed to. I checked the seams above me and the floor around me for leaks. I reached into the pouch and retrieved the bag of Betty's ashes, unzipped the entry flap, and scattered a few of the larger cream-colored bone fragments on the ground in front of me. A blessing for the threshold of my little home. I lay back down and winced at the soreness in my back and shoulders. We had paddled for nearly twelve hours — some thirty-two miles, a new daily mileage record for me. I set the small parcel of ashes on my chest and once again tried to remember that night four years ago.

The two of us had just finished a long paddling day. It was the first sea kayaking trip for both of us. Betty had done some white-water kayaking but had never been out in a sea kayak. "How are you doing?" I had asked, staring up at the close, dark ceiling of the tent.

"You know, Annie. I'm scared. Water is not my element. Lake Superior is so cold and so big and we're all such novices." I was amazed by her comment. This woman, who sometimes terrorized biochemistry students simply by the way she strode into a classroom, who had done triathlons and climbed mountains, who had lived alone most of her adult life, was telling me that she was scared.

I pulled my hand out of the sleeping bag on that cold August night and reached for hers, massaging it as I spoke. "I liked watching you today. Watching you challenge Paul on his interpretation of the weather forecast, watching you paddle those waves on Black Bay."

"You're not a half-bad paddler yourself," she said, rolling onto her side and putting her arm around my sleeping bag. I put my arm around her bag. We let the fear flow into the space between our bodies, be held, acknowledged, and disarmed.

Letting fear and terror show was the thing I would not do with Paul and Jon. Would not, could not. It would have gone against everything my father had ever taught me about being strong in the face of adversity. But I couldn't seem to purge myself of its poison when I was alone, either. I longed for the gentle understanding of my female friends. I awoke to the sound of rain on the tent above me. A light pattering. I felt happy, dry, and secure, was pleased that we wouldn't be moving for a few hours. Out of habit, I turned on the weather-band radio to see if the forecast had changed. It had. "Winds coming out of the east . . . building as the day goes on . . . rain continuing . . . small craft advisory." No sooner had I turned the radio off than Paul was talking to me from outside the tent. I unzipped the beige-colored door and saw him standing in his forest-green rain suit.

"Jon and I think it's wise to cross Black Bay this morning before things get worse. We can land on the leeward side of Porphyry Island and hole up for a couple of days there if we need to."

"Why can't we hole up here? What's eight more miles? This will be safe." I wanted to stay here, to have some time with my friend's memory, simply to rest my exhausted body.

"Well, this is a tiny island. Porphyry is much larger and gives us lots of places to explore if we're stormbound. There are trails on the island going to the lighthouse we visited on that trip with Betty." I knew the logic of his arguments. I didn't care. I felt so strongly about staying here that I muttered that maybe I'd stay and join them later. Paul left to begin packing his gear.

We had planned for moments like this at the start of the trip. We each had complete gear for being solo in an emergency or for personal reasons. I'd already done four days alone. The choice was mine. I zipped the tent up, rolled back into my sleeping bag, felt the damp chill grip my shoulders, and burrowed down until even my head was covered. In the safe, warm darkness a tiny tear rolled out of the corner of one eye. "Help me, my friend. I don't know what to do," I whispered aloud. "The men are leaving. I want to stay."

"Safety" was the only word that would come into my mind. My tears dried up instantly. I rose and began packing. Numbly, methodically, I pulled on my long underwear and wet suit, took down the tent, loaded the boat.

Push on, push on, keep moving, around the grief, around the pain. Paddle out onto the gray sea sky where nothing lives, where the neutral gray sameness presses down into my cells and squelches their breathing, where even sounds are a muted, muffled, melding of light mist and waves not yet risen. Move the body into the void. It moves efficiently, succinctly, when the heart has been left behind.

The eight days from the Minnesota border to Rossport, Ontario, were among the most brutal of the trip. From the time we left Middlebruin Island on July 1 until we arrived at Rossport nearly eighty-five miles later on July 5, we never saw the sun, another human being, or another boat. We passed spectacular hills, deep, fjordlike bays, and immense islands — all in fog, rain, and wind. Each day our weather-band radios warned, "Small craft advisory," but we managed to keep moving by ducking in behind the protection of islands or simply paddling despite big seas.

We may not have seen another human being, but we took advantage of one of the few signs of civilization we were offered. One hour after leaving Porphyry Island on July 2, we found ourselves in a driving rain, battling a head wind that slowed our forward progress to one-third our usual pace of three miles per hour. "We've got to stop. This is crazy," yelled Jon above the roar of the whipped-up lake. "We're getting nowhere and using tremendous energy." Paul was too far ahead to hear us. The thought of stopping and putting up a tent in the wind and rain and forty-degree temperature was more abhorrent to me than staying warm paddling. The rain was literally pouring out of the sky in torrents. My tent would be soaked inside before I ever got it pitched. Then I'd be stuck inside that cold, wet shell for hours, probably even overnight.

"What we need to do is to find a cabin," I yelled back to Jon.

"Yeah, right," I think he said as he pulled his rain cap lower over his brow. We rounded the back side of an island, got some relief from the wind, and spotted a cabin up ahead! Paul was already exploring around it when Jon and I landed our boats.

"It's locked and no one is home, but the sauna is open," he said. "I say we camp here until things let up." As it turned out, things didn't let up for twenty-four hours, and the two-room, seven-by-sixteen-foot wooden sauna became home. It took about an hour of blowing on wet birch bark and soaked twigs before the smoke had enough strength to push the cold air up the metal chimney and out through the dense drops of rain. It took another hour to get the sauna to room temperature.

The three of us alternately took turns coaxing the fire into action, gathering wood, and collecting water from the lake. Once outdoor chores were done, we began hanging our wet clothes up in the front seven- by six-foot dressing area. Using hooks and makeshift ropes, we succeeded in hanging up almost everything. Each of us took turns sponge-bathing ourselves and washing our hair in the main sauna chamber.

After a couple of hours of rest and confinement, Jon and Paul ventured out into what was now sleet to see if they could make their way to the other side of the island for a look at the open expanse of the big lake. When they opened the door, I was hit by a blast of cold air. I rose to check the fire in the barrel stove of the sauna. The large log inside was smoldering, refusing to ignite and release its heat. I looked at the pile of wood on the dressing room floor and picked up a large piece of birch bark, the miracle fuel of the north. Even though this birch bark was drenched, it would still catch fire. I peeled off a layer of the white outer skin, exposing the flesh-colored inner skin. I set the white paper skin below the log next to the few embers. It smoked for an instant, then burst into bright orange flame and slowly coaxed the larger log into action.

I wanted to peel back my own skin, too. My life felt as sodden and smoldering as the unburnt log. I had set together every condition for ignition, and something in me refused to burn. I was on this amazing adventure and I felt trapped. Not just because I was in a paper-thin clapboard shack. I felt trapped by this horrendous schedule that I had helped create so that we could include other people in our trip. A schedule that was like the life I had left behind, one that pushed us to keep moving regardless of what happened — bad weather, deep feelings, or magnificent scenery.

I carefully peeled off another layer of the birch. If I stuck too thick a piece of birch skin into the fire, it would be too wet, take too long to dry out, and not ignite the log fast enough.

What was the right thickness of my own skin to peel off to begin to free me from this overwhelming sense of oppression? I couldn't change the trip schedule. It was set. People had planned their vacations around meeting us at certain spots at certain times. I couldn't change the weather. I could only hope it would improve. I didn't have a clue how to begin effectively peeling away the forty-three-year-old skin of Ann Linnea Schimpf, Frank and Astrid's dutiful daughter, Dave's obliging wife.

We left our sauna home at 10 A.M. the next day in three- to five-foot seas, light rain, and patchy fog. I had carefully sprinkled some little glitter stars in the perfectly cleaned sauna, thereby thanking the absentee owners for their unknown gift. Twenty-four miles later, on Agate Bay Beach, I found myself again peeling layers of birch bark, coaxing a fire into life. Jon and Paul were off hunting for tourmaline intrusions. The moment we had pulled our boats onto the beach, Paul had begun to spot these rare and beautiful turquoise gems. He was a rock hound who believed he was driving an empty pickup truck, not a crammed-full sea kayak. At each of our six resupply places, Paul deposited a pile of rocks with whoever was meeting us so he could make room for fresh food supplies.

I didn't have the energy to look for rocks. I had just enough to put up my tent and make something hot to eat. I wanted to be sitting right here peeling birch bark, tending the fire, cooking a pot of rice and beans. I didn't understand why Paul and Jon weren't concerned with the details of setting up camp. I envied them their playfulness. I knew they were tired, too. Indeed, it was Jon who had suggested that we stop. He said he was cold, and ready for a rest. But they were off hunting for rocks without a thought about putting up their tents or eating.

I peeled off another layer of birch skin, carefully set it under the smoldering small logs I'd gathered from the beach, and blew steadily until the birch ignited. The water in the pot was now boiling, safely decontaminated. We purified drinking water with a handheld chemical filter, but we purified cooking water by boiling. Both methods removed bacterial and viral pathogens; neither removed chemical pollutants, which were a problem near the paper mills on the lake. I dropped in the dried rice and bean mixture Paul and I had so meticulously bagged a month ago, put on the lid, and rolled onto my side to stare into the flames.

I was making dinner for myself and these two men because I needed it, wanted it. But if I had been raised for forty-three years as a man, would my first thought upon landing on this beach be to cook, or to hunt for rocks? I wrote in my journal:

July 3

There is so much for me to learn. What I'm learning physically about the lake and weather and how to read waves occupies much of my thought process during the day. Clearly, Jon and Paul can paddle faster than I can. But I do think my skill level is equal to theirs in handling whatever rough paddling we encounter. Jon is a good teacher. He talks about waves wrapping around points or ricocheting off shallow bottoms as we're paddling in those conditions. I don't know if he means to teach or if he simply likes to chat while he paddles, but the conversation is very helpful to me.

But what I'm learning on land when I have some moments where I'm not focused on survival is the beginning of articulation about surviving the rest of my life. When we get to Rossport, I've got to talk to Paul about how exhausted I am, about some of the reflective things that are coming to me, about shaping this trip so those are a priority, too.

On July 4, I experienced both the exuberance of independence and the terror of nearly tipping. In the morning, as we rounded the corner between two islands just beyond Agate Bay and headed out onto an exposed stretch of open lake, we were greeted by five- to six-foot swells, the aftermath of the previous day's storm. A swell is a gentle, rolling, undulating wave. No whitecapping crest. Just a rounded, smooth top and a magnificent, concave trough. Troughs pull you down, down into their embrace, and then push you up, up to the next vista.

The ecstasy of swells is twofold: they are rare on She-Who-Is-The-Biggest, and even a neophyte paddler can handle big ones — five and six feet of pulsation. In the swells I was in control of every movement. It felt good to be so confident about paddling, and there was something about the sheer joy of smooth movement that knocked my emotions out of control. Tears came as I paddled. I let Her take me down, down — press me deep until I could not look up and see the heavens. Then I felt Her turn my face up again — lift my head from the azure water, to the mottled sky, to the broken depths of clouds. And just when I was highest, She sucked me back down into the trough of seduction. Over and over I was massaged deeper and deeper into the mystery of connection with this gigantic being.

The swells and broken sky lasted only thirty minutes before our course took us behind another large island. Then the skies darkened. Fog and heavy mist moved in. We stopped to listen to the weather-band radio and learned that another large storm was approaching, which could produce eight- to ten-foot seas on the open lake. We scuttled plans to paddle around the exposed south side of Saint Ignace Island and opted to head into the more sheltered waters of Nipigon Bay. By the time we reached the bay, strong, gusty northwest winds greeted us. Jon, with a rudder on his boat, happily played in the three- to four-foot surf of the quartering waves. Paul and I, without rudders, struggled to keep a straight course. Stroke, stroke, sweep. Stroke, stroke, sweep. Two quick, hard moves to set direction — one to the left, one to the right — then a broad, sweeping stroke to stabilize the boat from the sideswiping waves. At the time Paul and I purchased our Aquaterra Sea Lion kayaks, rudders were not commonly used. My decision not to have one specially added for the trip was foolish — a money-saving effort at the time, a body-beating decision overall. As one example, it's unlikely I would have experienced the stomach cramps that nearly took my life the first night of my solo had my boat had a rudder. Those cramps were produced by a combination of many large sweeping strokes (which wouldn't have been necessary with a rudder) and my lack of conditioning in the early part of the trip.

About twenty minutes into the routine, I reached to make the larger, sweep stroke when a huge wave caught the stern of my boat and turned it broadside. In the next instant I was engulfed in a wall of water. I do not remember bracing, but I must have because I ended right side up. My heart was pounding. My brain did not know if it should signal "paddle" or "rest." I had come within a split second of tipping over. I started paddling. Slowly. The panic raced, but my disciplined body went into athletic control again. Stroke, stroke, sweep. Stroke, stroke, sweep. My chant was now accompanied by a high descant, a voice that cried, "Paul, Jon, help me. I almost went over. God! Were you watching? I almost went over." Stroke, stroke, sweep. They weren't watching. They couldn't. They had to watch their own boats. I would have gone over and at least for a while they wouldn't have known.

I worked to keep up with Jon and Paul, but I had absolutely no confidence, no energy. I had almost tipped. Stroke, stroke, sweep. I was an animal now, disoriented, not sure where or how to land. I would keep going only because my instinct demanded it.

One moment the lake held me in ecstasy. The next moment I was in terror. This was no sweet lover. This was my father expecting me to learn by example, without instruction.

He had taken me high up into the mountains to fish with him when I was a six-year-old. I had watched him bait the hook, let the line glide into a calm pool, and then snap a trout into attention on the end of the line. I had tried to copy him, but fished in terror that my line would snag on a rock and I'd have to interrupt his concentration and ask for help. At age ten I had been the only girl on College Street allowed to cut the lawn with an open reel gasoline mower. I was proud. He criticized me for gouging down to the dirt on steep inclines. In my first year of high school I had brought home a report card with all A's, received a nod of approval, and was then admonished when I was caught still studying at midnight.

What had my father been doing to me? He was simply teaching me how to behave. He was trying as hard as he knew to be a good father. Teaching me to comply, conform, and obey, so that I might find safe passage through the immense, male-controlled world that I was growing into.

What was the lake doing to me? It was simply teaching me how to behave. It was neither evil nor good. It was demanding that I pay attention *all* the time.

Two teachers. One of my own choosing, one given to me. Both

stern taskmasters. Both unforgiving in their own way. One had launched me into the world of obedient wife and mother. Where was this one launching me?

I was less than one-third of the way around Lake Superior, assuredly considerably farther along than that in the decades of my life. I did want safe passage for the rest of both journeys. And I wanted something more. I wanted courage. Courage to live beyond a focus on survival and safety. Courage to claim the fullness that lay on the other side of security.

We paddled into the Rossport harbor about midday on July 5. Sunny skies and emerald-green waters delivered us back into civilization as though the past week of storm had been only another disturbing dream. As we stroked through the calm waters of the harbor, with its New England–style wooden homes neatly arranged on the hillside, the three of us talked about the trip. For Jon the journey was over. He complimented us on our skill and determination. We thanked him for his thoughtful presence and expertise. For Paul and me the journey was really just beginning.

5

Ancient Voices

*If one becomes utterly still, the earth will speak
in a language that can be understood.*

PAUL AND I WERE SITTING side by side on wooden chairs in
the hallway outside the dining room of the Rossport Inn. He had
just hung up the phone, ending our interview with Minnesota Public Radio.

"I couldn't help overhearing parts of your interview," said Ned,
the owner of the Rossport Inn, as he preceded us into the restaurant.
"It sounds like you guys have been on the trip from hell."

"It has been pretty rough," said Paul. "The weather hasn't given
us a single break."

"Well, it's got to get better, you know. It's July now." Ned handed
us menus and left us alone to select our dinners.

The dining hall was small, elegant. Numerous photos of the lake
hung on the walls. Each of the dozen or so tables was set with white
linen tablecloths and napkins and a full complement of silverware.
Paul and I, in our one change of rumpled, on-land clothes, sat in
contrast to the other diners, who had obviously taken their clothes out
of a suitcase instead of a stuff sack. "I'm treating," I told him. "We've
got to fatten up. Eat whatever you want. We're celebrating. We've
made it one-third of the way around the lake!" We ordered a pitcher of
dark Canadian beer and two Lake Superior whitefish dinners.

"I think Ned is right," began Paul. "Things have got to get better.
We've seen the worst of the weather."

Buoyed up by my first shower in eight days, I, too, felt optimistic. But I was also determined to share the fear and doubt I had experienced on the last leg of the journey. On my part of the radio interview, I had spoken about the grandeur and immensity of the land we had just paddled through. I had talked about our humility, about realizing our smallness in the scheme of things. But this was not a radio interview, this was a talk with a friend with whom I had chosen to share the most profound, dangerous experience of my life. I took a long sip from the huge mug of beer. "Paul, this last leg of the trip was so brutal, I began to doubt whether I'd be able to finish."

"Really?" His blue eyes looked at me, startled. I felt like the rabbit who finally musters up enough courage for the dash out of its hole and across the open expanse of lawn to the garden, but takes one step and finds a fox at the burrow entrance. I was trying to get past my long-held belief that trippers don't admit they have thoughts of failure in the middle of a journey, that to admit doubt is to open the door to failure. Paul was as stunned by my comments as the fox who has no idea he is resting at the entrance to a rabbit hole.

"At night, when we've safely made camp, my optimism returns. Like right now. I'm clean, off the water for a few hours, and ready to think about paddling again tomorrow. But, God, sometimes in the middle of the day when I'm so cold, when I see you and Jon off in the distance like two specks because I'm so slow, I think, I'm crazy to be doing this. I came for some leisure, some soul-searching time. My body aches constantly. I've lost fifteen pounds."

"I had no idea you were feeling that much doubt," he said.

A rabbit is taught not to trust a fox, to run when contact is made. I had been taught not to trust my feelings, to push through them if they tried to stop me. Paul and I stared at each other, held the gaze. We were meeting as friends of many years. This was our first moment alone together since June 20. For fifteen of the first twenty days of the trip we had either paddled solo or been in the company of friends. The moment hung suspended between us. It was another turning point in our friendship, a moment like the summer of 1987.

Paul and I had just bought a couple of used river kayaks from a youth camp where we had taught a family Sense of Wonder workshop. We knew little about kayaking. We were excited as we launched the orange and white handmade boats off the shore of Park Point that calm August day.

After an hour of paddling, Paul asked, "What do you suppose it would take to paddle all the way around the lake?" I threw back my head and laughed. Then I looked at him. His five-foot-nine-inch frame was comfortably resting in the kayak. Same kayak, same frame as my own. His blue eyes often have a mischievous smile. But his eyes were serious. He was not laughing.

"Paul, we don't know anything about kayaking. This is the most dangerous lake on the planet," I replied. He just held my gaze and smiled. Same look, same smile he had after our long talk about the possibility of home-schooling our children together. Same look, same smile he had given me after several years of unsuccessful searching to find a publisher for our children's book.

We did home-school our children together. Our book was published and has won several national awards. And here we are, paddling around the lake together.

I broke the silence. "I want to be able to do the whole trip, Paul, but I'm scared sometimes by how shaken my confidence gets."

The waiter appeared, balancing our dinner one-handed on a large tray. It was so luxurious to have someone place a fancy plate full of food in front of me. After the waiter left, Paul said, "So, can you remember what to do with more than one utensil?"

I laughed. "No, and I don't know how to eat a meal that has different courses to it, either." We fell silent for a while, relishing the good food, thankful for its careful preparation, grateful to be warm enough to eat slowly. After a time, I became conscious that I was nourishing myself for the next thought. The wrong thought, the wrong move, and we would again become fox and rabbit. It is so common in friendships to muster up enough courage to say the hard things and then retreat before the real change, the real essence, is reached.

"Paul, I want to keep going. I don't expect you to take care of me, but I do depend on you, like you depend on me. What

I'm trying to say is, I'm out on the edge of what is physically possible for me."

He leaned forward in his chair, moving closer to me. "I'm not sure why, but my body does seem to bounce back faster than yours. These long days have changed from being grueling to invigorating for me. But I hear you and I want to help you work this out." He reached across the table and laid his callused hand on top of mine.

I picked it up and stroked the palm. "I can't believe it! How can you have this many calluses already! Feel my hand. I don't have any."

He turned my hand over, stroked it, and said, "See, each of us is having a hard time in our own way. I've had to wear a wrist guard. Your wrists are fine. We bring different strengths. This is simply a damned difficult trip. We will help each other do this!" He reached for his mug of beer. I reached for mine. "To the rest of the trip!" he said as we clanged the steins together. And that was the extent of our communication. I had said I was afraid and exhausted. He had said he wasn't, offered a few sentences of encouragement. We went on with these few words as the only rope between us — our lifeline.

It was 9 p.m. by the time we finished eating. We retired immediately to our respective abodes: me to a one-room cabin next to the inn, Paul to his tent on the lawn outside my cabin. "This is where I belong now, Ann. I feel most comfortable outside. The one thing I will miss tonight, though, is the lake. I don't think I can hear her up here on the hill."

Lying in the cabin bed, I let myself moan with pleasure at its softness. My kayak had room only for a thin foam sleeping pad. Most of the ground we had been pitching our tents on was rocky and uneven. The hunched-over position of kayaking, the double S curve of the scoliosis in my spine, and the harsh sleeping conditions had put my back into a state of permanent discomfort. The soft bed was the luxurious embrace I could not get from anyone. It felt so good that tears trickled from the corners of my eyes.

The conversation with Paul seemed to have gone well. It was a start at breaking down the defenses between us. By most people's standards — indeed, by our own — we had an extraordinary friendship. But in the remaining weeks of the trip and the months following it, we would cross bridges together that we didn't yet know two people could pass over in tandem.

There had been no mail for me. The phone conversation with Dave and the kids had been mostly about the toxic spill in Duluth. An oil tanker railroad car had derailed and crashed off a bridge, releasing dangerous benzene gas that had caused a major evacuation of the city. I had thought little about their safety, had assumed the concern of their lives would be details like cooking, how to entertain themselves, whom to play with. I was shocked, drawn out of preoccupation with my own fear about the lake's brutality and into larger awareness of the world around me.

Life is fragile everywhere on this planet. There is no security in being a child living in a city where dangerous cargo is transported, nor is there security in being a fish swimming in a river beneath railroad cars carrying benzene. I thought to myself, we have no assurance that our dreams will be realized. No assurance even that we will be physically safe from one day to the next. All we have is right now. And right now I was on a search to come into enough of my own power to know how to claim this deep inner longing to understand my own life purpose.

And right now I was also away from my children. Far away. They were apparently safe in their own beds this evening, much as I was safe in mine. But I missed them tonight. This journey demanded that the focus of my life energy be on survival and claiming my longing. I had to let go of my lifeline to the children, had to trust their father to give them the protection and sustenance they needed. But on learning that their very safety had been in jeopardy, a storm-size wave of loneliness engulfed me. My eyes wandered to the little altar I'd made on the dresser next to my bed. A candle, the earth marble, a stone from an earlier campsite, pictures of the children. I rose, lit the candle, burned some sage, and breathed the smoke, letting it cleanse the dark thoughts and fears out of my body, feeling the invisible energy move around and within each cell.

I instinctively dropped to my knees and folded my hands together below my chin. The posture brought my childhood prayer to
mind: "Now I lay me down to sleep, I pray the Lord my soul to keep.
If I should die before I wake, I pray the Lord my soul to take." Not
the prayer of a woman determined to change the course of her life. I
had never been very eloquent about prayer. Christina led the prayers
in our women's circles, and we didn't pray in Quaker meeting; we
simply shared silence.

After the children's arrival, I had begun to search for a way to
return to organized religion so they might experience a formal faith
community. I looked first to the Methodist and Congregational
churches of my youth, but could not reconcile my own growth with
some of their formal liturgy. The Quakers proved to be a philosophi-
cal and social match.

But here I was, on my knees, wanting to pray. I felt as tentative as
I did paddling after the near tip yesterday. "Holy One, I have decided
to keep going. I'm scared about this. I'm scared for myself, for my
family, for my friends. I don't even know why I must keep going. I
just must. Help me to be safe. It is as important to me to be safe as it
is to find whatever I'm searching for. It won't do anyone much good
if I end up dead. And I could, you know. I have learned that in these
past few weeks. I proceed with new caution, but I do proceed. And I
need reassurance that I'm not alone. I thank you for the presence of
Betty's angel, for my ability to feel you in the beauty and wildness of
the lake, for the way you resonate in my belly. Help me to listen to
those signs, to grow in my own spirituality. Thanks. Thanks for
listening to me."

I crawled back into bed, pulled the covers up to my chin, and
slept the longest sleep of the entire trip. I awoke to the sound of Paul
knocking on my door eight hours later. It was his longest sleep of
the trip, too. Without the omnipresence of the lake breathing next to
us, keeping us alert and solely focused on when, how, and where to
travel, we both had been able to succumb to fatigue.

It was to be a wonderful day of paddling together: sunshine,
fifty-degree temperatures, only a slight amount of wind. Late

morning, Paul said, "Hey, what do you say we take a secchi disk reading?"

"Great!" I responded, looking at the map on my deck. "How about off the next point? Our charts say the water there is supposed to be more than a hundred feet deep."

For the third time on the trip we fulfilled our duties as Lake Superior Lake Watch volunteers. We were supposed to take a clarity reading on the lake every day between 10 A.M. and 2 P.M., but the reading required calm seas — a rare occurrence thus far. The procedure entailed Paul's lowering the one-foot diameter, black-and-white secchi disk over the edge of his kayak on a rope. I then leaned way over in my kayak, hanging on to his kayak for support, to peer into the water and discern the exact point where the disk became invisible to my surface-dwelling eyes.

On this day Paul said, "Ann, can you really still see that disk? I hardly have any rope left!"

"Yeah, it's still down there." When I could no longer see the disk, Paul marked the spot on the rope and hoisted it up. Fifty-five feet! The water was so clear that I could see the circular disk fifty-five feet below us. By contrast, our previous two readings had been twenty-two and twenty-four feet. The deepest reading from any of the hundreds of volunteer lake watchers in the previous two years of record keeping had been forty-five feet! Our journey was taking us to some of the most pristine parts of the lake.

About 5 P.M. we agreed to begin looking for a camp spot. As we paddled into a sheltered bay, Paul said, "Ann, something feels different about this place. Let's pull our boats up and look around before we unload anything."

He helped me muscle my boat up the steep, cobble embankment to a first small terrace, then I helped him with his boat. The light-colored granite cobbles had all been worn to cantaloupe shape by the wave action on this exposed beach. It was like walking up an inclined plane lined with huge marbles. The boats slid easily, but we had almost no footing.

I sat down to rest. "Let's go see what's on that upper terrace," said

Paul. We took off life jackets, paddling jackets, and spray skirts. The fifteen-foot-wide terrace we were on and the steep bank leading to the next bench were held in place by large-watermelon-size angular boulders that clearly had been beyond the reach of the waves' greatest eroding powers. Together we hopped gingerly from one boulder to the next until we reached the top. "Oh, my God!" I said, cresting the ridge.

A pile of rocks stacked ten feet high and four feet around loomed against the early evening sky like a miniature Stonehenge. We glanced at each other for permission to approach. I moved carefully across the ten yards of loose, ankle-grabbing boulders separating me from this ancient altar. If it hadn't been for the cloud of mosquitoes that descended on us as soon as we got over the embankment and away from the lake breeze, my demeanor would have been that of a pilgrim approaching a shrine. But even with the distraction of bugs, the sensation in my belly dropped me into the same prayer space as it had in the comfort of my little cabin the night before.

"I can't tell how old it is," said Paul, fingering the rocks. "Some of them are covered with lichens and some of them are not. These rocks are not the rounded, light-colored cobbles we pulled the boats over. They're clearly part of the darker, more angular rocks that are all over the top of this last terrace."

The mosquitoes and blackflies were so thick that it was impossible to stand still without constantly waving our hands. Our immediate physical needs took precedence over discovery and reverence. We scampered back down the steep embankment, began unloading our boats, and pulled out our bug head-nets.

We couldn't camp near our boats. There was nothing but boulders to pitch a tent on. The only place I could find to erect mine was a tiny, rocky niche wedged in the tangle of vegetation along the perimeter of the huge boulder field that held the giant stone altar. It took two trips across the treacherous terrain to ferry everything from my boat to the tent site. I laid everything neatly in a row: the clothing bag, the tent bag, the sleeping bag, the sleeping pad. The constant buzzing of insects outside my head-net made me feel as

though I was trapped inside a cylinder filled with a strange electronic field that emitted a relentless, high-pitched *hmmmmmm*. The
only exposed skin the irritants could bite was my hands, but that
was a minor assault compared to the constant pinpricks to my san-
ity. I kept swatting my hands against my thighs as I struggled to
bend the tent poles and thread them through their nylon sleeves.
Once standing, the tent didn't really fit between the small trees.

While I was struggling with branches, a thought came into my
mind: "Ask them."

"Ask them what?" I wondered.

The thought had come forward suddenly and boldly, almost like
some giant hand grabbing my jacket and shaking me to attention.
"Ask them what?" I said aloud.

The hum of insects grew louder because I was not moving. The
voice in my mind returned: "Ask them for permission to camp here."
I was shocked by the clarity of the thought, confused by its meaning. I stood still in the electronic buzzing, waiting for more direction. The next insight surfaced as intuition, not clear voice — I was
to ask permission from the ancient spirits of this place to camp here.

I bent to open the large yellow gear bag. The mosquitoes and
blackflies followed my every movement. I found the yellow altar
pouch, took out some sage, put it on a flat rock, and knelt beside it
with a match. "Please, may the ancient ones recognize the kinship of
our spirits," I prayed aloud. At first the buzzing outside my head-net
kept me agitated, made my mind race: Set up the tent, return to the
boats where the bugs aren't so bad, cook dinner, it's getting late. But
then I breathed deeply, closing my eyes and ears.

It was so quiet. No urgency of physical needs, no awareness of
time or place. Just quiet and darkness in the temple. Breath, there
was breath in the temple. Breath of life now and long ago. Air coming in, air going out. Waves coming in, waves going out. People
coming here, people leaving here. People then and now, not so different. Each of us finding our way the best we can: making altars on
the land, harvesting wood and berries, drinking water. Kinship. I
was not alone on this journey. Many before me had sought a right

relationship with the land. Many after me will seek the same. In the temple of my thoughts I prayed for steadiness of course.

While cooking supper over a driftwood fire, I told Paul that I had asked permission of the ancient spirits of this land to camp here. His blue eyes searched mine, then he said, "Thank you." We ate in the communion of silence. After a simple rinsing of dishes in warm water, we donned our head-nets and scrambled up to the immense rock altar. We paused again in front of it in silent tribute, then set about exploring the acre-size boulder field for other indications of ancient people's presence. The dark, lichen-covered boulders were illuminated by a nearly full moon. I wore heavy-soled hiking boots, teal wind pants, yellow waterproof parka, and head-net, but I imagined myself in moccasins, leggings, and leather tunic.

The only other time in my life that I could remember feeling connected like this to the ancient spirit of a place was in 1988 on my second three-month camping trip to the desert southwest with my children. Brian and Sally had been eight and five. We had hiked four miles down to the bottom of Canyon de Chelly in northeast Arizona. It was midday, mid-April. The children were sitting on the edge of a silt-laden river, gathering dark clay from the riverbank and molding a whole collection of bowls and pots. Several tourists wandered by and photographed the little dark-skinned, muddy Koreans. One of them said, "Isn't that cute. Indian children today are still making pottery."

I, the white mother, was sitting ten yards away in the shade of a giant cottonwood. Behind me scores of tourists were walking through the thousand-year-old White House adobe ruins. Across the shallow river was a hogan with a Navajo woman standing outside feeding her sheep. Looming above us on all sides were the eight-hundred-foot, sheer red sandstone cliffs of this reservation.

The red cliffs were washed with streaks of brown, beige, and ocher. Portions of the cliffs had broken off, leaving sculpted faces and forms that steadfastly watched over the valley. Cliffs that had stood guard over children making clay forms on the riverbank for thousands of years. Cliffs that held the clay adobe bricks of pueblos and kivas placed there generations ago by skilled brown hands. Cliffs whose comforting presence gave me the feeling that an old, trusted friend stood near. I felt that we were totally, utterly safe. A sense of gratitude as deep as the canyon filled my soul.

Here on this cold July 6 evening in southern Ontario I felt that same sense of companionship, comfort, safety, gratitude. That same connection to indigenous wisdom. I sat down on a large gray, lichen-covered boulder and looked back toward the stone altar. When I feel safe, when I arrive home in the womb of earth from which I was born, there is no filter between myself and universal wisdom. In this secret place beyond the reach of mosquitoes and night chill, I began to glimpse my life purpose, my connectedness to all things past and present. It was a fleeting glance, like a deer startled at the edge of a clearing who quickly disappears into the safety of brush. But I know I saw it.

Something was shifting inside me. It was barely discernible, like the wind shift from northwest to west, like the day from dusk into total darkness. I could not give voice to it. Could only become it — dusk creature . . . dawn creature . . . primitive self.

6

The Longest Day

When we are stripped of everything, and stand like a young tree
in the dead of winter enduring relentless subzero blasts,
the tether to life is tenuous. We must trust,
hold on, wait for the earth to warm.

TWENTY-FOUR MILES and one day beyond the ancient altar, we set up camp on a tiny rock island and were awakened by a severe, predawn thunderstorm. At first it was easy to ignore the rumbling as some distant figment of my imagination or ancient drumbeat in my dream. But a sudden loud clap of thunder followed by a flash of lightning and another loud report jolted me into an upright position. I couldn't remember where I was. Were the boats secured? Had we covered up some wood? What time was it? I was the firefighter awakened from deep sleep by the alarm bell, and I was instant action.

Check the watch: 5 A.M.

Assess the situation: Dawn, a thunderstorm that will pass quickly.

Make a plan: Take down the tent. Keep it dry. Get under the tarp and get a fire going for breakfast, because we have scheduled a long paddling day.

Within ten minutes I had my tent down and put away, my sleeping bag stuffed, my ground pad rolled up, and all spare clothing in gear bags. By the time rain was making the transition from big, intermittent, warning drops to serious, steady torrent, I had moved the last piece of gear under the tarp.

Such a simple piece of equipment that tarp was: a piece of navy-blue waterproof nylon, eight feet by ten feet, with a few grommet holes for tying. Properly secured to trees, the tarp provided a shelter as essential as a tent in this country of eternal dampness: a dry outdoor kitchen, a storage shed, an annex beyond the claustro-phobia of a tent. We didn't always pitch it; indeed, it was often too difficult to pitch because we camped on shores devoid of trees tall enough to hoist it. But when rain was predicted, as it had been last night, we usually took the time to raise it.

I easily started a fire with the sticks of dry driftwood we had stored the night before. Our fire ring remained mostly dry, while water ran off in a steady river on the low-pitched end of the tarp. I set the charcoal-blackened coffeepot on the ground below the rain river. It was full in minutes. It was a nice change to be collecting rainwater instead of filtering lake water. Virtually all of our water came directly from the lake. Our hand filters pumped the water through a microscopic screen that removed any bacteria, but yester-day paddling around a paper mill in Jackfish Bay, we had collected no water, had simply reduced our usual intake until we were miles past the plant. Hand filters do not remove toxic chemicals.

While watching the storm I kept feeding the fire. The rain was coming down so fast and the wind blowing so hard that only the tarp area next to the scrubby alders remained absolutely free of windblown rain. It was damp around the edges of the fire pit, but the fire was large enough not to be threatened. I reached to pick up the pot of rainwater and nestled it close against the orange-red flames. When the rain receded to a drizzle, I walked over to wake Paul in his tent.

He had been writing in his journal by flashlight. "I'll be right out," he said. His tent was perched atop a giant patch of sphagnum moss in a tight cluster of windswept fir trees about fifty yards from the rain tarp. In the darkness of the early morning storm I was careful as I picked my way across rain-slicked boulders dotted with slippery mosses. I had no sooner sat down on a dry, granite boulder next to the fire than Paul appeared.

I grabbed a handful of oatmeal mixture from a plastic bag, plopped it into the bottom of my sturdy wooden bowl, and set the bowl carefully down between two cobbles. Next I stretched the sleeve of Betty's gray jacket down over my right hand as a pot holder, lifted the hot water pot from the edge of the fire, and peered into it with a flashlight. It was boiling. I poured some water into Paul's cup and then into my bowl.

My round, broad spoon stirred the water into the oats, expanding and dissolving them. I was amazed how easily the oats and brown sugar united with truly hot water. They made a cereal, not our usual paste. Most mornings we didn't have a fire and simply poured the hot water from our thermoses into the oats. The routine we'd established was simple and efficient: fill our thermoses with hot water at night, make oatmeal in the morning, have some lukewarm water left for instant soup during the day. That way we didn't take more than five or ten minutes for breakfast and could be on the water paddling earlier.

But this morning we didn't have a choice. There was still lightning and thunder close by and it was raining. The elements were forcing us to eat in leisure rather than pushing us to get under way before they got worse. I was fascinated by the process of stirring and then chewing my oatmeal. I realized how little I had thought about the ambience of eating on the trip; mostly, it had become the automatic consumption of necessary calories to pour into an always empty tank. It felt so good not to rush. I made myself a second bowl.

By the time we each had stowed our dozen gear bags and were pushing our boats out of the tiny harbor in the middle of our rock island, it was 6:30 A.M. I felt cautious about the descending fog and three- to five-foot seas, but confident and optimistic.

"We need to take a compass bearing to cross this bay," said Paul. "The way the fog is swirling around, we may not be able to see the other side once we get halfway across."

I paddled over to raft up with him. We aimed our boats at the point on the other side of the bay we wanted to reach. Since our compasses were mounted on our decks, we could simply aim at

135 degrees south and east. With the waves we knew we could easily go off course ten degrees or more, so we decided always to keep the boats headed at 135 degrees or less. A direct heading of 145 degrees and we would miss the end of the bay and head out into the open lake.

Paul had been right. About twenty minutes into the crossing, the predicted blanket of fog descended and wrapped us in a gray cocoon. The distant shore became a wishful thought. We moved our boats to within twenty feet of one another and watched the compasses on our decks and each other as we stroked. Sometimes it was hard to keep the compass right on 135 degrees. A large wave coming in strong from the southeast would catch the bow of my boat, and the compass needle would swing wildly between 120 and 150 degrees. A steady course at the former reading and we would find ourselves too close to a shore with big waves breaking. A steady course at the latter and we would miss land altogether. Our lives depended on our eighty-dollar mounted compasses and our steadfastness in believing them.

"I think I hear waves breaking," said Paul after an hour. By our estimation, Ashburton Bay was five miles across and we were paddling at three miles per hour. I stopped stroking momentarily, to hear the waves, to have reassurance that this first open water crossing in the fog had not doomed us to the clutches of the open lake. I heard a distant but distinctive sound of waves breaking against something firm. My mind calculated: one hour, three miles per hour; we were little more than halfway across. Why should we hear waves breaking now?

"How are we going to know if those are waves on shoals or waves on the shore?" I yelled to Paul.

"Your guess is as good as mine," he responded. He stopped paddling and looked at the plastic-encased map fixed to the deck in front of him. "The map doesn't show any big shoals, but we have to keep our eyes open for the first sign of anything different from gray water and gray sky."

Since we were new at open water and foggy crossings, our ears were not yet trained to calculate distance by sound. However, in the weeks of foggy weather ahead, our senses of hearing would continue to become more finely tuned and developed, until they were like radar. This subtle evolution back into ancient wisdom would be as important to our day-to-day survival as plastic boats and metal compasses. We paddled for a long time, listening to the sound of breaking waves grow steadily louder, peering ahead of our boats for the first sign of something different from flat gray. Then, for an instant, I thought I saw the dark, looming silhouette of land. But as quickly as I saw it, the vision retreated. I looked at Paul; he was looking at me. We nodded. He'd seen it, too.

The gray-black images of rocky shore and trees appeared and disappeared and finally became clearly visible to us. We turned our boats southward (180 degrees) to follow the shoreline around Guse Point. Our maps told us this shoreline was Neys Provincial Park, but the fog was so thick, we could see no sign of roads or picnic shelters or overlooks. We kept peering straight ahead, hoping to see Pic Island, an immense, towering island four miles long by two miles wide, with hills several hundred feet high, that was located south of Guse Point. We had seen and admired Pic Island from our campsite six miles away the night before. But this morning the fog had devoured it.

We kept paddling in the choppy water, keeping the mysterious, swirling image of disappearing and reappearing rocks and trees on our left side. Shortly, I noticed that my compass needle was beginning to shift from south to east, that the waves were increasing in size, that there was wind on my right cheek. My eyes had not seen a point, had not told me we had gone around anything and switched directions, but the compass, the waves, and the sensation of wind on my cheeks clearly told of change.

On a sunny day, I can see where land comes to a point and then bends in another direction. Even if the point is large and round, on a clear day I know when I've gone around it because the scenery changes. I get a peek in a different direction. But in dense fog, when I paddle around a point, there is no change in view — just the same gray wall pressing in on all sides.

To have my eyes registering one truth — we had not rounded Guse Point — and to have my other senses registering the opposite — we had rounded the point — was disorienting and scary. I did not feel in control and I did not like it. My confidence was like the big rocks on the shore next to me: being smashed by relentless, cold waves and obscured by low, swirling fog.

A light drizzle began to fall. Water droplets collected on my eyelashes, further frustrating my vision and confidence. I became so impatient with the eternal imprisonment of the fog that I looked to Paul for some reassurance.

"Paul, now that we've rounded Guse Point you don't think we could miss Foster Island do you? There are so many islands here." I needed him to tell me that we had indeed come around Guse Point and that my reading of the map of what lay ahead was correct, but I did not say that. Instead I was pretending, bluffing, keeping us from really becoming a team.

We were paddling side by side, still about twenty feet apart. I looked over at his dark blue boat. Actually, it was never his boat I saw first — it was his bright yellow life jacket. He had a dark boat and a bright jacket. I had a bright boat and a dark jacket. I knew he was easier to see at a distance, that it would have been safer for me to have bought a new, bright jacket. But safety is as much a frame of mind as it is a piece of equipment. The faded green vest that had safely carried Betty through so many white-water kayak and canoe trips was like a good luck charm for me. It kept me safe from harm during the day; the old gray fleece jacket kept me warm at night. It was important to me to be companioned on the journey by more than her ashes.

Paul was checking his watch and looking at his map. Both our maps were covered with water droplets, making them difficult to read. He had his gray hat pulled tightly over his eyes, so I couldn't read his expression, but I felt his exasperation at me for verbalizing his own doubts.

He shouted his response above the wind and waves. "I don't think we'll miss Foster Island. By my calculations and our usual speed, we should be hitting the island's shore within the next twenty minutes."

It was the most assurance I could hope for, but it did little to mitigate my fear. My mind wanted to obscure the truth: I had never paddled in fog this dense, for this long, and neither had Paul.

Fortunately, the inland passage between Foster Island and the mainland turned out to be obvious: a channel nearly thirty feet across. We paddled our boats onto the rocky shore of the island, which was completely protected from the southeast winds. I was desperate to pee and rest. The feel of solid earth beneath my feet, the sight of smooth, wet, granite boulders scattered in the channel like grazing hippos, the sound of rain dripping from alder brush decorated with lacy spiderwebs all buoyed my spirits. I peed, pulled soup mix out of the lunch bag, measured a spoonful into my thermos cup, poured water made hot just six hours earlier. The euphoria was brief. As I finished the last drop of soup, I began to shiver. Ten minutes without the exertion of paddling and already I was cold.

I walked over to Paul, who was studying his map and drinking soup. He looked at me and shook his head. "We can't camp here," he said. "It's either bedrock or dense shrub, and we can't follow the contours of the bay's shoreline — too risky, with incoming waves. We've got to do another open-water crossing."

The bay separating us from Marathon, Ontario, was six to seven miles across. There were islands and shoals. The fog was dense and seas were building. It was a risky decision even for seasoned paddlers. I laid the edge of my map on his as a straightedge. We drew a line from the tip of Foster Island to an unnamed island near Marathon and determined its compass reading from the rose on our navigation chart. Once again, 135 degrees was the magic number.

"Okay, let's go for it," I said, and turned toward my boat. I stepped into the forty-plus-degree water, shivered as it filled each kayak bootie, put my weight on my paddle's shaft, and skillfully hopped into the boat. While fiddling with connecting the spray skirt to the lip of the cockpit, my eyes paused on the purple "Grace Happens" sticker on my deck. It made me think of Christina, of her christening ceremony for the boat, of her blessing for my trip. I was reminded of all the friends who were keeping us in their prayers this summer. I hoped they were praying this day — this specific day, when it was probably sunny in Minneapolis, Boise, and Tucson. I remembered the warm sleeping bag this morning, the tent I had so carefully kept dry, the fire, the two bowls of oatmeal. There would be a place like that this evening. My hope permitted prayer: "Holy One, keep me steady and alert. Paul needs me and I need him and we cannot make mistakes."

I backpaddled off the protected shore and pointed *Grace* into the narrow channel that led to the bay and the city our chart promised was there. I steeled myself for two more hours of holding concentration on keeping the boat upright, reading the compass at 135 degrees, and listening for the sound of breaking waves that could mean the opposite shore, a dangerous midcrossing shoal, or an island that signaled the proximity of the city of Marathon. Eventually, of course, my mind tired of the intense, exhaustive effort. It wandered to another long, gray, difficult day. The day I took Betty for the last mountain hike of her life.

It had been five months since her first liver-cancer operation in Salt Lake City. Five months, several surgeries, numerous radiation treatments, and many setbacks. But when we headed to Zion National Park in southern Utah in early February 1990, the disease was in remission and she had been walking a mile every day for two weeks.

We rose early in our motel room. She packed wool hats, gloves, down jackets, water bottles, peanut butter and jelly sandwiches on homemade pocket bread, camera, and binoculars in her green Frostline day pack. We set off up the "easy, one-and-a-half mile" trail to the lower Emerald Pool, rested and eager for our first adventure since the day before her first surgery.

The winter sun was high, but not yet high enough to radiate to the bottom of the narrowest canyons. The mouth of the canyon we entered, however, was ablaze with the sun's winter warmth — a tantalizing kind of heat that can only be caught by dark clothing or reflecting rock walls. We stopped often to identify birds, like green-tailed towhees and Steller's jays, and to admire verdant sprigs of growth emerging from late-lying snowbanks. Lunch was leisurely. We sat next to the aquamarine waters of the pool. Betty had been walking slowly, but steadily. She was optimistic, talking of possibly being able to take some more outdoor trips if the remission persisted. While we were sitting, afternoon clouds covered the sun, and immediately, the temperature dropped. We slipped on our down jackets and our gloves and caps, finished our sandwiches, and began hiking out.

The grayer the sky became, the slower Betty walked. Her mood and her stamina seemed to correspond directly to the arriving ridge of low pressure. Within ten minutes, she went from a normal walking gait to a labored placing of one foot in front of the other. Within fifteen minutes it became clear to me that she might not be able to make it all the way out.

"Betty, I can still carry Brian and he weighs one hundred pounds." (Her cancer had reduced her from 140 to 90 pounds.) There was no answer. She kept plodding along until she simply stopped. Her hunched-over, stocking-capped figure turned around. Hazel eyes gazed at me from behind professorial spectacles. They were not the eyes of confidence and challenge I had known and sometimes feared during the twelve years of our friendship. They were defeated, scared, lost.

"I can't do it, Annie. I can't go any farther."

"Will you accept a ride?" I asked.

"Please," she said. I set the pack down by the side of the dirt path, bent over, and she climbed onto my back. I staggered a bit under the weight, but slowly I gained momentum and began the half-mile trudge to the trail head. We were the only ones on the trail that bleak, cold afternoon. No words passed between us. I could not think of the weight, could not think of her frailness, just kept pushing on, pushing on, knowing her life depended on me.

As the steel-gray weight of fog and mist and waves pressed down on my paddling arms, I remembered that hike with Betty. I knew I had tremendous ability to endure physical pain, to push myself to do whatever was required. The memory boosted my confidence on this day when I would come to understand how Betty felt the moment she said, "Please."

The sounds of breaking water came to our ears about fifteen minutes before we saw land. Reasoning that we must find the southernmost island and then head east to the harbor of Marathon, Ontario, we paddled south along this shore until it ended. Seeing no more land, we guessed that this indeed was the southernmost island — a perfect piece of navigation, seven miles through dense fog and high seas exactly to the point we had set our compasses for. We then headed the boats southeast to find the mainland.

Within about twenty minutes we heard a low buzzing sound. Puzzled, I kept peering ahead into the endless, impenetrable wall for a vision to explain this strange noise. Almost instantly I saw the silhouettes of smokestacks. Soon I could see a bulldozer pushing at industrial debris. The acrid smell of sulfur permeated the air. The shore was littered with old railroad ties, steel cables, and slowly seeping streams of rainwater and sludge. The fog had delivered us to a paper mill!

Anger replaced my exhaustion. This wasn't on our maps. This could not be Lake Superior. There was no vegetation, no animals, no clear water. Who was responsible for this desecration? I wanted to know, wanted to exercise my years of skill as a National Audubon Society grass-roots activist, and get this place cleaned up.

When we had paddled by Jackfish Bay, we had seen the paper mill smokestacks at a distance. Almost scenic puffs of white smoke were coming from them. We were far enough away not to smell them and not to see any obvious clarity change in the water. We believed the cautions about the danger of organochlorines within a ten-mile radius, but our senses didn't sound ALARM as they did here within visceral range of the plant.

Lake Superior is the cleanest of the Great Lakes, a blue-colored gem. But there are tarnished spots along the perimeter of the gem where industry and population have gathered. Places where insidious, invisible chemicals linger out of reach of the lake's natural recycling mechanisms like rotten apples in the bottom of the barrel. Without careful attention by local and national/international groups, Superior will lose her "Shining Big-Sea-Water" status.

"We have the option of paddling up this shore toward what should be the town of Marathon or heading on to Pukaskwa," said Paul.

"I need a pee break. Let's stop and study our maps and then decide. All I know is I'm not stopping anywhere near here. This is horrible!" I peed discreetly behind a pile of scrap logs, about fifty yards from the bulldozer. Actually, it was so foggy I doubt the operator would have seen me if I had squatted in front of him. It made me feel contaminated just standing on the shore. Paul figured it was still well over a dozen miles to Pukaskwa Provincial Park — too far to go in the four remaining hours of daylight. Neither of us was optimistic about the possibility of finding a campground along the public waterfront of Marathon. Our only option seemed to be to continue. From the map it looked like we might be able to camp about halfway to Pukaskwa at a place where there was a small, protected bay with a river flowing into it.

We estimated two hours more paddling. I could do that. Paul was tired, too; we wouldn't be paddling fast. Seas were no longer building, just steady at three to five feet. We pushed off into the murky water and once again moved our bodies into cadence: Pull with the blade, push with the foot, pull with the other blade, push with the other foot. Pull. Push. Pull. Push.

As soon as the sound of the bulldozer and the sight of the smokestacks faded, the ache in my arms and back flared up again. Exhaustion overwhelmed my anger. I tried thinking of what the campsite might look like: a source of good water, trees for pitching the rain fly, flat, sandy places to pitch the tents. I imagined pulling out my completely dry tent, getting water boiling quickly, and having a big spaghetti dinner for supper. This little diversionary game would work for a while, but then my arms and shoulders would begin to throb and demand my attention. I would stop paddling, look at the swirling fog around the solid rock shoreline, see Paul paddling ahead, then say out loud, "You have no choice. Keep going." The cycle would begin again.

Finally we paddled into that promised little bay with the river flowing out of it. It was a mud-flat swamp. I stepped out of my boat. My kayaking booties sank eight inches into the muck. I struggled to pull the boat forward, out of the shallow, murky water. There were no trees, no boulders, just mud flats. No place to stoop and pee in privacy. It didn't matter, I didn't care. I had no modesty, no dignity. I just stripped off layer after layer and peed right next to my boat not more than ten feet from Paul.

"I don't see any option except to keep going to the park," he said in defeat when I looked at him.

"Shit. . . ." I turned my back and walked a ways down the mud flats. Tears were running down my cheeks. "God, help me," I said to the swamp. I remembered clanging beer steins with Paul just three days earlier. The clang of commitment. Paul didn't need me to cry. I'm sure he felt rotten, too. I turned around and walked back to him.

"I can do this," I said. "But I am really, really exhausted. I don't think I've ever been this exhausted in my life, so I need to be careful. If you can take the lead navigating in the fog, I'll hold my own paddling."

"I can do that." He didn't say how he was. I didn't ask.

As we pushed off, we began our eleventh hour of paddling. The only way my body would function was for my mind to shut down all its connections to nerve endings. Left with nothing else to do, my mind remembered another long, gray day I had shared with Betty.

She was visiting our family at Christmas. We had not yet adopted Sally. Brian had only been with us for nine months. A baby-sitting co-op enabled me to manage a part-time work schedule. One day a week I took care of six two-year-olds. Four days a week I had five hours to myself. Being the trouper she was, Betty had spent the day helping me change diapers, finger-paint, read stories, and put six snowsuits on to take a walk.

After the toddlers were picked up by their parents, Betty and I sat down to have a cup of coffee. Brian, who had shared me all day with five other children, was not about to share me with anyone else. He went into a full-blown temper tantrum that lasted for over an hour. Betty volunteered to fix supper so I could calm him down.

The little guy was not easily dissuaded from his neediness. He clung to me through supper until he fell asleep about 9 P.M. All the while, Betty was as steady a presence as Paul was, paddling his kayak through the fog ahead of me — never making demands, simply there helping in whatever way she could. When Brian finally fell asleep, I walked into the living room in about the condition I was in when I stepped out in the muck. Dave was reading the newspaper, Betty a book. He looked up momentarily. Betty rose and followed me into the kitchen. She said, "Sit down. I'll fix you a cup of tea and we'll talk."

I was so touched by this kindness, by attention I did not expect, that I fell into her arms and wept. Wept the tears of every tired mother, of every woman who is desperate for tenderness and understanding.

I don't know how long that memory held my attention, enabled me to forget my physical agony, but when I again became conscious of the waves and fog around me, the feelings of exhaustion and pain returned and I began to cry. Not just tears, but loud, wracking sobs. I knew I had to keep paddling or I would lose sight of Paul, but I paddled a very long time before I stopped crying. There would be no Betty and no cup of tea waiting for me at the end of this day.

After a time, I saw that Paul was not paddling. I caught up to him. "What's up?" I asked.

"We're really close to the park, but the map shows a complex series of inlets and bays to reach what I think is the campground. By the looks of all the rocks and cliffs on the shore, it's going to be the only safe place to land. I want to have you double-check my reading." We rafted up and I confirmed his assessment.

"How are you doing?" he asked, looking into my eyes with real concern.

"I'm going to make it, but there's not much left. How 'bout you?"

"I'm holding steady. It's 8 P.M. I don't think we have more than thirty minutes if we navigate this thing right." Just then a clap of thunder sounded and it began to rain hard. "Shit," said Paul. "We've got to get off the water. Follow me."

A surge of new energy poured into my body. The adrenaline of emergency. I stroked hard, kept the bow of my boat close to Paul's stern. Winds began to gust and the fog moved in even closer. It was nearly dark. After a time, Paul turned and yelled something, but I couldn't understand what he said.

Then I saw it — a light on the shore. At first I thought it was a mirage. But it didn't go away; it started getting bigger.

"The ranger's cabin!" he shouted. This time I understood. Thirteen and a half hours after we started paddling, we docked our boat on a sand beach next to the cabin. It was still raining hard. Paul studied my face. "How are you?"

"Not good. I'm cold and exhausted. I just want to lie down and sleep."

"Let's see if they will let us throw our sleeping bags on the cabin floor overnight." I followed my friend up the mud embankment and into the building, which was actually an information center. It was light and warm inside and filled with people. A young ranger was finishing a talk on the geology of the area. I felt woozy with fatigue, but there was no place to sit. I knelt in the back of the crowd and lowered my head until the fainting spell passed. People seemed oblivious to our presence, asking many questions of the ranger. Finally, the last visitor left and the olive-green-suited ranger walked over to where we were standing.

"Howdy," said Paul. "We've been on the lake all day and we're looking for a place to camp. Could we just rest here for the night and move tomorrow?"

"No," said the young man, who was probably holding his first job out of college. "Park regulations state that camping can only be in the campground, which is about a half mile inland."

I stared at him in disbelief. I looked at Paul. He still had his gray hat pulled low over his eyes. But even under that brim and above his curly beard, I could read the despair. The muscles under my eyes and in my cheeks began to twitch. I swallowed hard, trying to keep the tears from forming. I didn't know what to say. All I knew was that I could not carry eighty pounds of gear and a sixty-five-pound kayak anywhere.

"I have some Boy Scouts that need something to do," said a voice behind us. I turned around to see a smiling, balding, middle-aged man.

Paul managed to speak. "We sure could use help. We've been out on the lake for over thirteen hours. We're in pretty bad shape."

"I'll be right back. Meet you here."

I didn't care which bag I handed to which boy. I just opened my kayak's hatch covers and started giving anything to any pair of reaching hands. At one point I looked up and realized that the young ranger was one of the "boys" who was helping. Paul directed several of the kids to move our boats into the shrubs, and we all started walking up a gravel road. I followed the men and boys. I tried to feel gratitude, but all I felt was defeat. I watched my feet still in their kayak booties stumble up the dark path, tripping over small rocks and roots — an animal limping home.

When I caught up to where everyone had piled the gear, the Boy Scout leader was looking at me. I simply wanted to lie down in the mud, throw the tarp over myself, go to sleep.

"Please," I said. The man looked at me, waiting. "Can you tell me which way to the bathroom?"

"Sure, ma'am. They even have warm showers. Just head over there until you hit the building with the lights."

I remembered that the large yellow river bag contained all my clothes. I could see it in the dim light. My next memory was of pushing the shower button for the fourth or fifth or sixth time and thinking, "I should not be using all of this water." But I still wasn't warm. The inside of my very cells felt cold.

Bones were protruding all over my body. I could see my hip bones, my thigh bones, my entire rib cage. There wasn't an ounce of fat left on me. I think I pushed the shower button two or three more times after that. I pushed it until a thought came into the fog in my mind: "You still have to put up your tent."

It was totally dark by the time I returned to the campsite. Paul's tent was already up and he was gone, probably to the showers. I knew there were two things left for me to do before I could give up: put up the tent, and spread out the sleeping bag and pad. I fumbled in the dark for the river bag containing my flashlight, turned it on, and erected the tent and rain fly. I was just getting ready to crawl in when Paul came up.

"We did it, kiddo! We did it! I only know a handful of paddlers who could do what we did today. You are absolutely amazing."

I rose and hugged him, fighting back the tears. "Paul, you saved my life. I could not have made it without you. You did all the navigating at the end."

"Should we try and eat anything?" he asked.

"No, I'm going to bed. We'll cook a good breakfast." I unzipped the tent, lay down on the hard ground, crawled into my sleeping bag, and said, "Thank you, God, for letting me live."

The next morning, baking a coffee cake over a wood fire in bright sunshine, Paul and I rehashed the thirty-nine-mile day. "Could we have made any different decisions that might have kept us from pushing to such a dangerous level of exhaustion?" I asked. Just then the Boy Scout leader came over. We offered him a cup of coffee. "Thank you, sir, you really saved our lives," I said.

"Yeah, I knew you were in a bad way. That young ranger, see, he thinks he has to follow all the rules all the time. Rules don't apply in emergencies. Besides, all we're really here for is to help one another out, you know."

I reached for his hand and took it in both of mine. "Bless you, sir. Bless you. Won't you have some blueberry coffee cake?"

"Well, no, the boys and I are going on a hike today and we're nearly ready to leave. We'll come visit when we're back." He tipped his cap and walked away.

I turned to Paul and said, "He's right, you know. All we really are here for is to help one another out. Yesterday, I couldn't have helped anybody out. I was an animal, Paul. All I cared about was living. That's all. Nothing else! Maybe what we did is heroic in paddlers' eyes. Maybe only a handful of paddlers could have done this. But I don't feel like a hero. I was so helpless, so devoid of dignity, so stripped of self-confidence last night. I don't want to feel like that ever again."

I looked at Paul in his gray sweater and green wind pants. He looked healthy, recovered.

He looked at me in my purple wind pants and sweater. What did I look like to him? He looked at me like I was not speaking his language.

We were on the same trip, but it was exacting a different price from each of us.

I knew the first part of the trip was over — the part of adjusting to this rugged new life. I also knew the first part of my life was over — the part of always adjusting and accommodating to my surroundings. The second part of both my trip and my life were beginning — and I was still so sobered by the longest day that all I could register was fear.

7

She-Who-Finishes-Grieving

The cycle of grief has its own timetable.
Until that cycle is honored and completed we are moving
along life's path with an anchor down.

AFTER PAUL AND I finished breakfast dishes, I ambled along the dirt roads that meandered from one campsite to the next. It was a large campground — more than a hundred sites for tents or trailers, with a lot of privacy between spaces because of all the trees. The longest day had landed us in a miniature, forested village. The dwellings ranged from recreational trailers to large Sears, stand-up-style tents to a few scattered backpacking tents like our own.

Pukaskwa Provincial Park campground is at the end of a dead-end road a long way from any population center in Ontario. As far as I could tell, every site had a vehicle. Those that didn't actually have a truck or car parked there had a plethora of equipment, ranging from Coleman lanterns on picnic tables to huge, blue plastic rain tarps strung between pine trees, all of which clearly could not have fit in a kayak. We were probably the only ones who had paddled to the park.

I was looking for someone to talk to, someone to engage in friendly discourse about the weather or the scenery. I needed conversation that could help bring my shattered confidence back to some sense of normalcy. I kept walking the roads of my village hoping to make a friend, but since I didn't have a child in tow or a dog on a leash, I could think of no natural opening to a conversation, and no one reached out to me.

Next, I wandered up the dirt road that led to the entrance of the park. Perhaps there would be some mail for us at headquarters. Because we had written ahead asking for permission to use the park as a mail drop, the woman in the small wooden building was aware that we were expected, but reported that the park had received nothing for us. I asked if she was sure. She seemed to understand my urgency. "I'm sorry," she said. I thanked her and started walking back down the tree-lined gravel road to our tents; a dark, sad, slouched figure. Halfway to the first campsite, I had an idea. "Maybe Christina's in." As though wanting connection wasn't enough, I justi-fied the impulse: "I can find out if we have any teaching assignments lined up for fall, can talk to her about the trip." I turned and walked back to the pay phone outside headquarters.

Cars were driving in and out of the park, stopping to pay the entrance fee or to look for maps to their newly acquired campsites. I knew I would have to strain to hear anything from that outdoor phone, but I really needed to talk with someone. And once again, I was calling her the day after a traumatic experience. In Grand Marais I had totally fallen apart. I reassured myself that that would not happen again, that I was only looking for helpful articulation from someone with outside perspective. I dialed her number, then recited the well-memorized digits of my credit card to an operator. The phone started ringing in another country, six hundred miles away. The ringing stopped. I heard a click and expected Christina's an-swering machine, but a friendly "Hello" spoke to me.

"Hi," I said, trying to sound casual. "Am I interrupting anything?"

"Annie, where are you calling from this time?"

"Pukaskwa Provincial Park. It's in Canada, over on the far shore of the lake."

"What's all the background noise?"

"Well, I'm calling from a phone booth on the outside wall of park headquarters. Cars are driving back and forth."

"Cars, phone booth. I keep imagining you on some remote wil-derness shore and then you call me from a phone booth!"

I realized, again, what different worlds we were living in this summer. That even people following our progress by map had no idea of the conditions we lived in, on land or sea, or the impact of the relentless weather. "Well, mostly it is wild country and we don't see anybody for days." I tried to steady my voice. "When we come to a spot of civilization, I really look forward to mail or to talking to someone."

"I am writing. Did you get my package there?" she asked.

"No, I haven't gotten any mail in Canada."

"Shit. I mailed it by Express five days ago. Didn't you get my letter in Rossport, either?"

"No." I wanted to keep my voice calm. "What are you up to today?"

"Trying not to drive myself nuts," she said, and laughed. "I'm having a hard summer, too, in my own way. Something very basic is changing. I'm at the end of a cycle, and I can't see my way through."

"Like fog . . . ," I said. "We've been paddling blind a lot of days this summer." I held my breath, waiting to see if the city woman and the wilderness paddler could find a way to connect.

"Yes," she responded. "I feel a lot like I'm in a fog. Not a real one, like you are, but I can't see my way ahead. It scares me, makes me uncomfortable in my own skin. My life feels like a cold, soaked wet suit. But for me that's just a metaphor, for you it's reality. . . . How are you?"

Though she admitted to her own troubles, her voice sounded calmer and more steady than my own. I remained determined not to break down, but I felt tears rising in my throat. I guess I was quiet for a long time. The voice that came out of the black plastic phone hanging from the metal cord said, "I'm so sorry you haven't received mail. I want you to know that I'm listening as hard as I can as you share your trip in letters to me. You say things like 'four- to seven-foot seas' and 'small craft advisory,' and I, who have kayaked only a few times in relatively calm water, can't begin to comprehend what you're going through."

Her willingness to reach out, to have compassion and honesty, melted my resolve to remain She-Who-Stands-Strong-Alone.

"Well, I'm not doing very well," I said, and again burst into tears. "The weather is still gruesome, cold and stormy most of the time. The physical challenges haven't relented."

"Are you staying safe?" she asked in concern.

I laughed — an odd, checked chortle, considering I was crying at the same time. "There's no way to do this and stay safe. But we are being careful — and I am still alive. Yesterday we paddled thirty-nine miles."

"That sounds like a lot," she said. "Is it?"

"Almost unheard of."

"Why didn't you stop?"

"There was either no place to stop because of the fog, the dangerous shoreline, or the waves, or when we did stop it was all rocks and dense brush — no place to pitch tents. Christina, I don't know if I can take this anymore."

A car crunched over the gravel on the road next to the phone, reminding me that my level of vulnerability was public. I started openly sobbing on the phone.

"I'm so sorry that we're this deeply separated," she said. "Can you tell me what's wearing you down? Is it the exertion, the exhaustion?"

"I'm still in this internal battle between my absolute determination to take this life journey and the reality of what actually paddling and living in these conditions is doing to my body. I'm just physically battering myself. Hour after hour, I push on and keep asking, Why am I doing this? What am I doing?"

Now she paused before answering, "Do you get any answers?"

"All my life I've trusted my body. You learn through your mind — but I learn through doing things with my body, by moving until I have insight."

I heard concern in Christina's voice. "Well, that's fine, as long as it doesn't kill you."

"I don't know how to do it any other way. . . . This is my only chance. I've carved out this stretch of time and created this experience, and if I give up, if I just go home . . . I'll lose something important. And I don't even know what that something is because I haven't gotten it yet."

"Then you have to keep going," she said. "My first impulse was to tell you it's okay to quit — and it is okay, Annie. Your survival must come first. If you quit, you will live to make another time, to find another way. My second impulse is to tell you that your job is to find your wisdom."

In my mind's eye I could see the way she leans forward when she's earnest, almost felt her hand on my shoulder, trusted her to know the words my heart needed to hear.

"You are in some kind of race with time, with unbelievably harsh daily circumstances," she continued. "You must paddle with the questions that will most help you awaken into the next phase of your life. Your pilgrimage is to find the stamina to endure these questions, in addition to everything else you're enduring."

I knew this challenge was what I needed to hear, to be reassured that someone else understood what was driving me. The Longest Day had stripped me down to my lowest point of confidence and energy. I needed help remembering why I was on the trip, why all the pain might be worth it. I sobbed into the phone, "Please keep talking."

"You have left the shore of what you think you know about yourself, your life, your relationships, your direction, your purpose. You must ask God more deeply than you have ever asked: 'Who do you say that I am? What do you want me to do?' "

Though she couldn't see me, I nodded in agreement.

A man had gotten out of his car and was waiting behind me to use the phone. The lawn on the median strip of grass surrounding the entrance booth was a lush green. It was midday, July 9, and the sun was not yet warm enough for me to take off my wool jacket. Everything around me was common and ordinary and unchallenging, and I was still crying so hard I could barely talk. My friend continued, "You have not taken on an easy task. Nothing about this trip is easy. But be kind to yourself. You don't need to transform your life every day. Like today. You're taking a rest day, right?"

"Right."

"Well, don't spend it writing profound, difficult thoughts in your journal. Take those legs, which scarcely ever get to connect to land, and walk them to some beautiful, scenic overlook and just enjoy!"

"Thanks, thanks, that's a good idea." I felt some control returning. I knew the conversation had to end, that each of us had to return to our respective quests, but I didn't want to hang up, to let go now that I'd established a link to the outside world.

Again, my friend stepped forward with a bit of wisdom. "I'm thinking about you, Annie. All of your friends are thinking about you. Trust that. Feel the support you have."

"Thanks, I will. Your words have been helpful. Good luck with your own search. Talk to you again." I know she said "Good-bye" and maybe "Good luck," but I really didn't hear her. I just reached up and hung the black phone on the metal hook, nodded at the man waiting behind me, and began to walk slowly toward my campsite. Our five-minute conversation was like the shower the night before, a temporary emergency measure to pull me back from the cold edge of despair.

That night, as per our pre-trip schedule, a friend arrived from Duluth bearing letters, packages, and our next food resupply. Some of the packages held candy bars. There was a loaf of homemade bread for each of us from our dear friend Fran. Paul's wife, Mary, had sent the neighborhood butcher's best beef jerky. Clearly, word had gotten out that we were losing weight. I was especially excited to receive letters from Dave and the kids. I tried to remember what gift Brian and Sally would be opening tonight. Each of the six times we were resupplied they got to open presents I had wrapped before the trip with certain dates on them. Was July 9th a jump rope and a new baseball? or spending money for a trip to the movies? I honestly couldn't remember, my old life seemed so far away.

Sally had drawn me several pictures, and in her perfect handwriting had written a short note saying she loved and missed me. I studied the pictures carefully. One was of a lake with a rainbow and two tiny boats. The other was a mottled blue-and-green ball with these words written in crayon around it: "The World Is Our Home, We Only Have One of Them." She had just finished third grade, just learned cursive, and here she was, perfectly penning the few short messages she knew were important to me. I pulled out my sacred pouch, which held the children's photos. Tears started rolling down my cheeks when I looked at my beautiful, smiling daughter.

Brian's letter was the quickly scrawled note of a sixth-grader waiting to enter junior high. My solid boy, my buddy, the child with whom I'd had deep spiritual conversations since he was a toddler, smiled out at me from the wallet photo. Letters were not his medium of expression. We needed to be physically present with each other. I ached to see him.

Dave's letter was written in the neat half printing, half writing style that he uses to outline course notes on the university's blackboard. It was written on one side of a six-by-nine-inch sheet of white tablet paper. There was an acknowledgment of the fact that they were having cold weather, too; a brief reporting of kid activities; a wish for my good health.

As good as it was to get this one and only packet of written communication from my family, it was also hard. They were so far away, had so little idea of my reality, were simply doing the best they could to cope. I didn't detect joy or enthusiasm from their letters, so guilt settled over my sadness. All the words of people skeptical of the trip trumpeted into my ears: "How can you go away and leave a third-grader and a sixth-grader for the summer?" I had hoped that Dave and the kids would create their own adventure out of this time, but my heart now told me this was not true, that they, too, were having their own endurance test. Like the phone conversation with Christina, the words of my family brought only temporary sunshine into the fog of my increasing despair.

That night in my tent I held the little blue cylindrical flashlight in my teeth and wrote in my journal:

They don't understand. My family writes me letters like I'm off on vacation. Our friend delivers our resupply of food and letters from home, watches us react like kids on Christmas morning, and she thinks yesterday's grueling ordeal is little more than some athletic contest finished and won. Christina is the one person who seems to understand the urgency I feel about not giving up my quest, but I can't really convey to her the unbelievable strain of what I'm doing to my body. No one understands how desperate I feel. I don't know how to communicate what is happening to me.

The next morning a cold rain was falling. Our friend Sue drove us to Marathon for breakfast in a café. It was a blue-collar café. Men with heavy-soled hiking boots and wool, plaid jackets were sitting at several of the Formica-topped tables smoking cigarettes and drinking black coffee. Perhaps one of these men was the driver of that bulldozer we had seen shoveling debris on our longest day. Were they all paper mill workers? Did this town's livelihood depend on the presence of that plant and its pollution? What if we had chosen to find a place to camp in Marathon and had walked to this restaurant for dinner? I laughed at myself. I had written last night about people being unable to see any other situation except the one that is right in front of them, and here I was, warm, safe, and well fed in a place that two days earlier I had been convinced offered me only more cold, more wet, more misery. Surely there was a campground somewhere in this city of several thousand; surely someone — maybe even the bulldozer operator — could have offered us advice on a place to camp. The myopia of my own vision was a far greater threat to my safety than any external fog.

While we were in the restaurant, skies began to clear. The three of us returned to the park for a long hike. My spirits were buoyed by the beauty of a sunny, cool day and by the safety of being on land. Paul and I also spent some time studying maps and planning the next hundred-mile leg of our trip. We knew this stretch of shoreline had no roads, no cabins, no sign of human habitation, that it was the wildest stretch on the entire lake. When we had planned our itinerary some nine months earlier, we had given ourselves ten days to paddle from Pukaskwa to Lake Superior Provincial Park.

"Paul, that means no more thirty-nine-mile days, no more twenty-mile days." The thought of some leisure to our pace moved me back into excitement about returning to the lake. By the time we left the Pukaskwa harbor, on July 11, I felt the same renewed enthusiasm for the trip that I'd felt after our talk at the Rossport Inn. Doubt, then determination. Doubt, then determination. It was the pattern that would plague me for days.

After three hours of paddling in sunshine, we stopped for a break on a white sand beach. Clear blue sky filled with high, wispy white clouds had transformed the big lake into an azure sea. When blue water meets white sand, the allure is too great to pass by. We pulled our boats up onto the beach, unpacked our lunches, and headed for some driftwood logs. Paul was the first to lie spread-eagled on the sand in his blue wet suit, teal paddling jacket, and gray hat. "Great to be sunbathing in the Bahamas," he said.

"Paul, in the Bahamas they don't wear all these clothes!" I joined him on the sand, resting my back and shoulders against a log. It was unbelievably warm and wonderful. The radiant heat of sun on my wet suit relaxed my body as it had not been relaxed since that night in the soft bed at the Rossport Inn. I must have drifted to sleep for a while. Paul's voice brought me back to the sensation of a cool breeze on my bare face, warm sunshine on my covered body. "I'd say we're doing a noble job of adjusting to being lazy," he said. We both laughed, sat up, and began eating our lunches now newly stocked with candy bars, jerky, and homemade bread.

The entire shoreline of Lake Superior is spectacular, but the Pukaskwa coastline is beyond superlatives. At noon we were lounging on a white sand beach; by midafternoon we were paddling over immense red and gray submerged granite boulders that looked like exquisite marble sculptures. The next day we visited the largest waterfall on the lake.

There are not many places along Lake Superior where large waterfalls drop into the lake. Pukaskwa's Cascade Falls is one of the most notable. Root beer–colored water pours over black basalt, creating three simultaneous waterfalls. Paul pulled his blue boat along the shore of the south side of the falls. I landed *Grace* on the north side. After carefully tying my yellow boat to a rock and leaving it floating free in the roiling water below the falls, I scrambled through raspberry bushes and over boulders, working my way to the top, some thirty feet above. There I found a pool fed by yet another sizable cascade of water that had been invisible from the lake. I tested the water with my hands. It was warm; well, warmer than the lake. I realized I had been on the lake for more than three weeks and hadn't swum once. I slipped out of my wet suit and swimsuit and slowly waded into the embrace of the river. It was cool, clean, invigorating. Froglike, I did two short strokes into the center of the pool, turned quickly, and stroked back out to the edge, hopped out onto the warm, dark rocks, and pressed my cold body tightly against them.

The slight breeze raised goose bumps on my damp breasts. I pushed my back more firmly into the black rock reservoir of heat. When my front side had dried, I turned and hugged the rock. Oooh, the warmth massaged my cramped belly. My menstrual cycle had started the morning we left the campground. Given my weight loss and the rigor of our exercise, I certainly had not expected it to adhere to a twenty-eight-day schedule. But on schedule it was. I had all the necessary supplies and a plastic bag for stockpiling waste until it could be burned or added to a dumpster. To cleanse myself on the swim I had removed my tampon.

The combination of heat from these ancient lava rocks and the cool massage of breeze along my spine stimulated the flow of blood. I felt the warm ooze of menstrual blood flowing out the small crack in my woman-body into the fissures of the rock. I was earth woman draped over her mother, held, nurtured, accepted. Tears formed at the corners of my eyes. The same tears that formed at the corners of my eyes when I lay on the soft bed in the cabin at Rossport — tears of gratitude for momentary nurturing.

That night we stopped paddling at the Pukaskwa River. We had come fifty miles in three days. A faster pace than we had set out to do, but nevertheless, reasonably relaxing. Over a driftwood fire on a small spit of sand formed where the river ran into the lake, Paul and I cooked our favorite of the dehydrated dinners: pizza. It was a meal we could only cook with the coals of a wood fire on a night when we were not rushed. While the Bisquick crust was browning slowly in the well-greased iron skillet, we silently watched the pink-and-orange sunset. I liked how easy silence was between us.

Paul's words broke the tranquillity. "I've been thinking about paddling out to Michipicoten Island."

I stared at him in disbelief and said, "You've got to be kidding!"

"I've been studying the map. It's eight miles out and back, forty miles around the island."

Once again I felt like we were not on the same journey. I was savoring the first nice weather, the leisure of a slow-cooking meal, the quiet of the sunset, muscles that didn't hurt for the first time on the entire trip. And he wanted to keep pushing, to add an extra fifty-six miles! My whole life had been about pushing. Pushing to get good grades, a good job, a good home, good children. I couldn't push anymore. I just had to stay still, to keep up with nobody but myself.

"Are you excited about going?" I asked.

"Yeah, I am. Everybody says it's magical, partly because the fog makes it treacherous to get there. It's got an inland lake, steep cliffs, and few people." He looked at me. Our eyes remained locked. Lake Superior—blue eyes reflecting the soft orange sunset.

This time I was the one to break the silence. "It's okay with me if you go, but I don't have any interest in joining you. This is the only stretch of the trip where we scheduled ourselves shorter days. I really need to rest. Let's see what the weather is going to be up to over the next few days," I said, rising to get my radio.

Ten minutes later I was back from my twenty-foot walk. "Paul, my radio is missing! I must have left it at our last stop."

Virtually every piece of our equipment was indispensable. We constantly checked and rechecked the ground around us after lunch breaks and in the morning. But this time a black, hand-size radio set on a black rock had remained camouflaged. I would have to backtrack and find it.

The next morning Paul and I were on the water early: he to continue down the shore, to watch the weather, and to decide about venturing out to Michipicoten Island; I to circle back to Richardson's Point to find my radio. I would stay another day at the Pukaskwa River before moving camp. Paul would leave rock cairns at Red-sucker Point: "One if by land, two if by sea." If there were two cairns, I would know he'd gone out to the big island and I wouldn't see him until I got to the Michipicoten River. If there was one, I would look for him in the vicinity of Cairn Point the next day. It was the first time we had split spontaneously for solo time, had openly honored the differences in our journeys.

I was determined to paddle my nearly empty boat as fast as I could to retrieve the radio, and then enjoy a day to wash clothes, swim in the river, read, and write. I paddled as if I were swimming laps in a pool — an athletic endeavor with little concern about my surroundings. The radio was exactly where I had left it on the rocks near the Pukaskwa Pit we had stopped to explore. We had met a ranger in a patrol boat near Otter's Cove who had told us about the ancient site. "One of the most distinctive of these structures any-where around the lake: a circular depression three feet deep, five feet in diameter, with a three-foot-high wall around it," he had said.

We had read about the Pukaskwa Pits before beginning our trip. Once we reached the park we consciously began making rest stops on shores that seemed to hold potential for finding them. The areas are generally three to ten feet across and two to four feet deep and seldom have walls like the one at Richardson's Point. Archaeologists are just beginning to understand them, and speculate that they were used for ceremonies, rituals, rites of passage, or lookouts by native people just prior to the modern-day Ojibway. I kept looking for them, hoping to recapture some of the feelings I'd had at the stone altar and deepen my connection to indigenous wisdom on the lake. I had sat for a long time in the one at Richardson's Point, imagining myself a young woman off on a moon-time solo. Retrieving the ra-dio, I paused to look again at the structure, scrambled down the boulder field, and hopped expertly back into *Grace*.

The water was flat calm. The air was cool and beginning to warm. There was no sight of fog lurking anywhere. I felt strong and confident. Stroke, pull. Stroke, pull. Stroke, pull. I was a yellow dolphin cutting a path through the smooth waters of its own sea.

After a short time, I detected a movement out of the corner of my eye. Turning my head slightly, I saw a caribou standing on the shore of the island I was paddling by! The rack on his head was at least four feet across, a complex maze of bends and curves. Wrapped in brown-black fur atop the six-foot-high island, he towered over me like an ancient king. I stopped paddling and stared in disbelief. He returned the stare with complete disdain, walked down off his rock island into the water, and began swimming toward the mainland. Slowly, I pulled my camera and telephoto lens out of their stuff sack and paddled behind him at what felt like a nonintrusive distance. I started snapping pictures as he got to the shore of the mainland and walked out. He turned, looked at me, shook his great antlers free of water, and ambled into the forest.

"Holy shit," I whispered to myself, "I don't believe it." I had been looking for caribou ever since we left Rossport. And here, when I was not looking, was racing along paying no attention to anything, what do I see but the caribou I've been straining to find at the edge of every fog bank. I sat in my boat with the paddle across my lap, staring at the section of brush where this most magnificent of northern creatures had disappeared. "We are so far north," I said aloud to the still water, "that caribou still roam and ancient sites have scarcely been studied."

I resumed paddling. Slower now. Reminded once again that every moment holds the potential for magic. That those of too directed purpose can often pass by greater purpose.

When I got back to the campsite, it was noon. I stripped bare and swam out into the slow current of the Pukaskwa River. It was cold, but I did manage to do a half dozen strokes before walking out of the water. The invigorating swim, the warming air, the joy of the morning paddle, all straightened my spine. I emerged from the brown river water as the regal queen of this shore. I walked over to my collapsible canvas basin, returned to the river to fill it, and carried it two-handed to a spot ten feet from the river's edge.

After carefully setting it down, I unscrewed the cap of my shampoo, poured a quarter-size drop into the palm of my hand, and began to massage the biodegradable soap into my scalp, over my breasts, under my arms, up and down my thighs. The riverbank queen paused, looked up at the sun, looked down at her suds-covered body, and smiled more deeply and broadly than she had in many weeks.

Bending to pick up the basin of cool river water, I slowly raised it over my head, preparing for the baptism. Oooh, this cleansing waterfall felt so good! I opened my eyes to see sudsy rivulets forming all around my feet. The water flowed back toward its source, not quite reaching it. I had been careful enough. None of the soap went directly into the river. I dumped one more basin of water over my head to be sure all the shampoo was out before I waded back into the river for another quick swim.

Next I washed my clothes in the basin and pinned them to a rope I had strung between two driftwood stumps that the lake had deposited on this spit of land many storms ago. Paul always chuckled at my clothespins, teased me about bringing along something so frivolous, but I liked how the purple, yellow, red, and teal flags of my clothing flapped in the breeze. My tent, the boat, the clothesline clearly staked out this place as my territory.

I stretched my naked body out on my towel, wriggling myself into position in the soft sand underneath. Sand was my favorite natural bed. It molded to the unnatural curvature of my spine, comforting and cradling it. Sometimes after long days of paddling my back would be so stiff that I could scarcely climb out of my boat, but at this moment my back felt wonderful. I remembered a doctor's charge to my seventeen-year-old self: "We've discovered your scoliosis too late to use corrective rods. You're going to have to keep your body strong if it's to remain upright." That moment had begun my lifelong commitment to athleticism. At times I had been obsessive about that commitment — training for marathons to the point of injuring myself. In recent years, though, I had tried to seek a more moderate course with my exercise. This trip was, of course, a grand exception to that pendulum swing back to moderation. I knew it might be risky for my back to take this trip, but I also knew I had to take the chance, had to risk my life to save it.

Once my stomach was dry, I rolled over to dry my back. I didn't want to write or read; I simply luxuriated in the ecstasy of so much comfort.

Unwatched, while I was lying on my stomach staring upriver, the fog sneaked in from the lake and stole the sun. In minutes a cool breeze began to blow, the sun totally disappeared, and fog enshrouded my campsite. I walked the twenty-five sandy yards to my tent; put on the purple pants and sweater, which I had not washed; took out my sleeping bag, pad, and journal; propped myself up near the tent; and began to write.

For a brief instant I thought I heard voices in the fog. Couldn't be — not at this wilderness site — but minutes later two kayaks appeared and beached themselves on the riverbank I had so recently staked out as my own. Two men hopped out. Paul had asked me if I was worried about camping alone. "Not in primitive sites," I had said. "I'm not going to see anyone out here." I was shocked by this intrusion and felt a moment of panic at being a woman alone. As the men made their way past my clothesline and up to my writing spot, I breathed deeply and focused on sending them confident energy.

They introduced themselves with a heavy French-Canadian accent and asked if they might camp here since the fog had become too thick to travel in.

"Well, it's not a very big spit of land, but I think we can respect one another's privacy." We talked some about how quickly fog can move in and about its omnipresence on this part of the lake. They asked me how long I'd been out.

"Since June seventeenth."

"Where did you start?"

"Duluth."

"Oh, we heard there are two Americans paddling around the lake. Is that you?" asked the shorter, dark-haired paddler.

"Yeah," I chuckled. "That's me."

The other one tipped his orange baseball cap, displaying curly golden hair. They returned to their boats and began to unload them at a site not fifty yards from mine. They were perfect gentlemen, never spoke to me again except to come up while I was cooking dinner and writing in my journal to ask if I'd like some bean soup. Since I had plenty of food and was very much enjoying my solitude, I declined.

Once the water in my old black pot had come to a boil, I added soup mix and stirred it with my wooden spoon until the noodles and vegetables were fully rehydrated. Then I bowed my head in prayer. Each night Paul and I joined hands in some kind of grace. Since both of us are quiet people, often grace was just a matter of holding hands and nodding at each other. But tonight with the fog still swirling thickly around, my prayer was for Paul's safety.

"Holy One, I don't know where my friend is tonight. May he be safe, and may we reunite soon." There is something about absence that makes our feelings about a person more clear. For as much as Paul and I needed time alone, I realized how much he meant to me. I started to think about the risky crossing out to Michipicoten Island. What if he had gotten halfway out and then the fog moved in? What were the odds of hitting a target as small as an island, even a big one? Did I remember to tell him that I loved him, before he left? I made this entry in my journal:

Every day we make life-and-death decisions on this trip. We use the best judgment we can, but we are doing so with very little structure. There are no daily rules for living here: no guidelines for how far from the shore to paddle, how to set rendezvous spots in case we get separated in the fog, how long it is safe to paddle, where we should sleep at night. I know Paul needed the freedom to make this decision on his own. I pray he is safe. I cannot think about "what ifs." I just pray he is safe.

The lake had an eerie silence when I awoke at dawn. There wasn't even a gentle lapping of waves. It was dead still. I unzipped the tent and looked out at a river spit that had no fog, and to a distant horizon that contained a fog bank. Michipicoten Island lay hidden in the fog. I didn't need to get up and get an early start, but I had to get to Redsucker Point to find out if Paul had gone out to the island. The two paddlers were still inside their tent when I stepped into my loaded boat and stroked out of the mouth of the river on July 14.

On the map Redsucker Point is a distinctive landmark. When I paddled up to it in the morning sun, my heart dropped. The point was marked by a house-size granite rock. I realized that Paul would not have been able to land his kayak and make a cairn. I'd been expecting to see his signal easily, one pile of a half-dozen or so rocks stacked atop one another or two piles of stacked rocks. Now what was I supposed to do? There was no civilization between here and the Michipicoten River. Did I keep paddling until I reached the campground there, not knowing for three days where or how my friend was? I paddled around the point, looking for some other spot he might have been able to leave me a sign.

There! A single pile of rocks was carefully placed on a low-lying boulder next to the lake. He had not gone out to the island! "Thank God," I said aloud to a guardian seagull.

Paul was waiting for me at noon at Cairn Point, as happy to see me as I was to see him. We didn't paddle much farther, so we could take our time making camp, studying maps, exploring the land. It was a luxury to think about doing some hiking. A luxury we could afford, having come off a schedule of ten- to twelve-hour paddling days. To climb the hill behind our campsite we had to pull ourselves up and over tree roots, work our way around areas of cliffs, but finally we reached a hilltop several hundred feet above the lake's surface. Michipicoten Island was visible to the south. The entire eastern half of the sky was purple-black and dotted with intermittent lightning flashes. Paul pulled out his weather-band radio. "An area of extensive and severe thunderstorms preceding several days of thick cloud cover and rain due to hit the Pukaskwa Provincial Park area this evening."

For the next two days we paddled in dense, unrelenting fog, more three- to five-foot waves, and occasional rain. The physical challenge of the lake returned and so did my doubt. On July 16, I made this entry in my journal by flashlight:

> University River or Dog River, depending on whether you believe the navigation chart or the sign at the mouth of this river. Nine P.M. This is a lovely spot to camp, like so many places we make camp. But what do we see of them? We arrive late and leave early. And why *am* I doing this? Day after day of physical exertion that hurts. I hope I "come through to the other side," come to see this as more than just the most difficult, grand adventure I've ever attempted. But tonight, dear God, I'm not sure. I'm just exhausted.

The fog had again driven out my determination, returned my doubt. Where was the steady courage I needed? I had abandoned it, like the radio, at the sunny sand spit at the river mouth. There was no easy way to circle back and reclaim a mood. How could I get to a place of simply accepting what was and not wishing for something different? I turned off the flashlight in my little tent on yet another sandbar at the mouth of yet another river, and let the sound of rapids meeting surf pound the doubt out of my brain and make way for dawn and a return to determination.

However, the real transformation, the real movement out of doubt and into courage, happened on July 18. We were paddling out of the mouth of the Michipicoten River. It was warm and sunny. Our weather-bands, now tuned to Canadian stations, promised a whole day of sunshine and temperatures in the fifteen- to twenty-degree centigrade range (Fahrenheit translation: the sixties!). It was to be our first full day of summer paddling.

"Now this is the kind of day I signed up for!" I said to Paul.

He grinned. "Yeah, we might even be able to take off our long underwear today!"

Paul was to spend the night with a friend at Old Woman's Bay in

Lake Superior Provincial Park. The bay was named for the silhouette created by the headlands. I requested solo time on an island where I could view this impressive cliff face. By 1 P.M. we spotted the Old Woman — an immense, continuous wall of rock whose top edge held the silhouette of forehead, large nose, lips, and chin. We were paddling by a group of small islands. I wished Paul well and said I'd choose one of the islands and wait at my campsite for him the next morning. We were both so excited to be heading into our respective adventures that we didn't stop to think how difficult it would be for Paul to find my campsite if the fog rolled in. This time, though, the lake was kind to us. This *was* the kind of day we had signed up for.

"I don't know if anyone has a right to be this happy," I wrote in a letter to Christina that afternoon. I was alone on a cobblestone beach, totally naked on a huge white, body-size granite boulder smoothed by the waves. My freshly done wash was scattered on boulders all over the beach, beautiful in its wild array of colors. My tent was perched thirty feet up on the top of a small cliff, surrounded by ripe blueberries. The sky was cloudless. There was a light breeze. The waves were gently lapping against the shore. There were no bugs. I was neither too hot nor too cool. I was in heaven.

When the sun sank below the horizon, I put on my clothes, lit a fire for supper, and set out a candle, my children's pictures, and a feather on top of a boulder. I started to read aloud Martha Courtot's wonderful essay "Tribes," the last chapter of a book published in 1977 by the same title:

> We tell you this: We are doing the impossible. We are teaching ourselves to be human. When we are finished, the strands which connect us will be unbreakable; already we are stronger than we have ever been. The fibers which we weave on our insides will be so tight that nothing will be able to pass through them.

The water in the trusty old black pot over the campfire was boiling. It was time for me to drop the rice in. I couldn't. I just started crying. I bent over at the waist and wailed. I was finally safe enough for the terror, the fear, the agony, the confusion to pour out of me.

I was a lone woman on a lone island, howling to Old Woman. This journey to teach me my humanness was the loneliest journey of my life. But then I remembered another lonely night, the night Betty had died.

I had made many journeys from Minnesota to her Utah bedside during her five-month bout with cancer. When the call came that she had gone into a final coma, my friend Marge had said, "This time you're not going alone. I'm coming with you." We traveled by Greyhound bus. It took us forty-eight hours to get there, heading by stops and starts across the frozen plains of the Dakotas and Wyoming. In that time, three of her sisters flew in from New York and Betty was taken by ambulance from a Salt Lake City hospital to the Logan hospital, so she could die in her own town.

Her eldest sister greeted us in the hospital lobby. "Ann, we have been telling her you're coming. The doctor never believed she'd last this long. You know Betty; she's probably been cussing you out for being so slow. None of us has any idea what will happen once you go into the room, so we'd each like to take a moment with her first if that's okay." I nodded as Betty's three sisters and our mutual friend Rosalie filed one by one into the room with the closed door.

The door to the private room was huge and heavy. When it was my turn to go in, I struggled to push it open. There she was, the woman I had hiked with in Zion National Park not two weeks earlier. The woman who had recovered enough after being carried down from the mountain to hike several other short trails. Now she was a skeleton with sunken, glazed eyes and yellow skin. A sheet with a head, loudly inhaling and exhaling. A body clinging desperately to the cliff-edge of life. "Dear God, help me," I whispered.

When I reached Betty, I felt under the covers to find her hand and bent to kiss her cheek. Touch. Yes, touch. She is real. She is the same woman I love. I laid my cheek on hers. Rested in the security of our togetherness. And then the words came. "Hello, my friend, I'm here. I know you can hear me." I stood up and rubbed her hand and arm as I spoke.

"Betty, you are the best friend I've ever had. It is you that has made me alive, who has opened my heart and brought me amazing companionship.

"There are so many good memories between us. We have lived together so passionately. Climbed, skied, backpacked, kayaked, run marathons. We have explored mountaintops and deserts, lakes and forests. You have helped me change diapers, build Lego cars, mop up spilled Jell-O, and take toddlers camping. All of those things, at a time when I was far more interested in being a mom than being a good friend. You have taught me so much about love, loyalty, and devotion.

"I am going to try as hard as I can to be worthy of that honor, to love more deeply, to live more deeply. But I am going to miss you so much."

Betty's memory was bringing me out of loneliness, into companionship. I straightened up, resettled myself on the granite boulder, pulled on her jacket for warmth, and went deeper into the memory of that moment two and a half years earlier.

"I know how much you like to sing. I want to sing you the prayer I always sing to the children:

> *Mother we thank Thee for the night*
> *and for the blessed morning light,*
> *for health and food and loving care*
> *and all that makes the day so fair.*
> *Help us to do the things we should,*
> *to be to others kind and good.*
> *In all we do in work or play,*
> *to be more loving day by day.*

"Betty, I've come to give you Brian and Dave's love." And then I paused and leaned down to touch my cheek to hers, and said, *"And that of your daughter, Sally, for she is your daughter, you know. She bonded to you first.*

"You have battled this awful disease so valiantly. You lived your life with great courage and you have shown us all how to die with great courage. Betty, those of us here will try to take care of one another. I cannot hold your hand any longer. God has it. It will be peaceful, Betty. It's okay to let go. You deserve that peace so much."

Suddenly I became conscious of the hospital room, of Betty's labored breathing. It felt as if I'd been far away. I again became aware of my own *thought processes. And the first thought I had was, "A person could be in a coma for weeks. I am just going to sit here and hold her hand until she dies." I pulled up a chair and sat down.*

Almost instantly, her breathing was no longer labored. It was quiet and peaceful. I heard the door open behind me and felt hands on my shoulders. "Ann," Marge's voice said, "the doctor would like to talk with you."

"I'm not leaving. She's letting go." The hands left my shoulders and I heard the door close.

The door opened again and the doctor appeared at the other side of the bed. He took her pulse. He looked at me and nodded. The door opened and closed behind me again. Rosalie, Marge, and Betty's sisters all filed in around her bed. Betty heaved a huge sigh, and it was over. I let out a terrible wail, the same lonely wail I had let out into the darkness on the unnamed island where I was camped.

I had felt so alone that night, had never really recovered from the loss of my beloved friend until right now. I was still alone, but somehow I wasn't lonely anymore. I was glad to be here in only my own company. I looked around at my fire and tent and boat, and felt proud about how I did things. Confident about who I was. I reached over to the pouch holding Betty's ashes and sprinkled a few of them on the flames.

"I'm going to do this, my friend. I'm going to make it all the way around this lake. And I am going to come back so different, so changed that the fibers on my insides won't ever again allow doubt to come in and dissolve my ability to live life as fully as I can."

8

Confused Waters

The most vulnerable time for new truth in our lives is immediately
after the discovery. Like the emerging seedling, we have made the decision
to leave the seed's protective shell, but we are frail and unaware
of the cold realities of early spring.

WHEN PAUL PADDLED up to my solo campsite the next
morning, I was happy to see him. I felt a freshness, a newness about
my commitment to the journey that was more confident than our
night of clanging beer steins at the Rossport Inn. And I was determined to demonstrate this by being an enthusiastic and skilled
paddling partner.

"Did you have a good visit with Bob?" I asked.

"Yeah, it was terrific. Sorry to be here so late, but it was hard to
get away."

"I understand. I just finished my own closure in the journal.
Have you listened to your radio? This gorgeous, sunny day probably
won't be with us long."

"I know. That's why I tried to get away earlier."

Within an hour, we were paddling across Bushy Bay into strong
southwest head winds and rapidly darkening skies. After the crossing, we stopped to listen to our radios: "Severe thunderstorm warnings . . . locally heavy wind . . . rain and hail . . . small craft
advisory."

"Let's continue along this protected shore until we get to Grindstone Point, where we can look to the south and assess the situa-

tion," said Paul. Neither of us wanted to stop after just a few hours of paddling. We were rested and ready to put on some miles. At Grindstone Point the east-west shoreline dipped southwest, straight into the wind. The entire western sky was dark purple. The shoreline ahead was steadily rising cliffs. Seas had been building while we were in the protected lee of the shoreline — they were now at four to five feet. Lightning was flashing in the distance. The Master Scheduler would have Her way; it was clear we had to stop. We made camp on the rocky, brushy shoreline, struggling to eke out tiny places to pitch our tents in the thick alder and aspen forest. Since rain appeared imminent, we exchanged a few words about checking in with each other at six and then crawled into our respective tents some hundred yards apart.

The four-foot-by-seven-foot tent felt like a cage, barely big enough to sit up in. My options for self-entertainment while sitting out the storm were limited. At times I liked the tininess of my shelter — it felt like a safe cave. But other times, like right now, it felt claustrophobic. I didn't want to write in my journal. I had done that for the last twenty-four hours. The book I was reading seemed hopelessly boring. I had recommitted myself to paddling, to making mileage. And now I was asked to sit still.

On the island I had decided to make it all the way around the lake, to let go of the doubt inside myself. That had seemed like the big issue facing me, the issue that would open the door to an easier trip, but the Aha! of transformation was short-lived. Another invisible wall loomed before me — the one that demanded rigid goal-setting, the one that kept me from being fully present to the moment. The one that kept me twitching in my tent, pacing in my mind until my watch finally registered 5:30 P.M.

I put my hiking boots on, unzipped the tent, made my way through the thick brush to the beach. It had not rained, but it still looked threatening. I could see Paul in his green rain suit sitting on a boulder near the point. As I sat down on a black lava rock next to him I said, "What do you think? Is it going to lighten up enough for us to paddle a few more hours?"

"I don't think we can chance it," he said. "It still looks pretty unsettled. The map shows the area beyond Cape Chaillon, beyond what we can see, to be all cliffs, and I can't get any radio reception. Let's eat some supper while this rain is holding off and get a real early start in the morning."

"It's amazing, isn't it? Last night we had gorgeous weather. Tonight it's working up to be the biggest storm of the trip," I responded. We sat for a bit watching the clouds building up to black again, listening to the waves pounding on the rocks in front of us. "You know, Paul, one of the tough lessons I've had to learn on this trip is the one of being She-Who-Can-Never-Keep-Up. Does it bother you that I'm so much slower than you?"

"No, I just factor it in. I take it into account to make decisions safely, like right now."

I was trying to open the door to a conversation about the transformation I'd felt recommitting to the trip. His answer felt cold and distant to me. I was surprised and hurt and not sure how to proceed. "Is something bothering you?"

"I thought you told me day before yesterday at Michipicoten Harbor that you had a good talk with Dave. When I called Mary from the campsite last night, she said Dave hadn't heard from you." There was a long pause while the fox and the rabbit sized each other up. "Ann, my life depends on you out here, and lately I haven't trusted you. That's why I bring up the thing about Dave."

I looked at him like I looked at him the morning after the longest day. Who was this person who was experiencing things so differently than I? How could we be at such opposite poles of perception when we were partners committed to the same journey?

"Paul, when you came to pick me up at the phone booth I said I'd spoken to Dave to protect myself. I had tried to call him three other times that night. No one was home. I desperately needed to talk to him, to have that connection, but nothing was working. I haven't talked to him for a week — not since Pukaskwa — and as far as I know it will be another week until I can call again. I was disappointed, on the edge of tears. I didn't want to talk about it in front of you and Bob. I didn't even write about it in my journal because what's really going on inside me is that I'm terrified that I'm not connected to him anymore."

Paul's shocked blue eyes mirrored my own. What could I say now? Where had that statement come from? He held my gaze, waiting for more. I perceived him as the omnipresent male authority figure: my father, my husband, all the professors and bosses I'd ever had. I didn't want to invite him further into my vulnerability because experience had taught me that I'd be invaded, attacked, destroyed. I had said too much; the strain of his accusation had disarmed me. I looked steadily at his serious, penetrating eyes. Why had he not been trusting me for a while? That was the rest of the question I needed to respond to.

"Paul, I'm having a hard time communicating. Except for the calls we make to Minnesota Public Radio where I've thought ahead about what I'm going to say, whenever I call home or to a friend I either end up crying or feeling misunderstood. I'm lonesome. I'm confused. I'm in the middle of big change. Change bigger even than this trip or this lake." I looked at him expectantly. If this was a woman friend, there would be a rising empathy, shared story, puzzling together over our similarities and differences.

But Paul just kept staring out over the lake as I talked. He was so far away. As far away as all the voices on the phone. As far away as all the letters that supposedly had been mailed that I hadn't received at any of our Canadian stops. He made no response, and I plunged on with my self-explanation. "If what you haven't been able to trust in me lately is my commitment to the trip, you've been right. Until last night on the island, I wasn't sure if I was doing the right thing to continue when I feel so beaten every day. But something switched for me and I want you to hear that I have the optimism, the enthusiasm, that I had on day one of this trip." I dropped my head and waited.

Soon I heard his familiar voice with the hard edge tucked away. "Ann, it really doesn't bother me that you're slower. You bring incredible strengths in setting up camp, in cooking, in journal writing."

His softness made mush of any clarity I had about maintaining aloofness or distance. I threw my arms around his shoulders and cried. He embraced me and let me sob until I realized he was as uncomfortable holding me when I cried as Dave was. I slid back to my composure and my sitting position as easily as I had slid into the placating position in our conversation. I'd done all the explaining, all the adapting, and then had been grateful for the tiniest hint of understanding from him. Still, the tension between us had eased.

Paul moved to set up his backpacking stove, asking me what I'd like for supper. "Let's just heat up some water for soup. I'm not that hungry," I responded. While he fired up the stove and filled a pot with water, I pulled the dried soup mix out of its plastic bag. By the time we had put the mix into our cups, it had started to sprinkle. The sprinkles quickly intensified, so we filled our cups with the lukewarm water and scampered back into the isolation of our tents.

I finished my soup, ate a piece of bread, and made this entry in my journal:

> I'm expecting a highway of water to start rolling through the tent somewhere soon. The noise in here is terrifying, intruding, unnerving. It is so unlike last night. Last night for the first time on the trip I slept without the rain fly up so I could see the stars through the mesh top of my tent. Tonight there are no stars; there is no light save this little flashlight. I want to offer a prayer ere I try to close my eyes and rest: Holy One, help Paul and me. Guide us not only to be safe, as we are in our tents tonight, but also to grow in our friendship as this trip progresses.

When my watch finally said 5 A.M., I knew it was okay to get up. I had been like a caged cougar since 1 A.M. — waiting for enough light to emerge. Hunched over in the four-foot-high tent, I struggled to pull on rain pants and jacket, hiking boots, and rain hat. I carefully unzipped the rain fly, slid out, and rezipped it without knocking much of the water from the overhanging brush into the tent. Even though my tent was only fifteen feet from the rocky shoreline, it was fifteen feet of tangled, dripping alder and downed aspen trees.

It wasn't until I could stand upright on the shore that I realized it was actually still raining — not hard, but a dense mist squeezed out of the fog. I made my way down the nearly dark shore to Paul's tent. "I'll be right out," he said.

I went and stood on the point of land where we had had our conversation last night. In my yellow rain jacket and dark pants I looked like a miniature lighthouse on a fog-enshrouded point. I held my weather-band radio in many different positions but got no reception. It was not a good day to have no weather report. There were miles of cliffs ahead and no safe landings if the weather changed abruptly.

Paul tried his radio. No luck either. "Probably the headlands here are blocking our reception, but it looks to me like a weather system that will hold. Fog, drizzle, seas of three to five feet. I think we can do it." Our lives depended on each of us paying full attention to each paddling decision. I did an inner check to be sure I wasn't just agreeing to avoid tension like that which came between us yesterday. "I really do want to paddle today," I said. "We made only six miles yesterday. I agree that it seems safe enough to go."

And it was not so bad to be out paddling, certainly better than the preparation — pulling on icky wet suits, wool socks, and booties; or rolling up soaking-wet tents; or trying to load a boat on a rocky, slippery shore. Once on the water, I sang my blessing to the morning, feeling confident in my ability to paddle in these waves and fog, rested and strong for the day's journey.

We didn't want to be too near to the cliffs. The confused water created by waves breaking on the rocks and then ricocheting off into incoming waves was very difficult to paddle in. Sometimes incoming waves can unite with ricocheting waves and create a wave twice as high as either the incoming or outgoing waves. The thing of it is, we never knew when that big wave might rise. So, to paddle confused waters, we had to always be ready for anything from any direction. It is the most unnerving water to be in — not unlike the waters our friendship had moved through last night.

We remained far enough out to be beyond the greatest area of confusion, but close enough so we could still get occasional glimpses of the cliffs in the fog. A steady but gentle wind was pressing mist into our faces from the southwest. Once or twice I thought I noticed a gust from the west, but mostly I just focused on keeping Paul in my vision, the boat upright, the confused water to my left.

Paul motioned me over to him. "I don't like what's happening," he said.

"What do you mean?" I asked.

"These occasional gusts from the west signal some kind of weather change. If this system gets blasted out of here by a huge high pressure ridge moving in from the northwest, we're in big trouble."

"Well, if it does come in from the northwest, there's nothing we can do," I said. "That place we camped last night would be a death trap, with northwest seas pounding on boulder beaches. We've got to keep going." He nodded. I felt my stomach tighten, the grip on my paddle intensify. We started stroking again. Harder.

I began paying more attention to the occasional gusts from the west. Within minutes they were regular gusts not just from the west, but from the northwest. They kept building and became more frequent.

Over on this side of the lake, Superior is known for her nor'westers, sudden high pressure systems that come racing across the full expanse of the lake, picking up momentum and pushing waves as they come. It was the nor'westers on this shore and the nor'easters on my home shore of Duluth that made Superior infamous for her shipwrecks.

A kayaker's head sits just three feet above the water. One wouldn't think strong surface gusts of wind would have much effect on someone sitting that low to the water, but they do. The wind, blowing along the surface, goes into a kind of frenzy when it hits a small boat, a frenzy of pushing, tugging, battering. When the first big gust hit me from behind, I realized that Paul's worst prediction was coming true.

I looked over at him. He was not there. I panicked. In my intense concentration on the shifting winds and seas had I gotten too far away from him? His boat suddenly appeared. It had been down in a wave trough, out of my vision. He was about twenty yards in front of me, and then his boat disappeared again. Experience told me that if his boat was disappearing like that, the seas between us had already built to the five- to six-foot level. That alone would not have been too much to handle, but the seas were an erratic mixture of southwest waves and northwest waves — accompanied by those terrifying gusts. From the time Paul and I rafted up to discuss the possible weather change until we were engulfed in its maelstrom could not have been more than ten minutes. She-Who-Is-The-Biggest had created one of her infamous sudden blows.

The fog bank lowered and deepened, and suddenly it was dark. So dark, the water seemed black. Paul's boat looked black. The cliffs were black. I was holding on to my paddle so tightly, bracing to the right or left when a wave or a wind gust came in, that I wasn't moving forward. I knew I must keep paddling, but where was Paul? He was farther ahead of me now. We were each on our own. Alone. He could not rescue me. I could not rescue him. "God, please don't let us tip!" I said aloud. A sudden gust of wind tipped me dangerously far to the left, mocking my prayer. My skilled brace-stroke righted me, and just as quickly a wave from behind hit and engulfed me in water. There was no boat. Just me and water and a paddle in my hand. In the next second, there was the yellow boat again, and I was still in it and right side up.

"Paddle, Ann, paddle," I shouted to myself. "You must keep paddling forward, don't just brace." I would stroke two or three times and then have to brace. Stroke, stroke, brace. I dared not look up from my boat long enough to try to find Paul. I just kept the looming blackness of the cliffs in my peripheral vision, making sure I was not getting closer to them. But it was all confused water. Near the cliffs. Around me. One mile out from the shore. A thought crept into my mind: "What if I go over? I'll never be able to get back in the boat and pump it out before the waves drive me into the cliffs."

Another trailing wave devoured my boat and I gulped a breath just before it engulfed me. When it had passed, I paddled three more strokes. Another gust of wind and I braced on the right side. "Upright, Ann, that's all you can think about. Stay upright." I was shouting instructions to keep myself company. The aloneness and separation were as terrifying as the storm itself. I do not know how many braces or gusts of wind or douses from trailing waves I battled, or for how long before my arms began to ache. I had long since given up keeping track of Paul. It was just me, the wind, the waves, and the cliffs. There was no other reality. No dry or wet tent. No campfire. No beautiful thoughts or revelations in journals. No friends. No family. Just me and the wind and the waves and the cliffs. And I was the one thing that didn't belong out here.

The more my arms ached and my breath quickened from the exertion, the more I felt a thought rise up from some depth inside myself I had not known was there. I was being pushed at by the wind, engulfed by ice water, and squeezed by a seductive thought: "Give up. It would be so easy. You're so tired. Just relax and the fight will be over."

The thought was so soothing, so calming, so inviting that I did relax and rest in its assurance for an instant. But just then She blasted me with a gust from behind and tried to rip the paddle from my hand. Her sneaky lunge for power freed the anger in me from its cage. "No! No!" I yelled into the darkness. "I will not go over! I will not go over!" Brian's and Sally's faces appeared on the waves in front of me. I would not go over. I could not go over. Now my fury matched the storm's. I stroked. I braced. I was not afraid even when the waves came up from behind and buried my boat. "Grace Happens," the purple bumper sticker Christina had given me to christen the boat, emerged from the torrents of water, flashed before my eyes, and disappeared — but I held the thought. Rage and grace fueled me. I was in control of this boat. Now there were me and the children and the cliffs and the wind and the waves out here. And all of us belonged.

I had never been so angry in my life. Me, the soft-spoken, gentle teacher, the aunt and mother and neighbor that all kids loved, the daughter and wife who tried to obey and please, was yelling. Was screaming. Was claiming my right to live. And nothing was going to take it away from me — not this storm, not any person, not any structure, not any rule. I, who am a woman, had a right to claim the fullness of who I am.

After a while I noticed that the waves were not as high, that it was easy to see Paul again. He was paddling closer to the cliffs and it felt safe to join him, so I paddled in his direction. He yelled something to me, but I couldn't hear, so I moved still closer.

"I think the worst is past," he called. "We're in the protection south of the cape. The northwest winds can't get at us as well here." I was amazed by my friend. He already had the situation figured out. All I knew was that I was feeling more in control, more relaxed, but I could see he was right. I turned sideways in my boat to look behind me. The wind was clearing out the fog, so I could see quite a way beyond the cliffs. The size of the seas was much bigger behind us. We *had* gotten ourselves to a safer place.

"I'm okay. I can keep going, but we should probably try to land somewhere in here. Once this shore bends around to Ryan Point we'll be back in full exposure."

"Let's just stay in close to the cliffs and see if we can't find a small cove or something," said Paul. I was so relieved to be out of immediate danger, so happy to have survived the terror, that I really didn't care if we landed or hung out in our boats until the storm passed and we could continue. That level of relief was short-lived, though. My arms ached. I needed some rest soon.

We paddled by several protected rocky coves, but in three- to five-foot surf any landing on rocks was too dangerous. Finally we came to an area of large cobbles, a flowing river — the Red Rock River. Just beyond it was an extensive sand beach. Paul and I had practiced a lot of surf landings on Park Point in Duluth, but we had always practiced when we were well rested and knew that the entire shoreline was free from protruding boulders. Today we were neither well rested nor knowledgeable about the shoreline.

"What do you think?" Paul asked me as we rafted up about a

hundred yards off shore to assess the beach. We watched the breaking waves for a while. They seemed to break pretty evenly, not re-
vealing any large rocks under the surf.

"I'm nervous, but we have no choice," I finally responded.

"I'll go in first. Give me time to land. I'll catch your boat and help
you." I let go of his blue boat, pushed him toward shore, and began
to backpaddle so I could hold position. I watched him approach the
edge of the surf line, knew he was counting sets of waves, waiting
for the smallest one.

He let three sets pass. That told me he was nervous, that he really
wanted to be sure of the wave patterns before he went. Finally, he
started stroking fast. "Go," I whispered. "Go!" He landed on the
shore, hopped out onto the sand, and started to pull his boat away
from the water when a large wave came in and filled it. He couldn't
move it. I knew I had to go, to get there to help him pull his boat up.

"Steady, Ann, take your time." It helped me to hear my thoughts
spoken out loud. I waited at the edge of the surf, looked over my
shoulder, saw no large waves coming in, and began paddling fast.
Paul caught my boat the moment I hit the sand. He pulled it up out
of surf's reach with me still in the cockpit. I pulled up my spray
skirt, hopped out, helped him pull my boat the rest of the way off
the beach, and then we ran over to his boat. Even with two of us
pulling, it was hard to move the water-filled craft far enough out of
surf's reach to be able to pump the water out. When we finally had it
far enough up beyond the surf, we stopped to catch our breath, to
look at the lake and the waves pounding in. I stepped around from
my side of the bow of his boat, put my arm around him, and said,
"What does cold and wet matter; we are alive!"

"No shit," he said.

It had taken us two hours to paddle three miles. We had started
at 6 A.M. It was now 8 A.M. In the time it usually takes me to get up,
feed the family breakfast, and be off for the day, I had come as close
as I had ever come in my life to letting go of it. I stood staring at the
lake and the surf and the clearing skies until I started to shake. I was
soaking wet, the wind was howling at forty miles per hour, and

though the sun was beginning to break through the clouds, the temperature was in the forties. Once again survival determined right action.

Paul and I got out of our wet clothes by dressing in the shelter of scrubby pine and fir trees just beyond the sandy shore. We emptied our boats, then unrolled our tents and, using my clothespins, hung them out to dry in the raging wind. "Hey, what do you say we have spaghetti for breakfast?" yelled Paul above the roar of surf and flapping tents.

"Great, I'll get the stove going over there in the shelter of that big boulder. Would you gather some water from the river?" We were each wearing every piece of clothing we had along. I was wearing long underwear, wind pants and rain pants, long-sleeved polypropylene top, wool sweater, wool jacket, windbreaker, wool socks, hiking boots, wool stocking cap, and gloves. And I was trembling uncontrollably the whole time I was lighting the stove, boiling the water, and stirring the noodles.

We paused and held gloved hands before eating the first bite. "For life," I said. "I give thanks for life." Paul nodded, and we ate in silence. It would have been impossible to talk. The feel of the warm spaghetti going into my nearly hypothermic body, massaging its way down my throat, releasing its heat into my frozen interior, was so amazing, so intense, that I could focus on nothing else. I was making love to my body, bringing it back to life.

By 2 P.M. we could see that the wind was subsiding. While we were eating, Paul had placed a stick in the sand marking the high point of the surf. The surf line was several feet below that now. We reasoned that we could paddle a few more hours before setting up camp.

"Paul, it's important to me to be the last one to take off. You took the risk by being first to come in. I want to take the risk going out." He looked at me, smiled, and nodded. I wanted to prove myself in this way, to know I was an equal partner again.

I pushed him and his loaded boat out into the surf in a small set of waves, moved my boat to the water's edge, climbed in, and secured the spray skirt. We had spent a lot of time watching the waves break while waiting for the wind to subside. The waves on this beach broke quite differently than they did on Park Point. There the bottom was shallow a long way out. Here it was obvious that the shore dropped off quickly, because the incoming waves curled and hit with some force, since they only hit a small area of shallows. I knew any one of those waves would tip me if I timed my takeoff wrong.

Myself, my boat, and my gear weighed about 260 pounds. All of that weight was sitting in one spot on the beach, and I had only my arms to budge it into the water. I counted three big waves, two small ones, three big ones. Yes, go for it! I pressed both of my neoprene-mittened hands into the sand and began to push my boat to water deep enough to float it. I could see the next big wave moving in. Push! Push! Yes, I'm floating. Now paddle! Paddle!

The wave hit me in the face, but it didn't matter. My boat was heading straight into it and I was far enough off the shore not to be pushed back onto the sand. I did it! I did it! I paddled out to Paul. "Nice job, kiddo!" he shouted.

"Thanks, I needed that."

"Hey, you're tough! Let's see how many miles we can still make today." And miles we did make. We paddled for five more hours that day, past Cape Gargantua and its four-hundred-foot hills, past Devil's Warehouse Island with its huge cave, and into the trailing seas of a late afternoon sun, to a campsite on Buckshot Creek.

I don't have much recollection of those five hours. We did pass through a spectacular maze of rocky islands. We did stop once on a small, unnamed island and find a magnificent band of quartz marbled into red and purple lava rock. There were big seas pushing us along. Late in the day the orange-red glow on rocks and distant hills moved me to sing. But mostly, I was in the post-euphoric high of an athlete who has just accomplished the greatest feat of her life. I felt invincible, undefeatable. It was not until the next day when we paddled into the immense three-hundred-plus-unit Agawa Bay Campground that I was able to gain some perspective on our feat.

When we landed on the shore, a couple and their two sons were walking on the beach. Strangers always seemed to be attracted to us, curious about two small boats paddling in from the big lake. "Were you out yesterday?" asked the mother.

"Yes," I responded.

"Holy smokes," said the father. "We didn't even dare walk on this beach yesterday — you could hardly stand up!" We talked to them awhile and learned that they lived in the same town as my in-laws and, indeed, he worked with my mother-in-law! On the planet's largest lake, at least a half dozen times we spontaneously met people we somehow knew. The earth is so small, we are all so connected.

With the help of these people, we eventually located our friend Bob, who had decided to follow us by land through Lake Superior Provincial Park. "Hey, I'm glad you guys are all right," Bob said. "I wanted to reserve us a campsite on the shore of the lake, but yesterday no one had tents pitched on those lakeshore sites, because they simply wouldn't stay up in the wind."

That afternoon I lent them my boat and Paul took Bob for a long paddle. At each stop where friends met us on the trip, the weather had cooperated, so we were able to accomplish our pre-trip dream of getting people into boats and out on the lake. By this point in the trip it had become a joke: on our rest days the weather would be wonderful, on our paddling days the weather would be horrendous.

I sat on the sand beach, leaning up against a driftwood log, writing in my journal and watching the great sun ball sink lower into the calm lake horizon.

July 21, 6 P.M.

It's fun to watch Bob and Paul play with each other. This paddle they're doing together is no small feat. Bob is terrified of the water, of small boats, but he trusts Paul — just like our friend Sue trusted me to take her out on the lake in Pukaskwa. Enabling, that's what we're doing with this trip. Enabling others to share our dream, to be

challenged, expanded in their lives. Well, yesterday sure expanded
my life! I am damn lucky to have lived. I do not want to be heroic
about it. I want to understand what happened out there. Paul called
me "tough" after I paddled out through the surf unassisted. It made
me feel good, accepted, especially after our misunderstanding of the
day before. I paddled the rest of the day feeling "tough," one of the
guys. But the lesson I want to/need to learn is NOT about being one
of the guys.

I set down my journal, walked barefoot to our campsite, retrieved my yellow pouch, and returned to the warm sand, still
dressed only in shorts and a T-shirt. I pulled Brian's and Sally's
pictures out of the two-inch-square "Tribes" booklet and reread the
lines: "We are doing the impossible. We are teaching ourselves to be
human."

I held the pictures in my hands and spoke aloud to my children:
"I am coming back. I won't let anything happen to me. I'm going to
be a different person, someone better able to help you open the
doors of possibility for yourselves, a woman who is going to claim
her own possibilities."

That night I had a dream that unnerved me. I was back home in
Duluth in our cedar-sided house. My parents were visiting. Dave
and my folks were giving me a terrible time about traveling so much
for my work, about how I was never home, about how the bathroom
floor hadn't been washed in months. We were all sitting in the living
room on chairs, watching Brian and Sally build houses out of decks
of cards on the carpeting. It was a trick Betty had taught them. I was
feeling very uncomfortable, so I slid down off the sofa, where I had
been sitting next to my mom, onto the floor to play with the children. But within minutes I exploded in a torrent of words and rage,
smashed the kids' carefully constructed houses, and stomped out of
the living room and out the door.

How could I do that? Destroy the children's card houses, walk
out on Dave and my folks? I pushed the dream out of my mind and
sat up in my portable home, feeling the cold air on my body. I pulled

on the rest of my clothes, unzipped the tent, and walked the two blocks to the campground bathroom.

No one was up yet. Sunlight was beginning to stream through the forest. The picnic tables, the lawn chairs, the parked bikes were all empty. No generators were on in the campers, no boom boxes were playing from tents. The world was sleeping, but I could not. I walked briskly past a grassy meadow, stopped, and gawked. "Frost! My God, there's frost on the grass!" I could not believe my eyes. It was July 22. I walked to the beach after visiting the latrine, still lost in thought about the dream.

That rage in my dream was impotent — it accomplished nothing, got me nowhere. In the dream my husband and parents harassed me to conform, to stay the traditional woman. As a traditional woman, I couldn't lash out at those in authority over me, so I lashed out at those I was in authority over — my children. Though I'd seldom expressed it, this form of rage was everywhere in the world around me.

Yet it was rage that had saved my life the day before, so rage was not always impotent; sometimes it was life-giving. In the storm it was the energy I had needed. My feelings were translated into action that was pertinent and real. Rage was fuel that allowed my paddling skills to function at full force. It only barely dawned on me what an unusual occurrence this was for a woman — to experience full-blown rage and release it in a way that managed to save her life.

There are moments when we experience self-evolution, when the structure of who we are is changed by choice and circumstance. For that moment on the beach, I sensed my own maturity growing. A mottled brown gull flew by. A juvenile bird. I remembered the gull rock and the baby fluff balls on sticks I had chuckled at one month ago so many miles back in Minnesota. One month ago this gull could not fly. It, too, was maturing. In that month it had grown from a ball of fluff awkwardly hopping on rocks to a bird with wings and webbed feet that could paddle in cold seas for hours, and finally to a bird that could fly.

I wanted to be like that gull. Flying. Free. There were changes coming in my life that my forty-three-year-old being couldn't imagine, standing on that sandy beach on a cold summer day. Changes that had to do with the dream reality and the storm reality.

9

Windbound

Listen. The earth speaks wisdom. Tells when and how to move.
Sets a cadence for the rhythm of our days, our lives.
Unleashes the wildness within.

THOUGH THE MORNING of July 22 was frosty cold, it was the beginning of our first stretch of calm and warmth, a prolonged relaxing of the trials dealt us by She-Who-Is-The-Biggest. After thirty-five days of mostly cold, wet, windy, and foggy weather, we would be given four warm, calm days for crossing the dangerous shipping lanes of Whitefish Bay.

When I returned from my solo walk to the beach, Paul had a fire going and navigation charts spread out on the wooden picnic table.

"What's up?" I asked. "Are you finding a way for us to shortcut Whitefish Bay?"

There are some places on She-Who-Is-The-Biggest known more for their treachery than their beauty. Whitefish Bay lies at the top of that list. A tiny bulge in the far southeast corner of a map of the lake, it is more than eighty miles in circumference — with twenty-three of those miles being the mouth that opens into the main body of the lake, and two miles on the opposite side being the mouth of the Saint Mary's River that leads into the Sioux Locks and the other great lakes. Every large ship entering and leaving Lake Superior must pass through this shallow bowl infamous for nor'westers that can whip waves into thirty-foot foes in less than an hour.

At the mouth of the Saint Mary's River, shipping lanes are one and a half miles wide. From there these lines, drawn so clearly on navigation charts, fan out until the swath they cut is seven miles wide at the mouth of the bay. Big ships, five hundred to a thousand feet in length and carrying iron ore, grain, or bulk goods, must travel within the confines of the lanes as they move cargo from one city to the next. The "lanes" are not, of course, clearly delineated on the water's surface. And therein lies the challenge for small craft. The freighters and some of the larger sailboats and motorboats carry Loran navigation equipment, which charts their precise location using sophisticated satellite technology. However, most small boats that need to cross the lanes must simply guess their location and proceed with caution. While in the shipping lanes, small craft are extremely vulnerable because they do not have the right of way. Even if they did, it would be meaningless. The large, lumbering freighters can't "see" small boats, nor could they stop if they did. It takes nearly a quarter-mile of reverse engine braking to bring these giants to a halt.

"With any luck, the day after tomorrow we'll be back in the States," said Paul.

"You sound like a Canadian," I responded.

"I feel like one," he smiled. "People have been so good to us along this shore of the lake, the scenery has been so wild, so unspoiled. I have some ambivalence about returning to the more populated U.S. shore."

"I agree, but there's going to be something about paddling across that border that is incredibly reassuring to me. I will feel a giant step closer to knowing I'm going to make it all the way around."

We studied the charts, mapped our route, and began paddling the last stretch of Canadian shore. When we passed Batchawana Bay and Rudderhead Point on July 24, it was sunny, warm, flat-calm. We made a stop on Maple Island and looked at Ile Parisienne through our binoculars. The five-mile-long island looked so inviting, floating out there nine miles away in the middle of Whitefish Bay. The sky was too hazy to see beyond it to the Michigan shore, but I thought about short-cutting our way across. It was only 9 A.M. I reasoned that we could easily do the nine-mile crossing to the island and then the fourteen-mile crossing to the U.S. shore in one day. The weather was so good, so clear. It would save us two days of paddling!

Do hawks, with their phenomenal ability to soar and flap, take the shortcut from Canada across the widest part of the lake to the United States? Of course not. They slowly work their way down along the shore, using the easy drafts of thermals created by the high hills, stopping to rest on land when fog or adverse winds come in. Wild creatures know their limits, their vulnerabilities.

I didn't speak my temptation aloud. If Paul shared it, he said nothing. This summer particularly, we could not trust the weather to stay calm for a whole day. And we certainly could not count on no ships passing through the shipping lanes during the two hours it would take us to cross them. We had read that traffic through Whitefish Bay could be as frequent as one ship every forty-five minutes. Wild creatures who do not recognize risk and respect it do not live.

From Maple Island we paddled along the shoreline, with its mixture of cabins, homes, and resorts, sixteen miles to Gros Cap, our last stop in Canada. We arrived at the small cluster of buildings, which had put this spot on the map, at 2 P.M. on a warm Friday. Paul and I both dove into the water near the small, wooden dock. Oooh, cool release from heat and sweat! The lake served as a giant cold pack for every tired muscle in every part of my body. The dive propelled me some distance from the shore. I let my body go limp, surrender to the marvelous coolness, float to the surface like a fresh-water jellyfish. The buoyancy provided by my wet suit enabled me to roll over on my back and lie spread-eagled on the water's surface, toes pointing skyward, arms reaching straight out, floating on the ultimate water bed.

I swam back to shore, sat down in the sand, pried off my wet suit, and walked to the Blue Water Inn in my swimming suit, carrying a change of shorts and a T-shirt. The sign on the outside of the little café read, "Friday Special: $6.95 — All the fish and chips you can eat."

"Boy, are they in trouble," I said laughingly to Paul. Our French-Canadian waitress was delighted when we asked for second helpings of the batter-covered whitefish, the fries, and the coleslaw. I knew I wasn't full after those seconds. "Paul, do you think I dare ask for a third helping?"

"Hey, go for it!" A third helping and a malt later, I finally felt full. I had not felt this full since dinner at the Rossport Inn. Each and every cell in my body felt satiated, happy, alive. Paul got up from our little booth to go to the bathroom. There weren't any other customers in the café so early in the afternoon. I closed my eyes, leaned back in the plastic-padded seat, and consciously imagined the nourishment making its way to cells damaged by the abuse of too much exertion, too little food. To them I whispered a small prayer: "Thank you. I appreciate what you've done. I am trying to be careful."

Like two gorged wild creatures, we wandered outside to find a shady place to rest and digest our meals. I went first to my boat and pinched open the clamp holding the front hatch in place. Everything was so easy when it was warm. Canada had delivered many finger-numbing days when I could not even manage to open the clasps without first blowing warm air on my fingers. A man and woman and their two children waded into the water next to my boat. One of the little girls peeked into the open hatch. Her mother admonished her, but I encouraged her to look further, asking for her help finding the yellow bag. She was delighted to find it and pull it out.

I walked a short way to a birch tree and took some sage from a little plastic bag, carefully laying it in the grass below the tree. A car drove up and parked on the gravel in front of the Blue Water Inn behind me. A family of three emerged and walked past on the way to the beach. This was not a setting for a private, introspective cere-mony, not the time to reflect on memories of the harsh, rugged, Canadian journey. So I simply lay on my side on the lawn and stared out across the glass-calm waters separating me from the United States. After a time, I wandered over to Paul's resting spot. "Could I interest anyone in a nice, calm paddle?"

"Is that a promise?" We both chuckled. We had planned for and worried about crossing these shipping lanes for days. Now it appeared the final push would be easy, but I couldn't rest until the goal was really completed.

We picked up our things, got back into our wet suits, and paddled out to the buoy station at the edge of the shipping channel. Using our binoculars, we looked down toward the Sioux Locks and out into the expanse of Whitefish Bay. Nothing was approaching from the bay, but there was a freighter coming up from the locks, about a half-mile away. We floated peacefully on the water. I was busy taking pictures. Then Paul spotted another ship coming up from the locks behind the first one. If we let both ships pass before going, we'd be here an hour with no guarantee that more ships weren't in line behind these two. We decided to cross behind the first ship. Since it was moving at nearly triple our speed, we reasoned that if we began paddling immediately we should pass exactly behind it. So off we went, paddling at what initially looked like a crash course toward the oncoming freighter.

I was sprinting, paddling at a tempo well beyond my normal cadence. With these big metal monsters bearing down on us, I couldn't relax into any kind of rhythm, couldn't think about pacing myself, could focus on only one thought: "Get across."

After fifteen minutes I could see we were going to pass behind the first freighter, as planned. Then I simply shifted my fear to the next approaching boat. It seemed to be coming faster than the first and was farther over in the shipping lane, closer to the U.S. shore. Paul was well ahead of me. Stroke, Ann, stroke. The boat is heading right toward you. The adrenaline of fear pumped strength into my arms, until I could clearly see that I had passed safely in front of the oncoming black-and-white U.S. Steel ship. That's how close I had gotten: close enough to read the insignia on the bow of the boat.

Then I gave up. Quit. Couldn't think of paddling another stroke. My will was gone, desire had been sucked out of me, I couldn't paddle. I lifted up my arms, did a few strokes, but that was all. I was boatbound. Immobilized. Paul's boat was far ahead, waiting for me, but I couldn't move. My mind said, "You must paddle." My body said, "I can't."

"Must."

"Can't."

"Must."

"Can't."

I saw Paul turn around in his boat and look at me. Once again my mind won the battle. I started stroking slowly toward my friend.

"What do you say we try and put in some miles before dark?" he said. "My weather-band says a big storm will be moving in tomorrow out of the northwest. We want to be as far over on the west shore of this bay as possible when that hits."

I couldn't believe he was saying this. I must have stared at him for a long time.

"Well, what do you think?" he asked again.

"I think I can't go any farther. I think I don't want to go any farther. We started paddling in the dark eleven hours and thirty-two miles ago to do this crossing safely. We have just finished the Canadian leg of our journey. I need to stop and honor this passage." I was as stunned by my words as he was.

He rubbed the stubble of his beard with his hand, turned, and said, "Okay, let's find a place over there." We were on shore in ten minutes. We chose spots several hundred yards apart to set up our tents. Sitting on the sand beach in shorts and a T-shirt, grateful that the day's hot sun was too low in the sky to burn me further, I tried to write something in my journal:

July 24, 8 P.M.

I have been up since 4 A.M. Paul and I rose in total darkness and began paddling in the barest of dawn light to increase our chances of being able to cross the shipping lane today. The weather held, so we were able to cross. I should be feeling joy at completing it safely, at finishing the Canadian part of the trip, but I don't. I'm still feeling this awful lethargy that hit me as soon as we made the crossing. I don't know what this is about.

I laid down the pen and began digging trenches in the sand in front of me with my feet. Straighten the leg out, pull it back, straighten it out, pull it back. My heels excavated neat leg rests. I had created an earth chair. The earth was holding me. I was no longer moving or pushing. My mind and body could finally rest together in the same place.

The thought that came to me was, "I don't want to be heading home. I'm not ready." The sun had slipped below the horizon. The white, leading edges of the predicted storm, wispy trails of clouds I call mare's tails, had turned magenta and orange. The day was done. My old life was not. It was somewhere at the base of that beautiful sunset. Same house, same people, same patterns waiting for me to rejoin them. But I was not the same, I had no intention of simply slipping back into the old routines. Here, on this beach, in this earth chair, I really began to think about returning home. The first half of the trip had been about survival and stripping down. This second half of the trip had to be about preparation and rebuilding.

With the threat of a nor'wester hanging over our heads, we again rose early in hopes that we could paddle the full thirty-six miles to the tip of Whitefish Bay in the lee of northwest winds before the storm hit. About midday we nudged our boats up onto a sand beach that we thought was the community of Paradise, Michigan. An older couple walked over to greet us and began asking questions. We learned that this was their beach, that the man was a retired fishing captain from the Department of Natural Resources. As he watched us pull our boats safely off the beach and tie them to trees he said, "You do know what you're doing. We always tied our boats up, too. Even on a pretty decent day like this you never know when the lake will come up. Why I remember . . ."

And so it went. This balding, jovial man regaled us with tales about his thirty years of boating on the lake. While he talked we were fed pasties at the Paradise Cafe, watched his wife finish making fudge, and met the neighbors. After our midday rest, when we finally climbed back into our boats with packages of still-warm fudge, we had forgotten our fears of an impending storm; but within an hour the wind kicked up, and we remembered.

By the time we reached Whitefish Point at the mouth of the bay, the sky had grown black with clouds and the fading of the day's light. Winds were now strong out of the northwest and were creating a wraparound effect — that is, even though we were on the leeward side of Whitefish Point, there was still considerable wave action. We carefully counted waves before we landed in the small surf, relieved to have a safe end to a long day. We were not prepared for what we found on shore. Everywhere were signs: "Private property, no trespassing." "No public camping allowed." We tried knocking on several cottages to ask if we might camp the night on their beach to avoid the storm. No one answered at the first two homes. An older man opened the third door. "We're kayakers who've just come off the lake. There is a storm coming. Might we camp on your stretch of beach this evening while we sit the storm out?" He turned his head and looked into the room, probably seeking his wife's opinion.

"Sorry, we can't let no one camp here," he said, already beginning to shut the door. Paul and I turned to walk back down his wooden steps. It was the first time our request for help had been denied. Apparently, travelers in need of shelter in a storm were not a novelty here.

On the wilder shores of the lake we had only the elements to contend with. We had barely survived their challenge. Now it appeared that part of our preparation for returning to civilization was to deal with some of its harsher realities. I felt angry and defeated. In Canada, even in more populous areas, we had always been welcomed, indeed, often treated as celebrities. This rejection deepened my ambivalence about aiming toward home.

At 8:30 P.M., fifteen hours after we'd pushed off from our campsite, we still had no place to pitch our tents. "We've got to backtrack," said Paul. "We can't go around that point. Seas are huge out there."

Backward. For the first time on the trip we had to lose mileage! I sloshed out into the water with my booties and did a clumsy takeoff in the small surf. We paddled back about a mile to a clearing that had no homes and no signs posted. Paul landed first, quickly and skillfully. I was busy thinking about how I'd put the tent up in the dark and the rain, had my plan for unloading and setting up camp all rehearsed. A wave picked my boat up and carried me in sideways. I braced and rode it in, but I'd already pulled up my spray skirt, so a lot of water went into my boat.

Paul ran over to help. "Are you okay?" he asked.

"Yeah, just dumb, not paying attention." By the time we had unloaded our boats and carried things up and over the dune, it was totally dark. I found my flashlight and put up the tent by holding the light in my mouth. The weather was still warm, but I had to put on my rain parka and tie the hood around my face to keep the mosquitoes away. Paul pitched his tent a considerable distance from mine, but walked over to make sure I was all right before retiring.

"You did a heck of a job paddling today," he said, reaching to give me a hug.

"Thanks," I said, opening my arms. I knew he was just as exhausted as I was. I put my arms around his neck and clung to him as long as I dared.

It was too warm to lie inside my sleeping bag, so I lay on top of it. I was numb with exhaustion. That's a powerful phrase — "numb with exhaustion." Earlier in my life I had known the meaning of it a number of times that I could recollect — long days of backpacking, the end of a marathon, several days of fighting backcountry forest fires. But never in my life had I endured this kind of utter physical depletion day after day after day. How can a body exercise hard for ten or eleven hours a day, on and on and on? I knew it wasn't good for me. The pain in my back as I stepped out of the kayak every night was harder and harder to ignore. Somewhere, many days ago, I felt I had moved from the point of peak physical conditioning into a regimen that was more about long-term depletion than maintaining extreme physical conditioning. Lying here I literally felt like a mind without a body.

Then I felt a warm tingling at the corner of my nostrils and at the top of my nose. My face made a few minute twitches. I closed my eyes. Tears were rising, reaching, looking for release. I opened my eyes. One neat tear rolled out of each eye and down my cheeks. It was so lonely to cry alone, so wonderful to be nurtured and held through sadness or fear.

I remembered the first time Betty did that for me. We were standing on opposite sides of an eighteen-inch-wide ledge that was six feet long. We were each wearing fifty-pound backpacks. On one side of us was the mountain. On the other side it was fifteen hundred feet straight down to the valley below. The wind was gusting. We were on a five-day summer backpacking trip in the Colorado Rockies. Either I kept going or we had to completely retrace the trip. I was frozen there. Terrified. The only thought that would go through my mind was, "We just adopted Brian. He's so little. He needs me."

She came scampering back across the ledge and said, "It's okay, Ann, we don't have to go this way. Come on, I'll find another route." That night in this same little tent she had said, "Do you mind if I ask what froze you out there?" I was lying on my back looking up at this same close, dark ceiling. She was lying on her back. I started to tell her about Brian, but it came out in an explosion of tears. She rolled over in her sleeping bag and put her arms around me, held me until the storm subsided. I let her hold me like I let Paul hold me, but somehow the tears came with her. And now I reached for her gray jacket, curled up around it, and let the tears come again.

The next morning it was raining lightly and blowing hard, down in the little pine forest where we'd pitched our tents. Our weather-band radios confirmed the storm's arrival: "Four- to seven-foot seas, small craft advisories." When we clambered up the dune, we were standing on nearly the most northwest point of this big basin. We looked out across the bay whose shorelines we had paddled these last two days. It was a sea of whitecaps. Waves weren't breaking on the shore below us, because we were in the lee of the nor'wester. But even a half-mile out from our shore it was plenty choppy. And back where we were camping yesterday morning there were undoubtedly seven-foot waves obliterating the earth chair I'd made. "Let's walk to the museum so we can look out on the open lake," said Paul.

"Yeah, maybe we can find a café and get a cup of coffee," I added. Two landbound adventurers left the challenge of their wilderness, choosing the omnipresence of civilization. Most of the time on the trip this option was available to us. Today we took it. It felt good to stretch legs, to feel their strength, to be upright instead of bent in half, to be heading toward people.

The museum at Whitefish Point contained an impressive array of old buoys, anchors, and lights. There were maps and sagas of shipwrecks. "Graveyard of Superior," one sign called this immense bay. More shipwrecks have occurred here than at any other place on the lake. The reasons listed were: all ships entering or leaving the lake had to pass through here; the area gets northwest winds that have had the fetch of the entire lake; the shallow waters of the big bay catch incoming waves, ricochet them off the bottom, and create waves twice the size of the old ones. There were photos in the museum of forty-foot waves.

I walked out of the neatly painted, white-sided museum building and followed a paved path to the shore of the lake. There weren't forty-foot waves out there, but there were at least some ten-foot waves. It was very cold standing up against the constant pushing of the wind's frigid hand. I found my way to a sandy spot, dropped to my stomach, propped my head in my hands, and watched the action. It was an enormous relief to be on shore simply admiring the waves, not counting them to figure out when and how to go through them. I looked around at the beach. Despite the cold of the day, there were quite a few people out walking. None of them were dressed to be out very long. Some of them even wore shorts. After all, they could simply walk to their cars, close the doors, and flip on their heaters. I took the journal out of my jacket, sat up, and penned the first poem of the trip in my journal:

Windbound

Torso and trunk cloaked in wool and wind shell
that ward off chill gusts and purple/gray sky.
Rooted. Windbound.

Not shorebound like a tourist idly wishing for better weather.
But windbound. Studying She-Who-Is-The-Biggest,
waiting out her moods, venturing out when it feels safe.
Ah, but She's a trickster, this one.
Some days I venture out and
> *in comes the fog . . . or*
> *the wind shifts and builds . . . or*
> *skies darken and a thunderstorm approaches.*
Again and again I venture out in hope, in caution, but not today.
Today whitecapped, angry waves bite at the bow of a big freighter,
hurtle themselves thirty feet up and over the deck.
Graveyard of Superior . . . not today for that freighter,
not today for this windbound paddler.
Today I rest and give thanks that one more day finds me safe.

It was a day for phone calls. I called my family, Christina, several other friends. All the phone calls felt different than they had from the fog of the Canadian shore. I could feel my enthusiasm, my storytelling powers, my interest in *their* stories. This was the same old Ann coming through — the optimist, the concerned and connected friend, the confident adventurer.

This time when I called Christina she was in Duluth teaching. "Now where are you calling from?" she asked.

"Whitefish Point, Michigan, from a shipwreck museum."

"Well, I know I don't have to worry about you shipwrecking today," she said cheerfully. "It's gorgeous here. The lake is like a giant mirror."

"Actually, it's so windy and stormy here we're staying put on shore."

"You're kidding!"

"No," I responded. "How's your class going?"

"Pretty well. I seem to have moved through some of that fog and staleness we talked about last time. You sure sound different! You have great energy!"

"Yeah, I do. I had another long, tough day yesterday, but I have some perspective now, have gotten enough glimpses of wisdom that I bounce back faster after the crashes."

The wind was howling so loudly that I had to press my hand hard over my left ear to block out its incessant whistling, had to force the earpiece deeper into my right ear, pushing my body against the leeward side of the building to better fit into the three-sided phone booth.

It felt wonderful not to be in trouble, not to be grasping the phone cord as a lifeline. I shared some of the anecdotes from yesterday's trip — the package of warm fudge, the rejection by landowners, the collapse at day's end. "The really important thing is that I'm letting myself have feelings, not beating myself up for them. And as a result, they contribute to my strength, rather than draining me."

When we finished talking, she said, "I'm so glad you're on land, that you're safe today. When it's time to paddle again, remember, paddle like heaven."

"Yeah, paddle like heaven. Not 'paddle like hell.' I like that. You take good care, too. Talk to you soon."

I stepped out confidently from behind the building. The full force of the wind hit me, pushing me backward a step. I returned to the shelter of the building. First I crammed a wool stocking cap over my head, then I pulled up the hood on my rain jacket and tied it tightly. Then, once again, I confidently stepped into the wind, pushing my body forward in a kind of dance with this invisible partner.

I found a birch tree that had a sitting space about three feet off the ground from which eight arms emerged in all directions. It invited me to come rest awhile. Certainly I hadn't done much sitting still on this trip, but I remembered some of the times I had: my friend's cabin on the Minnesota shore, the field of boulders near the ancient stone altar, the Pukaskwa River, the island off Old Woman's Bay. And what I remembered about each of those times was the insights that had occurred for me.

I leaned back on one branch, dangled my feet around another, put my hands behind my neck, and just stared at the lake. This was not a time for writing or reading or talking with anyone. This was about seeking communion. I don't know how long I was reclining there or even exactly what communication I was expecting. All of those other times of quiet and insight I had not been actively looking for anything. It simply came to me. Here I was looking, but nothing save the roar of the wind, the pounding of the surf, the swaying of the tree came into my awareness.

But then came the memory of a conversation Betty and I had about one month into her illness. She and I were sitting on the couch in the living room of her home in Utah, listening to music, waiting for dinner to finish cooking. She had just gotten out of the hospital after her initial, unsuccessful surgery.

"What do you think happens after people die?" she had asked. My agnostic, scientific friend sat looking at me waiting for an answer. I had begun reading some books on death as soon as I learned of her tumor, but my theories were as vaguely formed as her skepticism was entrenched.

"Well, the only thing I do know is that there is more to you and me than our two bodies on this sofa. I know that, because I feel your spirit when you're not with me. Sometimes when I'm disciplining Sally your voice says in my ear, 'Don't be so hard on her, Ann.' And so, I know that if you don't live through this you'll always be with me — the memories, the feelings, the shared wisdom."

She seemed satisfied by my answer, but I wasn't. I really didn't have a clue what happened after death, except that I was sure it didn't have anything to do with ascending to some big hall full of angels in white robes. I couldn't imagine Betty being happy in a place like that.

The insight faded and I again became aware of the wind and surf. It felt good to be cradled by this tree, but I was getting cold and hungry, so I climbed down, thanked it for holding me, and began the mile walk back to our campsite.

"Do you feel like having some soup if I fire up the stove?" I asked Paul, who was reading in his tent.

"Sure," he said.

I walked the hundred yards back to my tent, following the grassy clearing and the line of pines. I pulled the stove out of its river bag,

assembled it, primed the pump, and finally lit it despite the gusti-
ness of the wind. Paul came over carrying a plastic sack of food and
his mug. "When you walked back, did you see that sign advertising
fresh fish?"

"Yeah, but it looked so weather-beaten I couldn't imagine it was
for real."

"Well, it is. I walked down the road and talked to the owner. He
said his boats come in at about five with fresh whitefish. Want to
walk down with me later and buy one for supper?"

"You bet! Hey, did you get through to anyone on the phone?"

A cloud passed over his eyes. He bowed his head to focus on
opening the plastic bag of his soup powder. "Yeah, to Mary and the
kids. It's hard sometimes, isn't it? I want to call home, but it's so hard
to catch them at a good time."

His honesty and vulnerability surprised me. His fear had tiptoed
out of the forest into the clearing. I did not want to say anything that
would frighten it away.

"Yeah, it's hard for me, too. Dave never has much to say. Sally
seems to be having a pretty lonely summer. Only Brian manages to
talk much."

"Ann, how are you feeling about going home?"

"Uneasy, scared."

"Mary told me she's taking off on a short trip as soon as I get
home. I understand she needs time away after the summer, but I was
hoping she'd want to spend time with me first."

The wind was howling through the tops of the trees around us.
The song was wild and beckoning, not comforting or gentle. "Paul,
mostly I have been totally out of sync with everyone I've called.
What we're living through is way beyond anyone else's wildest imagination. We seldom go indoors. They seldom go outdoors. We make
day-to-day decisions that are mostly about physical safety. They
don't worry much about physical safety. We get lonesome and sit
quietly with the trees or the lake. They get lonesome and turn on the
radio or TV or call someone. We are becoming some other kind of
creatures, Paul. Reentry is not going to be easy. Don't take Mary's trip

personally. Give her the space she needs so that you can come to-gether, both ready to be at home."

His blue eyes stared at me. I held his gaze. Then he nodded, reached for the pot of hot water, and poured it into his mug.

That night he cooked dinner for me: fresh whitefish, potatoes he had secretly bought in the Paradise store, and onions — lots of on-ions. He built the fire in a swale slightly above the beach, but still below the crest of the dune that sheltered our tents from lake winds. It was a hallowed little spot free from blasts of wind and sand that surely would have ruined our supper. The warmth of the flames reflected back from the banks around us. I sat with binoculars, watching the steady stream of freighters moving in and out of the bay through the waves.

"I'm glad seas are big enough that we're not even tempted to be out there," I said.

"What do you mean? Why do you think I'm cooking this grand supper? We're heading out after we get stoked up."

I looked at him in disbelief. His eyes were full of mischief. He winked and laughed. "That's what I like about you, Ann, you always believe me. Come on, it's ready," he said, reaching for my hand. We both bowed our heads. "I'm grateful for good food, for safety, for a good friend," he said, and then squeezed my hand before reaching for the spatula.

It was the most delicious dinner we cooked on the entire trip. The fish was so tender, so juicy, that I didn't have to chew it. I placed it on my tongue, moved it around in my mouth, savored the soft texture, swallowed it, and felt its richness all the way down. To a wild creature food is the highlight of the day, the most sought after treasure. We did not dilute our pleasure with words.

We washed the dishes, talked about whether we would be able to paddle tomorrow, allowed many spaces in our conversation. When it was time to retire to our respective tents, I said, "Thanks chef, that was a hell of a meal."

He grinned and held his hand up in a high five sign. I reached up and slapped my hand against his. We both laughed and turned to-ward our tents. That night I wrote in my journal:

July 26, 9 P.M.

This is some kind of turning point on the trip. Paul and I have been honest and open with our feelings today. There is something about heading west, about beginning the journey back toward home that is opening us up. I cannot imagine how it will be to see Dave and the kids again in three days at Grand Marais, Michigan. I certainly cannot think ahead beyond that to returning to a lifestyle of living indoors, of driving cars, of listening to the news. I am going to need Paul when we return home. He is going to need me. No one else will know the language we are learning to speak.

The winds continued, so we stayed another day. One of the strongest memories of that day for me was my early morning walk on the beach. The sun was shining. The wind was still making big waves off in the distance, away from the protection of this shore. The red-brown sand was blown free of tracks. No one was on the beach, even though there were homes less than a mile from where we had pitched our tents. I stopped and photographed several pieces of driftwood in the orange-red light of early morning. The lake near shore was mostly quiet. I paused to skip a few rocks and then continued to saunter down the beach toward the small harbor where we had bought the fish.

Suddenly some strange tracks appeared in front of me. They were not bird tracks. They almost looked like the skittering tracks crabs make next to the ocean. I wondered if some large insect had traveled this way. Then I looked ahead to the end of the tracks, and there rested a pine cone. Ah, the mysterious tracks of the many-toed, white-pine wanderer!

I carefully followed the pine cone tracks, lay on my stomach, and focused my camera. The back lighting of the morning sun, the sparkling of the sand crystals, the immensity of the lone pine cone on the empty beach filled my viewfinder with the most spectacular shot I took the entire trip. After I snapped it and put the lens cover back on, I lay there awhile.

The sand felt so good beneath me. Soft, enfolding. I wriggled my body against it and liked the feel of being touched, of being held.

Oh, it had been so long! I took the camera off my neck, put it ins
my wool cap, and carefully laid it by my side. I wriggled some mc
Snake woman.

The wriggling aroused me, excited my body in a way it had
been alive in nearly a month. I smiled in recognition, laid my h
down, and gazed across the water to the rising sun. "Yes, I am alive
whispered. "I am alive." I slipped my hand through the layer:
clothing to stroke the softness. Gently. There had been so little gen
ness in my life this last month. Gently, steadily. The heaving of
lake on the shore next to me set the pace. She and I in rhythm w
each other.

All of these nights I have lain next to her. Always she breatl
heaves, sighs. On this morning I came alive to her presence. I
sound, her rhythm stirred me. I closed my eyes and felt the whisp
of breath on my cheeks, her fond fingers tousling my hair. I
alive! I am love! And I came into the full wildness of She-Who
Teaching-Me-To-Be-Human.

10

Dune Jumping

In the circle of our family, truthtelling is often the most difficult.
But if we cannot start there, where do we start?

AFTER TWO DAYS of being windbound on Whitefish Point, Paul and I were bobbing up and down in our kayaks, photographing a rainbow rising in the barest of dawn light over the campsite that had kept us safe. It was time to begin moving again. The sun was rising behind us, the storm was moving off to the west, the rainbow was a magnificent stream of colors against a purple-black sky.

For a moment, I was the little white-haired girl with the Dutch-boy haircut who would lie down on our freshly cut, still damp, southern Minnesota lawn after a thunderstorm and imagine what it would look like at the end of the multicolored band that arched over my white wooden house. I believed that at either end of the rainbow you could find a place that looked a lot like the pictures of heaven in my Methodist Sunday School book: happy people in white gowns smiling and helping each other.

Lying on the damp earth, I could feel the slow seeping of warm wetness through my shorts and cotton T-shirt. The earth felt so alive. I pretended it was my friend sending a magic potion into me, trans-forming me into someone who could fly to that place at the end of the rainbow.

The liquid earth beneath was rocking me now, surrounding me with the energy of belief that at the end of the rainbow there still was a magic place. Not the white-robed heaven of my youth, but a place of light, of understanding, where I was going to be at the end of my journey.

My childhood daydreaming sessions on the lawn often ended with being discovered by an inquisitive little sister or nosed by a neighborhood dog; this session was interrupted by the reality of waves that were slowly pushing my boat back toward the beach. When I was a child and the interruption would come, I would whisper to myself, "I'll get there," and then I would jump up, pretending I was ready to play. It was my special secret I shared with no one. On this warm, stormy July morning I turned my boat and began paddling west. I started thinking about seeing Dave and the children in two days. "I'll get there," I said aloud to the lake.

There are three things I remember about the two-day paddle from Whitefish Point to Grand Marais, Michigan, where I met my family for the first time in a month. One was the rainbow. The second was the stop at Hemingway's Big Two-Hearted River. Northwest winds built after the rainbow disappeared, and eventually forced us off the lake at about 2 P.M., still twenty-seven miles from where we were to meet family and friends the next day. It was not so much the beauty of the winding, root beer–colored river that I remembered as it was the descent into paranoia about seeing Dave again. After Paul and I put up our tents, I announced that I was going for a walk to see if there was a phone where I might call and let Dave know the weather was kicking up again.

"Why do that?" Paul asked. "We don't know what will happen. We might still make it there tomorrow."

"I don't know. I just have to call." There was no phone in the primitive campground at the mouth of the river, but a half mile up the dirt road that led into the heavily forested campground was a gas station and convenience store with a phone booth outside.

It was about 4 P.M. when I closed the glass door to call, creating a barrier between me and the cool, gusty winds. Brian picked up the phone after the first ring. "Hi, Mom! Where are you?"

"Oh, about twenty-seven miles from where we're meeting tomorrow. How are you doing, buddy?"

"Pretty good. Do you want us to bring the little kayaks?"

"Yes. Will you organize all the life jackets, paddles, and spray skirts for the boats?"

"Sure, Mom. No problem. Want to talk to Dad?"

"Please. See you tomorrow!"

"Hello," said Dave.

"Hi, hon, how are things going?"

"Not so great. There's so much to get ready." Guilt seeped into every crack of the phone booth. My husband was already taking care of the children so I could be on this trip, and here he was, organizing food and gear for a camping trip designed to resupply me.

"Is the equipment list I left helpful?" I asked.

"Somewhat."

"Is there anything I can do?"

"I don't think so. Do you know for sure what your schedule will be?" We were engaged in the kind of communication most comfortable between us — sharing information about tasks done or undone. When the conversation moved beyond detail into feeling or emotion, we got stuck. So when he asked what our schedule would be, instead of speaking the hard-earned truth of forty-two days of paddling in constantly changing conditions, I deferred to detail and my desire to be helpful, to please. "We have twenty-seven miles to paddle. We should be able to make it for supper tomorrow night."

"Do you want us to wait a day before coming?"

There was no oxygen supply in the tiny phone booth. The glass walls started to press in on me. Of course, I wanted to see them. No, I did not want them to wait a day. I slipped into automatic reassurance. Shut out the churning inside and stayed focused on the plan. "No, just come. We'll get there."

"Okay, see you tomorrow night."

"Drive carefully."

I hung the phone back up on the hook, pushed open the glass door, heaved a sigh of relief when the cool wind blasted in. Each step I took back to my tent felt heavy. I did not feel the attention-getting blasts from the wind, did not notice the sun filtering through the tall pines, did not look up when people passed by me. I had fallen into the world of a marriage that was unemotional, businesslike, and efficient. It was a long hike to the world of the lake.

The third thing I remember about those two days was the night paddle. Strong northwest winds held us windbound until early the next afternoon, July 29. When we finally pushed our boats off the shore near the Big Two-Hearted River into three-foot surf, we knew we could not make it to Grand Marais unless we paddled into the night. "Well, Ann, you've been saying for the entire trip that you wanted to paddle at night. Looks like this is going to be your chance. There's no moon, but at least we won't have trouble finding a target as big as a whole city."

By 9 P.M. the sun was setting, so Paul and I pulled our boats onto a sandy shore to put on warmer gear, eat some gorp, and don our headlamps before it got totally dark. We were not planning to stop again until we got to Grand Marais, which we estimated was still three hours away.

"How are you feeling about this?" asked Paul.

"Good. I'm strong, the sky is glorious. I'm ready." I didn't feel scared.

"This is the point of no return. It's going to be really hard to land on any shore between here and the city without the help of moonlight." I appreciated that he was voicing the cautions. All I was thinking about was getting there, seeing my children, making sure they were all right. I wasn't thinking about the dangers. He continued his instruction: "Remember, waves may have died down to nothing, but paddling at night is tricky, disorienting. We've got to be careful." I watched Paul push his boat off into the orange sunset waters and felt a huge surge of gratitude for his companionship.

We paddled by some people having a campfire on the beach. I wondered what we looked like to them: two purple silhouettes on a sea of orange. The lake's surface was a watercolor painting, transformed with each brush stroke of the sun's diminishing rays. Orange gave way to orange-silver. When the entire sea became liquid mercury, I knew I had been transported to the magic place beyond the end of the rainbow. I was the lake. I was silver. I was sky.

Finally, the Master's brush turned the entire scene black. To onlookers, two paddlers, the boat, the lake, the land, the sky were no more. All was simply black.

But *we* were not onlookers. We were nocturnal animals capable of seeing the shore, of hearing one another's paddles, of sensing how and where to move.

We did not use our headlamps, because they destroyed our ability to see the faint silhouette of shoreline. However, without headlamps, we could not see how we were placing our paddles in the water. It was like walking a trail in the dark. On a path, I place each foot down carefully because I do not know if the next step will contain a rock or a root. On the lake, we placed each blade down carefully because we did not know if we had placed it in a wave or in a trough. If a tug back on the paddle was mostly air and we were not prepared, the imbalance could have flipped us over.

At first it unnerved me that I couldn't see Paul. But after a time, I began to trust my ability to "hear" how far away he was by the sound of his paddle stroking. As I slowly began to trust my paddling steadiness and my radar ability with Paul, my focus expanded to the whole of the night world around me. It was so immense! An infinite dome of endless, tiny white lights. A place of exquisite beauty and latent danger.

The Big Dipper greeted us. It is one of the grandest patterns across the dome. It looked to us not so much like a ladle or spoon as a protective hand that kept nudging us toward the shore, making sure we didn't venture out on the open lake. It was a friend. Were I to have paddled many nights under the stars, a story would have emerged for me, a story that explained my relationship to this friend in the sky. It would not have been the Ojibway legend or the Greek legend, but the night paddler's legend.

And on that night, which grew cold and dark and long, there was this magic, this return to primitive knowing.

We spotted the lights of Grand Marais long before we got there.

We hadn't a clue how far light travels across the water at night, so when we saw the lights, we speeded up our pace thinking we'd be there shortly. But lights on water at night are like mirages in the desert. Elusive. False tellers of good fortune. The harder we paddled, the farther away the lights seemed to get. Minute after minute we stared at those lights, listening for the sound of each other's paddles in the water, keeping the Big Dipper to our right side. This journey was like neither long paddles in the fog nor long paddles in daylight. We could see where we were going, but we never seemed to get there. After a time, the magic of the night faded, just as the magic of the first fog paddles had faded. We became two cold, exhausted animals whose lives depended on moving stroke by stroke toward the only safe place there was to lie down.

By the time we reached the Grand Marais harbor, it was midnight. In this town of five thousand, we reasoned, it would not be too hard to find the Woodland Park campground. We pulled our boats onto the first sand beach we found. "Let's jog, Paul. I'm freezing."

Twenty minutes later, two skinny-legged, wet-suited creatures were walking through a campground full of tents, campers, and cars, looking for a yellow Volvo and a large beige dome tent. No one was awake. We passed row after row of tents, trailers, campers. My mind raced: "What if they didn't get here on time either?"

Under one of the campground light posts, I spotted the car. I walked over next to the tent, dropped to my knees, and unzipped the flap. I peered inside and could see Dave sleeping between Sally and Brian. Paul's son, Galen, was on the far end.

Dave woke up. He laughed in disbelief. That woke up Sally. "Mom!" She shot upright in her sleeping bag and grabbed my neck.

"Oh, Sally, Sally." I held her and rocked her and the tears streamed down my face. "Sweetie, I have missed you so much." I reached out one hand to invite Dave's hand into mine. It was so good to be with my family. So good to be home.

Brian and Galen never woke up. Dave and Sally were able to get back to sleep. Paul and I took the car back to the waterfront, loaded up our things, and returned to set up tents.

Our first day was a day of laughter, of storytelling, of exploration. At 11 A.M. Dave and I were still sitting at the picnic table drinking tea, talking with good friends who had come to be part of the rendezvous, when our kids and their kids all came running up.

"You've got to come see the dunes, Mom!" said Sally. "They are totally awesome. Come on!" I looked at Dave, at the pile of dirty dishes on the table, at our friends, and was held captive only for a brief moment.

"Okay, let's go!" The sun was out and the temperature was climbing. After a while, all the children and I stopped to take off our shoes, sweatshirts, and long-sleeved shirts. We left them in a pile and continued walking down the beach to the bottom of an immense sand dune.

"You climbed all the way up there?" I asked, pointing to the top of the two-hundred-foot hill.

"Come on, Mom!" yelled Brian, already on all fours and climbing.

The five of us scrambling on hands and feet must have looked like a small herd of exotic sand insects. I kept looking at the two youngest children, who were four and seven. They were laughing, confident, as competent as Brian and Sally. Certainly more competent than I. When we got to the top where some trees were growing, we turned and looked to the lake far below. Our pile of clothes and shoes was the size of a pin dot. The huge boulder the kids used to mark the climbing-up place was the size of a racquetball. Sally didn't give me time to get nervous. She grabbed my hand and said, "Okay, jump your way down."

We leaped straight off the side of the sand mountain. Free fall. The split second we were airborne, out of control, was too short for me to finish being scared. Before my scream subsided, the solid, grabbing power of deep sand held my legs and firmly perched me eight feet below where we had started.

"Isn't it cool, Mom?" asked my grinning daughter. "Watch this." Before I could open my mouth, she was flying through the air in a headlong dive. She landed spread-eagled on the sand another eight feet below me, giggling.

Brian and the younger children were a bit more cautious than Sally as they jumped their way feet first down from the dune. All of us became free spirits making leap after leap into the void. Leaping and being caught. Leaping and being caught. Over and over nearly twenty times until we reached the lakeshore. We went up and down the dune a half dozen times before we got hungry enough to return to camp for lunch.

Dave had cleaned up all the dishes and left a note that he had gone hiking in the Nature Conservancy tract of forest adjacent to the dunes. I pulled apples, oranges, cheese, and crackers out of the cooler for the five of us. Our friends the Passineaus returned from their walk and decided to take their children exploring by car. Brian, Sally, and I headed back to the beach with swimsuits, life jackets, my kayak, and the small river kayak from home. Paul and his son, Galen, had taken off on an overnight kayaking trip of their own.

And so it went, a day of pure play in the sun and sand and on the water. I didn't worry about Dave, because he was off doing what he loved best: botanizing, collecting specimens for the university's herbarium. And I was happy just being the mom who loves to play with her kids. More friends arrived from Duluth that evening, and we all carried a picnic dinner down to the beach for a cookout.

Adults drinking beer, kids eating hot dogs, driftwood fire burning late into the night. It felt so good to be a regular person, to be with family and friends, not to be alone. I reached for Dave's hand as we were all walking back from the beach to our tent sites. "Did you have a good time today?" I asked.

"Yeah, I enjoyed the hike," he said. I waited for him to say more, to mention the evening campfire, but nothing was forthcoming.

"So tell me, honestly, how has it been."

"Pretty tough. I just go to work, come home, clean up the mess the kids have made, and cook supper."

"What do they do during the day?"

"As you know, the weather hasn't been great. They've been inside watching a lot of TV, reading, sometimes playing with friends."

"You haven't done anything together, no outings?"

"No, it's more than I can manage just keeping things running at home." His hand felt cold, lifeless, in mine. I was devastated by what he was telling me. The kids had been left mostly alone, hadn't been taken on their summer schedule of picnics and treks to the beach. I saw now that everyone had been in some kind of endurance test. I kept holding his hand, but only because I didn't know how to let go.

When we reached the two tents, Brian asked if he could sleep alone in mine. I knew I didn't want to sleep next to Dave, but I also knew I couldn't refuse this request. "Sure, but let's switch sleeping bags. Mine is pretty grubby from the trip. I don't think you'd want to sleep in it."

Sally put her sleeping bag between Dave and me. The two of them fell asleep quickly. I lay awake staring at the large dome of the family tent for a long time. I knew I should appreciate the fact that I had gotten to go on this trip, that Dave was willing to spend a summer single-parenting, but I was angry and disappointed. The flexibility of his job at the university didn't demand that he go to work every day. He went because that was his priority and his escape. He didn't appear to be using this as an opportunity to get closer to his children. He was just doing his duty.

I remembered my sexual arousal on the beach at Whitefish Bay three days earlier, and the similar awakening prior to seeing Dave one month ago. Then I had not wanted to be sexual, despite his interest. Now, apparently, neither of us had any interest.

The next day, the last day of July, was as beautiful as the previous one. Brian and Sally and I returned to dune jumping, kayaking, and swimming. Sometimes the three of us were alone, sometimes we were joined by our friends, sometimes Dave joined us. I figured he was grateful for time alone and didn't push anything, but all day a tightness grew in my stomach.

We repeated our beach bonfire for supper. Some fireworks added to the festivities of storytelling and eating. I watched Dave across the campfire. He appeared to be having a good time, talking with friends, singing when he knew the songs, helping kids roast marshmallows for s'mores. A good man, an honest man, my partner for nearly twenty-one years, a man who did the things he was supposed to do. A man I seemed unable to connect with intimately.

After midnight, we started the trek back to our tent. Brian and Sally came up beside me, each taking an arm in theirs. "Mom," Brian started.

"Come home with us," Sally continued. "Summer is no fun without you."

I was stunned. Completely unable to speak. My children were asking for help. We walked up the wooden stairs and across the length of the campground in silence. When we reached our tents, I said, "Get your toothbrushes and let's go to the bathhouse." I looked around. Dave was busy talking with one of our friends. I knew the children were waiting for an answer. I had no idea what I was going to say.

Sitting in one of the metal stalls of the bathroom, I felt caged, afraid. My brain kept trying to say, "They are your children, you should . . ." Brian was waiting for us in front of the bathhouse. The three of us were standing under a light. Both children turned and looked at me. I took each of their arms in mine and started walking back toward the tent.

"Do you remember the long trips we took to the desert, when you were toddlers, when you were five and eight, when you were eight and eleven?" They nodded. "Do you remember what we used to tell people when they'd ask how long we'd be gone?" They shook their heads.

"We said we'd come back when we had learned what it was we were supposed to learn. I need you to remember that, because it's the same way for me right now. I'm going around the lake to learn something, and I know I haven't learned it yet. I'm sorry your summer is not good, but I have to keep going. It will just be two more weeks this time." I drew them in closer to my body.

When we got to the tents, twelve-year-old Brian reached for a hug. "It's okay, Mom. I understand." Then he turned and climbed into his tent. Sally just clung to my arm, refusing to look at or talk to me.

"Do you want to stay up with me a little bit?" I asked her. She still said nothing, simply kept grasping my arm. We sat at the picnic table for a while, me talking about the stars, about plans for what we'd do when I returned. By the time Sally and I unzipped the tent door, Dave was asleep. I pulled her sleeping bag next to mine. She climbed in, curled up next to me, and was breathing heavily in minutes.

Tears started streaming down my face. "God, please let this be the right decision," I prayed softly.

The day dawned windy and cloudy and there were sprinkles in the air. I helped pitch a rain tarp over our picnic table and then busied myself repacking gear for the next leg of the journey. Brian and Sally woke in good spirits, willing to be helpful whenever asked. Brian put plastic bags around each new package of food. Sally alternately played with our friend's children and helped Dave prepare scrambled eggs and bagels for breakfast.

At 10 A.M. I hugged everyone good-bye. First, the good friends who had brought so much camaraderie, second, Dave. "Thanks, hon, for everything. Take good care of yourself and the children."

"You be safe," he said, kissing me on the lips.

Brian was not one to show emotion in front of a crowd of people, but he grudgingly gave me a hug. Sally grabbed me around the waist, refused to look at me, and again clung tightly. I bent down and kissed her head. "It won't be long, Sally. You'll see. There will still be summer left for us to go to the beach and play."

"It must be time to go," said Dave. "The weather is turning bad again." Everyone laughed. The two friends who had come to paddle with us for a few days pushed their boats off the sand beach first. Dave helped me attach my spray skirt. I asked him to let Paul know we had gotten a late start when he picked up Galen at the next campground down the shore. Dave pushed my boat. I turned and waved one last time and then started stroking back into the life I was trying to find.

By the time we got to where Paul and Galen had camped, it was midafternoon. Dave had picked Galen up hours before. Our new paddling comrades were tired from battling head winds all the way. We decided to stay and get an early start the next morning. Camp felt awkward to me that night. I was not yet back on the lake. I had been pulled back into my other life, the one I had left the shore of so many weeks ago, the one whose ways had kept me from being fully present on the lake for weeks. Part of my heart wanted to be riding home in the car with the children, but I didn't say that to Paul or my friends, didn't let them feel the magnitude of my grief, because I myself was afraid to feel it. And so, I tried to be a part of cooking, of storytelling, of planning.

I later learned from all three of them that they knew something was bothering me, they just didn't know what. For six weeks the importance of truthtelling had been hammered into me by the lake. For two days I had left Her classroom, and already I had forgotten. The message I'd given to my children was correct, there was more I was supposed to learn.

11

Spirit Song

The instruments of our bodies, when fully tuned and aligned,
move with a grace and rhythm that is holy. In that holiness we are capable
of our greatest actions. In those actions our lives become Spirit Song.

THE SOUTH SHORE of Lake Superior has more sandy beaches and warmer water than the north shore, but it is not necessarily easier to paddle. To a kayaker, what is important are coves — little indentations in the shoreline where the land juts out or dives inward to provide a barrier to incoming waves. A strong wind on a straight shoreline offers nothing but difficult surf to land in. A strong wind on a shoreline with lots of indentations offers small refuges that are not subject to the direct onslaught of the wind. The north shore has many more coves than the south shore.

On August 3, the day after we bid our paddling companions farewell on a white sand beach in Pictured Rocks National Lakeshore, a cove created by a point of land jutting out into the lake rescued us from the lake's fury. And it was this bout of paddling the lake's fury that rescued my heart from a twenty-one-year silence.

Seas had been building steadily from the northwest all day. There was a one-foot chop at our dawn launching. Two-foot waves crept up to three-foot waves by noon. By midafternoon we were moving through three- to four-foot waves. At 3 P.M. we did a tricky landing on a cobble shore, hoping to find a place to camp. We helped each other pull our boats beyond the surf line, tied them to a sharp-edged boulder, walked gingerly along the tops of cobbles, and found a sunny, wind-free place behind a huge, smooth black rock. I pushed my back into the warmth of this massive boulder, poured myself a cup of soup, and drank in silence. Paul's elbow was touching mine. He was studying his map. This little island of calm and warmth was an ecosystem unto itself, a haven where our beleaguered bodies and overstressed minds could recuperate.

Paul said, "We're four miles from Shot Point. The lee side of that point might create a cove with enough protection for a safe landing." He wanted to keep moving. I looked around me. The entire shore was a tangle of big rocks and driftwood tree trunks. The adjacent vegetation was dense alder brush. There was no place to camp. The island of comfort on this shore consisted only of this little three-foot-square space. "Let's listen to our radios."

"Winds building out of the northwest . . . waves four to seven feet by afternoon . . . small craft advisory."

Nearly two months into the trip we were no longer neophytes conferring about the weather. We knew exactly what the forecast meant. We knew the consequences of staying: no place to pitch a tent, sleeping upright against this rock. We knew the consequences of leaving: building seas that would be tough to paddle through even if we were well rested.

I leaned over and studied the map. "I agree with you. Shot Point looks doable. Leaving here won't mean we're doomed to no place to land again if we're right about that point."

Ten minutes later I questioned my judgment. The seas were so large that I could no longer see Paul most of the time. Those northwest winds moving across hundreds of miles of open lake all day now had the water in full momentum. Neither the lake nor the air was as cold as it had been the day the winds switched and nearly took our lives off Lake Superior Provincial Park, but we were in trouble again. Each stroke of the paddle had to be swift and strong, always poised to do a quick brace. Stroke, stroke, stroke, stroke. There was a cadence here. Not the quick moves of the sprinter, but the measured moves of the marathoner.

The tempo lured me into song. At first the songs were things that came out of my memory — musicals, camp ditties, pop tunes. My voice was timid, quiet. But the more I sang, the better I felt. As my confidence grew, my volume increased, my paddling became more rhythmic, like a dance. I was dancing with the waves, singing to their tune. Paddling like heaven. That was the phrase Christina had used. Yes, paddling like heaven.

The next song that came out of my mouth had the tune of "The Impossible Dream," but the words were different, were about this moment, these waves. I smiled at what I was doing. As a child, I had often made up words to tunes I knew. Words that sang my young heart's joy. And then I remembered the last time I had known Spirit Song.

It was the first year of my marriage. Dave was a biology graduate student at Washington State University and I was getting my teaching certificate at the University of Idaho. We were driving the winding mountain roads outside Moscow, Idaho, in our green Studebaker station wagon, Fern. It was night and we were driving home from some event that had made me happy. I started singing as I drove, singing my love for this new life, this new person.

"Stop that," said the voice from the seat next to me.

"What?" I asked.

"Don't do that. I don't like it."

I was crushed. He didn't like the love songs I was making up for him. He was angry. I didn't understand, couldn't understand, but as a young bride of twenty-one I did as my mother taught me. I was silent in the face of this demand from my husband. The silence cemented the first piece of armor between our souls.

Not until this moment did I recapture that song. And it was so easy — the songs, the stroking, the ecstasy. *Grace* and I went careening down the side of a wave, almost like a frictionless sled on a snowy hillside. Hitting the bottom of the trough, hitting the end of a song's phrase, I would dig my paddle in, sing the beginning of the next phrase, and up we'd go to the top of the hill we could not see over. Stroke and sing. Stroke and sing. Stroke and sing.

Then there would be the top of the wave and down, down, effortlessly *Grace* and I would glide to the bottom to begin the next climb. Even when the waves would skip a beat, would come in bigger or at a different angle than I was adjusted to, my cadence would not falter. It was strong enough to absorb change. Flexible enough to be fueled by variety. I made up song verses and sang to the children, to Christina, to Betty. I made up verses about my life and the work I'd do, the freedom I'd found. I was Lake Superior Spirit and I could have paddled around Shot Point to Marquette, Michigan, thirteen miles away, but in the one quick glimpse I had of him, I noticed that Paul was paddling much closer to shore than I was. I altered my course and angled toward him. Once both of us were more in the lee of Shot Point and the northwest winds, he said, "Ann, where have you been? I thought you were going to paddle all the way to Marquette. I'm getting off this lake. It's too dangerous out here."

The lake became shallow quickly. There was some surf on shore, the effect of waves wrapping around the point. Paul carefully paddled in and landed. In my newfound confidence I paddled in too quickly, was picked up by an incoming wave, and found myself surfing along at breakneck speed. First the boat leaned precariously left. I leaned with it and braced hard. Then the wave threw me to the right. Another hard brace. Shift and brace. Shift and brace. In one minute I did a half-dozen strong braces. When the wave finally let go of me, I had succeeded in keeping the boat pointed straight into the shore, had not succumbed to turning sideways and being dumped. Minutes earlier I had been confident and singing. Now I felt humbled and shaken. Mindfulness is so important. Whether in ecstasy or storm, we must be totally present to the moment, ready for the sudden shift of wind or mood or energy.

We pulled our boats onto the cobble beach and then walked across the lush green lawn of a new, two-story cedar-sided house and rang the doorbell. A middle-aged man with dark hair and a strong, slim body answered. He seemed startled to have his dinner hour interrupted. "May we use your phone?" asked Paul. "We've been stranded in this storm and would like to call a friend in Marquette to see if we could stay with her tonight."

I watched him study Paul, wondering if he would ask us to move our boats off his property. But when Paul hung up the phone, he asked, "Is there anything I can do to help?"

"Well, if we could stash our boats on your beach so our friend doesn't have to carry them into town we'd sure appreciate it."

"No problem. I've got a big garage. You can store anything you want in it." He followed us out the door, across the lawn to our boats, which were safely tucked in some high grass beyond the cobbles. The man zipped up his light jacket in the wind. "Geez, this really is a blow. How'd you guys paddle in those waves?"

We looked at each other. I spoke up. "It wasn't easy."

After our night on land in the company of Paul's friend in Marquette, we set off from Shot Point about noon the next day, rested and well fed. We decided to head straight across Marquette Bay to regain some of the time we'd lost by starting late. The distance was fourteen miles. At my three-mile-per-hour speed, that meant nearly five hours without a pee break — a feat I'd never attempted before, and haven't since. By the time we landed, I literally jumped out of my boat and ran to the marina rest rooms. As Paul said, retelling the story later, "At that moment I knew Ann was going to lay claim to being the only woman to paddle all the way around Lake Superior without ever once peeing in her wet suit."

The sun was low in the sky when we rounded the giant thumb of Presque Isle and began heading to our evening stop at Little Presque Isle Point. The intermittent clouds of the day were gathering to create a menagerie of parading purple creatures against an orange glow. Each movement of my paddle blade forward over the top of the orange-silver sea released dozens of droplets of water that hit the lake and bounced briefly like water beads across a hot skillet. The kayak moving forward, carving a V across the smooth skin of water, the gentle sounds of blades entering and leaving their liquid home, the magic of miniature glass beads bouncing along beside the boat, all cradled my heart in a very tender, magical place. The place where Spirit Song lives. For the second day, Spirit Song came forward. Strong, but not loud. A slow, quiet ecstasy that matched the lake's quiet mood. Private whisperings from me to the lake, from the lake to my heart.

I had noticed a tenderness in my left wrist before we landed at the marina. Even as I sang, I was aware of more pain. When we reached our campsite an hour later, my wrist hurt so much I could hardly finish paddling. I told Paul immediately.

"Geez, you haven't said anything before."

"It didn't start hurting until an hour ago, and then it hit fast," I replied.

"I have an extra wrist guard, a backup for the one I've been wearing on my right wrist the whole trip. You should wear it tomorrow."

We had landed next to a magnificent white pine forest on a narrow isthmus of land that would enable us to enjoy both this sunset and tomorrow's sunrise. We cooked dinner in the dark, simple fare of packaged pea soup and some whole-grain bread our friend Jo in Marquette had given us. The mosquitoes quickly drove us into our tents. Holding my tiny flashlight in my mouth, I made this entry in my journal:

Aug. 4, 9:30 P.M.

I do believe we have a guardian angel. We were so lucky that Jo was home in Marquette to host us, that the home owner let us store and dry things in his garage. Paul's comment to me at Jo's really meant a lot: "Ann, this was an awesome day. You are one hell of a paddler." I want to be able to push these next seven days, go all the way to the Porkies at a thirty-mile-per-day pace, see the wildness of the end of the Keweenaw Peninsula. But my left wrist started hurting today. Please don't let this be anything big.

The next morning over a quick oatmeal breakfast, Paul commented that it was good we were starting in flat seas, that maybe not having my paddle feathered for a while would help my wrist.

Our paddles, like all good kayaking paddles, could be taken apart at the middle. The two halves slide neatly together and are held firmly in place with a metal button. In calm weather the paddle blades on either end face the same direction. In windy weather, in order to have the leading blade angle into the wind, rather than push flat against it, I would rotate the two blades so they were at nearly a ninety-degree angle. This feathered position requires a more strenuous rotation of the wrist than the unfeathered position when the blade is lifted out of the water and brought forward. Over time, a feathered paddle takes a greater toll on one's wrist than an un-feathered paddle. Unfortunately for us, conditions were so windy on most of the trip that up to this point we had been forced to keep our paddles feathered much of the time. Undoubtedly, my wrist's seem-ingly sudden flare-up was the cumulative result of overuse.

While we adjusted our paddles into the unfeathered position, we reviewed our plans for paddling around the Huron Mountains. Lo-cated on Michigan's remote Upper Peninsula, these large hills have little road access except that created by owners of the Huron Moun-tain Club. We were cautioned by a number of people to stay totally away from that shore, not to land under any circumstances. Sup-posedly, all the land in the area was owned by wealthy people intol-erant of trespassing. We had heard stories of young college students trying to sneak in on dares, being caught, and then being trans-ported blindfolded to a remote site and released. I had images of someone pulling a gun on me.

When we stopped for lunch below some steep cliffs on Salmon Trout Point in Big Bay, we again studied our maps and ate gorp. Kayaking friends had pointed out that this was the last stopping place before hitting the stretch of private property. The next "safe" spot to stop was some nine miles away. We figured we had come more than twenty miles since dawn. My wrist wasn't hurting. We were determined to camp at the Huron River, still sixteen miles away. The sky was blue, temperatures were in the seventies, winds were light. Paul propped himself up on a rock, tipped back his hat, and prepared for a nap.

I knew that he could afford a nap, but my calculations told me I needed at least six hours to finish this paddle. It was already one-thirty. I wished Paul a good rest and said I was going to head out, so I could get to the river before dark.

Keeping my boat a respectful distance from the shore, I could glimpse large, rustic homes. Periodically, I stopped and looked through my binoculars. At one point when I was looking through the binoculars, I spotted a small motorboat leaving a dock. I worried that someone was coming out to chase me away.

By the time I reached the area where I knew it was safe to land, my right wrist was aching. It disturbed me. My left wrist yesterday, my right one today. I had had no chronic pain on this trip, nothing that signaled "Problem. Caution. Injury in the making." The back-to-back wrist problems made me uneasy.

After pulling my boat out of the calm water, I took off all my clothes and dove in. It was still too cold to swim comfortably, but on a seventy-degree day the quick dive was renewing to a tired body. The Huron River was still a long way away. It would be dark and cooler and probably buggy by the time I got there. I needed a hair wash so I pulled out the collapsible canvas basin from the back hatch, along with the shampoo. About ten feet from the lake, I carefully balanced the freshly-filled basin atop a reasonably flat rock, soaped up my hair, and then dumped the basin of cool water over my head.

The minute the last drop of water rolled off my hair onto the black rocks I heard a loud noise and looked up. In the next instant an immense, windowless silver plane flew low over my head. I crouched in my nakedness. The plane flew out over the lake, banked, and headed back toward me. I was sure I had violated some rule of the Huron Mountain Club, was sure the plane was returning to take pictures of my intrusion. I wrapped my arms around my legs and lowered my head. As soon as it flew by, I scurried to put on my swimming suit, wet suit, and shirt.

The plane never returned, but I hurriedly repacked the boat and paddled away. Paul caught up to me the last couple of miles before the Huron River. The sun was setting on another cloudless, almost wind-free day — a rarity on Lake Superior. A gift we had earned but could never expect.

We landed on the sand spit at the mouth of the river. By the time we had both tents up, the food hung by a rope over the limb of an immense cottonwood to discourage night-foraging bears, and our boats pulled safely up to the dune grass, the half-moon was rising. Paul handed me a loaf of bread. I chewed off a piece.

"Now you're talking!" he said, taking the loaf from me and tearing off a chunk with his teeth. We laughed and shared a hunk of cheese in exactly the same fashion. "God, I love this. I could live forever this way. Exploring all day, stopping only when the sun goes down."

I learned that he'd had quite a different experience with the Huron Mountain folks, that a local kayaker had actually paddled out and taken him ashore. He couldn't stop laughing when I told him about the mysterious plane and my exaggerated fears.

"Paul, I have bad news about my wrists. Today the right one started to hurt. When I wasn't worried about silver spy planes, I thought a lot about my wrists. One of the things I did was figure how many strokes an hour we take."

"Yeah?"

"Three thousand. On a thirteen-hour day like today that's thirty-nine thousand strokes!"

"Geez."

"I'm worried enough about them that I want you to go ahead around the Keweenaw. I'm going to paddle through the channel, save myself some eighty miles."

"Are you sure?"

"Yeah, I want to finish this trip and I don't want permanent wrist damage."

We were standing barefoot on the sand, under the moon. A wild-haired, bearded man at the peak of his immersion into the journey. A clean, straight-haired woman as fully immersed in her own journey. Nothing came between us. No denial, no false caretaking. Simply understanding. We reached for each other simultaneously. "Thanks," he said, wrapping his arms around my waist. "Thank you," I said in return.

On August 6 at 9 A.M. we hugged each other on the tip of Point

Abbaye. Again it was warm, calm, sunny. The forecast was for these conditions to hold for twenty-four hours. Paul was heading due northwest to intercept the long, extending thumb of the Keweenaw via Traverse Island. The island, which we could not actually see, but which Paul had taken a careful compass reading for, lay nine miles away, floating somewhere between him and the much-fabled remote peninsula. The stories we had heard about the Keweenaw rivaled those about Michipicoten Island: Remote. Rugged. Foggy. Dangerous storms. Numerous shipwrecks. Unforgiving shoreline. It was easily the wildest stretch of shoreline on Lake Superior's southern edge.

As I watched him make preparations for the long crossing, I felt a twinge of regret at not being able to accompany him on what was clearly the more adventurous route. But I looked down at the flesh-colored wrist guards on my arm, remembered the purple discoloring this morning, and knew I was making the right choice. Besides, I really was ready for extended solo time. We hugged one last time, reiterated our plan to meet in Porcupine Mountain State Park in six days, then Paul pushed off from the rock ledge we were on. It seemed like only minutes before he turned into a barely discernible speck.

My plan was to paddle down the west side of the Abbaye Peninsula before crossing over to the Keweenaw. I was trying to find the shipping channel that had been cut through this largest of the lake's many rugged peninsulas. If you look at a map of the entire lake, there are two features that immediately jump out at you — the Keweenaw and Isle Royale, both claimed by the state of Michigan. There's no real logic to why an island some fifty miles off shore and only fifteen miles from Canada should belong to Michigan, but it does. And locals would say there's no logic concerning why the entire Upper Peninsula, including the Keweenaw, should belong to the state of Michigan, but it does. In fact, there is an ongoing effort to have the Upper Peninsula secede and form the fifty-first state. It is the Keweenaw, that seventy-mile-long boot jutting out into the lake, that harbors some of the most fiercely independent, isolated, and charismatic characters that have chosen to call Lake Superior home.

The shipping channel that makes a northwest/southeast cut through the lower third of the Keweenaw gives inhabitants of this sparsely populated land water access from one side to the other that is much less hazardous than traversing around the end of the exposed boot. By the navigation chart on my map, I guessed the mouth of the channel to be opposite a point about nine miles down the nearly featureless Abbaye Peninsula. The only way to guess where that nine-mile point might be was to gauge distance by time paddled. After three hours of steady exertion on relatively flat water, I stopped for a pee break, figuring I should be nearly opposite the channel opening.

Gazing through binoculars across the big bay that separated me from the Keweenaw, I could make out the silver roof of a barn. When I set my binoculars down, the silver roof faded from view. I looked at my chart and saw a barn marked just three miles to the south of the channel. I took a reading with my compass to the approximate place the opening should be: 290 to 300 degrees. I laid the compass on the map and took the reading several times to be sure. I was nervous about my first large open-water crossing alone. In those eight miles of crossing anything could happen — the wind could come up and whip the bay waters into a frenzy, the fog could roll in and I'd not know if I'd landed north or south of the channel.

This felt like the real beginning point of my journey alone. I pulled my sacred pouch out of the front hatch, retrieved a large piece of chocolate from my lunch bag, prepared an altar on a flat granite stone in front of me. Then I sat on a boulder in the warm midmorning sun wondering how to begin this ceremony. I sat a long time in silence before I began to hear an inner whisper that instructed me how to drop from navigator mind to prayer mind: "Take and eat the chocolate. . . . Feel the blessing of the breeze. . . . Look to where you are going and where you have been. . . . Smell the freedom of your journey. . . . Sing the truths of your heart."

Softly, shyly because there were some cabins not too far away, I began to sing. First, a blessing to the four directions. Second, a chant I'd learned from a friend: "I will not be afraid." When I sang the verse "I will not be afraid to say what I know anymore," I stood up and sang in a loud, strong voice. Each breath in made me feel taller. Each word out felt as if it were being heard. By what or whom, I didn't know. I just knew I felt the earnestness of one who had someone near and dear listening.

When I ended the Spirit Song of beginning my solo, I felt connected — to the lake, to the trees, to the rocks, to everything in my field of vision. I was like a gong whose tone has slipped beyond hearing, yet still the metal vibrates. Lone kayaker on the small cobble beach in view of no one but She-Who-Is-The-Biggest, I bowed my head. Waited until the message was fully absorbed. Then the euphoria of readiness bubbled up and I said aloud, "Yes! Yes!"

My passage across the bay was easy, uneventful. The next morning, however, I awoke to a driving rain that intensified as the day progressed. The early part of the canal opened up into Portage Lake, a large body of water whose shores were speckled with homes and cabins. By the time I found the lake's opening into the narrower shipping channel, the fog had descended, wind was blowing hard from the east, and cold rain was being driven through my paddling jacket into my wet suit and my long underwear. On either side of the channel, cement walls separated me from buildings and from roads where cars were driving with their headlights on to make their way through the downpour. Once or twice a small motorboat passed me, but mostly I was the only vessel making my way through the artery that separated the small cities of Hancock and Houghton, each with a population of more than ten thousand.

My lunch break was in an abandoned boathouse beyond the two cities. I surreptitiously squeezed myself through the half-opened door into a room cluttered with old newspapers and furniture. I sat in a paint-splattered wooden chair and carefully poured myself a cup of hot soup. The rain was battering the old roof overhead, but it couldn't get at me. I felt grateful for this respite from the storm's onslaught, but my comfort was short-lived. Without the exertion of paddling I became chilled quickly. The time from when I stepped out of the boat until I returned was not more than twenty minutes.

That night I camped at McClain State Park, on the western edge of the canal through the Keweenaw. I wondered where on the wild, rocky eastern edge Paul was, and said a prayer for his safety on this cold, windy day. As I sat alone under the log roof of a picnic shelter at the campground, wearing every piece of clothing I had, I watched the people around me.

No one else was taking advantage of this dry place. They didn't need to. They had driven here in warmth and comfort. They had either trailers or elaborate tarps and large stand-up-style tents. My tiny tent without a car parked beside it looked like the fishing shanty on a lane newly built up with bigger and fancier houses. Out of those bigger and fancier tent and trailer homes came the sounds of boom boxes blaring and generators whirring. I didn't fit in this faster-paced, noisy world. I missed Paul and the reassurance that someone else was on a similar journey. Thoughts crept into my mind: "My children always have a radio on at home. Duluth is a city big enough to have traffic jams. Phones will ring. Headlines will blast violent news."

I wasn't ready to go back. Something important needed to come from this solo time, but I didn't know what it was. . . . Something that would help me feel eagerness about returning.

I took off from the campground about 6 A.M., well before anyone else was stirring. It was still raining lightly, there was enough wind that I had to feather my paddle, and there were intermittent patches of fog, but by noon the sun was beginning to make an appearance. I was feeling tired when a bald eagle flew in front of me and made its way into a large dead tree on a deserted sand beach. I took this as my signal to stop. I followed and set up camp. That night I made this entry in my journal:

Saturday, August 8

The sun is setting, but I still haven't put my clothes on. The warmth from the fire will delay that for a while. I walked naked on the beach all afternoon looking for feathers and rocks. Swimming often. My body is so strong, so skilled. I am so happy to be with myself, so grateful to be alive.

I do not have false pride. The lake will humble me tomorrow and the next day and the next. What I do have is an enormous growth in confidence . . . and that is the transformation that will enable me to return. I cannot plan how I'll implement that. Cannot even know how it will disrupt the status quo of my life. But it undoubtedly will.

August 9 was the first day on the trip when a wet suit was too hot. I actually was forced to stop hourly to dive into the refreshing coolness of the lake. Unfortunately, the heat also forced the first hatch of biting sand flies on this coldest, wettest summer in nearly a hundred years. And so, despite the heat, I didn't take my wet suit off, because every time I stopped paddling the creatures would descend on me in a swarming, biting fury. Smaller than houseflies, they are a lot quicker and meaner during their intense twenty-four-hour life cycle. My routine for stopping that day became: land, pull the spray skirt off the boat, step out, slide off the spray skirt, dive into the water, swim, climb out, grab a handful of gorp while still wet and inaccessible to the beasts, put on the spray skirt, reenter the boat, paddle away. If I paddled quickly enough, I would leave the monsters behind on the shore in search of a more helpless mammal.

A real dread of kayakers is getting one of these awful pests in the boat with you. Several times I'd be quite far from shore when I'd feel the quick flash of pain around my ankles that signaled a sand fly trapped in the hold beneath my spray skirt. The routine for extricating myself from the misery of repeated ankle attacks was to curse, remove my spray skirt, and then paddle as fast as I could hoping to blow the critter out of the hold. One place I stopped for a swim was actually labeled Misery Bay on the map. It was about halfway between the opening of the ship canal and the first community of any size along that stretch of the Michigan shore — Ontonogan. Perhaps some luckless explorer had discovered this bay on the day the sand flies hatched.

As the day progressed, the wind picked up and high, fast-moving clouds started to move in. My weather-band radio talked about temperatures in the eighties and a chance for severe thunderstorms or tornadoes in the evening. It was 3 P.M. I had promised myself not to do more than twenty miles a day, and to stop when my wrists hurt. My wrists weren't yet hurting, and certainly at this point on the trip seven hours of paddling seemed like a short day. But I was nervous about getting caught in a sudden storm, so I steered my boat to shore near the Flintsteel River, about eight miles from Ontonogan.

Picking a campsite on the more populous south shore required a different set of criteria than choosing one in the wilds of Canada. On the north shore, the main issue was whether or not we could safely land our boats and whether or not there was a flat, non-rocky place big enough to pitch a tent. On the more sandy south shore, the main issue was whether or not the land is private property. I landed my boat at a place where the closest cabin was a mile down the beach. The area I landed on had no fences, signs, or buildings.

The wind had come up enough so that if I remained on the beach, away from the forest, the pesky sand flies could not land. The sand and dune grass part of the beach was about thirty feet wide. To avoid the flies I would have liked to pitch my tent right on the sand. However, the size and number of storm-tossed logs littered everywhere cautioned me against carelessness. A small, downed forest of forty- and fifty-foot logs scattered like so many toothpicks all over the beach had been placed there by a storm from the northwest. The predicted thunderstorms were to come from the northwest. I pitched the tent in the forest while sweating in my bug protection, wind pants and hood-tied parka, but I cooked my dinner out in the open in the wind wearing shorts and a T-shirt.

About midway through boiling the rice for a curry dinner I saw a man on a three-wheel all-terrain vehicle approaching from the vicinity of the cabins on the Flintsteel River. As he got closer, I could see that he was carrying an open can of beer. My heart started beating fast. I stroked it with my left hand and said aloud, "You get what you invite. Be centered. Be calm."

"Howdy, what you doing?"

"Camping."

He paused and looked around at my boat and tent. "What kind of boat you got there?"

"A sea kayak."

"Ain't you afraid of the lake?"

"Sure, I'd be a fool not to be. But I'm careful and I'm skilled." He remained seated on his three-wheeler, but turned the motor off. All he was wearing was a pair of tattered, cut-off jeans. He was about my height and size, and I estimated him to be in his mid-twenties.

"I've lived here all my life and I've lost a lot of buddies to the lake. I can't swim, so I stay away from her, spend my time cruising the shore," he said as he looked at me, then toward the fire.

"You been out long?"

"Yeah, since June seventeenth."

"You're fooling me."

"Nope, I started in Duluth and I've paddled all the way around to here."

"No shit! Well, have a good dinner." He gunned the motor and started off down the beach, showing off his ability to maneuver the machine up and over the downed logs.

He returned an hour later en route back to his home. This time he climbed off his machine and took a seat near the fire opposite me. I offered him some of my food, but he shook his head.

"I got some good stories about this part of the lake," he offered.

"I bet you do," I replied.

For the next hour he regaled me with stories about friends who'd gotten drunk, gone out in motorboats, and fallen overboard. He talked about how much respect he had for the lake, about sunsets he'd seen, about northern lights, dense fog, and frozen waters. I didn't say much, just kept nodding and eating my dinner. Then, as suddenly as he'd sat down, he got up, and walked back to his machine.

"Well, have a good evening and watch out. There's supposed to be a whopper of a storm coming." He started up the motor, but this time he drove away slowly. I was glad for his company, for the genuineness of our connection. This was not how I'd felt in the campground two nights earlier. Yes, I had felt fear and estrangement when he first drove up. But I had stayed in my own place of centeredness, had invited him to join me there. Had not compromised my own confidence. And he had responded to my invitation, respected my energy, and in his own manner had chosen to be in heart space with me.

This was the strength I was seeking to be able to return home — enough confidence to claim my own truths, the ability to invite others into my space rather than always accommodating myself and trying to fit into theirs.

As it turned out, there wasn't much of a storm in the night — some gusty winds, distant thunder and lightning, a brief patter of rain. I rose to an overcast dawn and cooked a leisurely breakfast, baking myself a small cinnamon Bisquick coffee cake in my iron skillet. By 8 A.M. I was paddling in partly cloudy weather in one- to two-foot waves. The forecast was for winds to pick up and create four- to seven-foot seas by afternoon. Since I was less than two hours from the Ontonogan harbor, I wasn't worried. I was confident about my paddling, knew I was not ending each day exhausted. I felt the beauty of moving into my tasks strong and ready for anything. Such a different feeling from ending every day depleted, beginning every day afraid.

Across the infinite horizon of gray water and gray sky, on the Canadian shore of this lake, was where I had made the marathoner's journey of moving through agony day after day. Over and over I made that journey, losing pound after pound of flesh, layer upon layer of doubt and denial. My friend Annie had been right those many days ago on the shore of Lamb's Campground: "We keep doing things over until we get them right." For much of my life I had been running and skiing and swimming and paddling, pushing my body through pain, past pain, looking for truth. This testing and pushing of limits had been a powerful tool for me.

But over here on this side of the lake, on this new side of my life, I was trying to learn in a new way: Wait. Rest. Listen. Move forward out of the confidence of your own well, not out of the desperation of depletion.

The wind started to pick up. At first it seemed like a game. Some sudden, playful-puppy gusts to get my attention. But very quickly my senses became alert. The waves *were* building. I stopped to move my paddle into the feathered position. I looked to the shore about a quarter mile away: all rocks. Even in these moderate waves, landing there would be tough. I looked to the distant northwest horizon: blue sky. Damn! She-Who-Is-The-Biggest was doing it to me again — a sudden clearing out of a low pressure system by a high pressure system from the northwest. When this had happened in Lake Superior Provincial Park, it was cold and I had had Paul with me. Now it was warmer, but I was alone. Then I had gotten angry, had saved myself with that adrenaline. Now what would I do?

I fidgeted in my plastic seat, moved my feet firmly against the kayak pedals, leaned slightly forward, and consciously began to dig each blade of the paddle in more firmly. Christina's phrase again filled my mind: "Paddle like heaven, Ann." "Yes!" I said aloud, and began to use my own breath as a chant, as rhythm.

I guessed that the breakwater wall of the Ontonogan harbor extending out into the whitecapping waves was about forty-five minutes away. I stroked and stroked and stroked, and each pull of the blade had my entire body strength behind it. Within minutes the waves had built to a level over my head. Four feet. Seven feet. What's the difference? The only thing I knew was that I had to keep pushing through them. Again I was the athlete. Being strong and competent was my skill, but this time I knew it wasn't my only skill, that it was only part of the strength I would bring to this emergency.

When a storm comes up suddenly, the waves look like upside down V's. They are steep and sharp and extremely challenging to paddle through. Time after time I found myself staring at a huge wall of water towering over my head. I would speed up my paddling, reach the top of the wave before it broke over my head, and . . . WHAM my boat would slam down the back side of the wave with such a noise, with such force, that I was afraid it might crack. Then there would be a set of shorter waves, so I could correct the direction my boat was heading before another giant pressed down on top of me. Stroke, stroke, stroke, stroke, WHAM. Correct, correct, correct. Stroke, stroke, stroke, stroke, WHAM . . .

There was a rhythm here. Paddle like heaven, Ann. I started to sing, timidly at first. I was still focused on my fear that the boat might actually crack. But slowly the music eased me into the rhythm of it all. I was fighting with all the strength and wisdom and courage of forty-three years of living. And I was beautiful out here in the wind and waves. A woman of the sea, a veteran of sudden blows on this biggest of lakes. Each song verse I made up, each stroke I took, pumped energy and confidence into every cell in my body. And I needed them all, needed to bring to bear a power as strong as the rage that had saved me near Lake Superior Provincial Park. But this wasn't rage. This was confidence, skill, experience.

I was close enough to the breakwater now that I could see the individual boulders that overlapped and intertwined to create these two parallel walls extending a thousand feet out into the lake. I could see that the waves at its mouth were HUGE, much higher than anything I'd come through, and that they were a muddy brown color. My mind snapped into instant analysis. Body moving. Mind moving. There were thunderstorm warnings last night. It had probably rained heavily upstream on the Ontonogan River. Now the river was spilling muddy rainwater into the lake where it met incoming waves, feeding their height. Can I make it in? Should I turn and go to shore?

I looked to the shore between forward strokes. It seemed to be mostly sand now, but if there were any rocks, I'd be dashed to bits. I stared at the huge brown waves. The mouth of a river is the most dangerous place to land. If I can get to the opening between the great rock walls, I'm going to have to turn sideways to the waves before I can run in. Neither the shore nor the breakwater looked like an easy option. Stroke, stroke, stroke, stroke, WHAM. Correct, correct, correct, correct.

I prayed out loud, "Okay, God, help me." I leaned forward.

Stroke, stroke, stroke, stroke, WHAM. Correct, correct, correct, correct. My momentum was forward. I would seek the safety of the harbor.

I inched *Grace* forward. When I guessed my yellow boat's position to be fifty yards out from the mouth of the breakwater walls, I glanced over my shoulder. Dirty, angry water was smashing into the piled-up rocks, flying up into the air, blowing over the tops of the huge boulders. If I tipped, there would be no rescue. I paddled in place, letting several big waves go by, counting sets so I could turn on a small wave. Two big ones, two small ones. Three big ones, two small ones. Two big ones — yes, the next one looked small. I began to turn the boat immediately after it passed. Stroke, SWEEP. Stroke, SWEEP. Stroke, SWEEP. Each time the blade entered the water it was perfectly placed, and pulled with every cell in my body working in total harmony. *Grace* turned quickly, nimbly. Now I was pointed bow-in to shore, was located exactly in the middle of the two breakwater walls, about forty or fifty feet of angry water separating me on either side from the walls of rocks. NOW I had to paddle as fast as I could. Get inside the walls, away from the angry, trailing seas.

But there was another problem. The seas were so large, they were breaking over the top of the wall on the right and creating an area of tremendously confused water next to that wall. I inched my boat as close to the left wall as I dared and kept stroking as hard as I've ever stroked in my life. My arms ached, my shoulders hurt, but I didn't care. Safety was at the end of this long tunnel, and I *was* going to get there. It took me less than ten minutes — the wildest ride of my life.

When I reached the end of the breakwater, I kept paddling until I got into the harbor. Only when I saw a marina over to my right did I stop, lay my body over the top of my spray skirt, and heave a huge sigh of relief.

"My God, I did it. I did it. Thank you," I said, hugging my boat. Slowly I sat up. Ahead, the small marina held mostly sailboats. The wind was wildly bending the trees on the shore, but it was flat calm on the water in the marina.

I paddled. A man signaled me from the wooden dock high above my boat. I felt like a toy amidst these thirty-, forty-, and fifty-foot yachts. I paddled closer, took off my rain hat, and said, "Howdy." He stared down at me in utter disbelief. I realized that he had thought I was a man.

"I seen you come in through there. That was a hell of a job paddling, young lady. Bring your boat over there by the brick building."

12

Guardian Angels

*There comes a time in our lives when we are called to believe
the unbelievable. If we allow ourselves to believe, we open the door
to the infinite possibility of who we might become.*

BY THE TIME I paddled my boat over to where the man had
pointed, there was a crowd of a half dozen men waiting. Landing a
kayak on a steep, rocky embankment in deep water is no easy trick.
I pulled up my spray skirt, carefully placing the paddle perpendicular to the shore, resting one blade on a rock, the other on the boat
deck directly behind my back. Then, with the most grace I could
muster, I leaned on the paddle shaft and carefully stepped onto the
uneven shore. I grabbed the towline from the front of my boat and
tied it to the pier timber next to me.

The men, who were watching my every move, stepped back to
make room for me on the sidewalk. The man who had spoken to me
said, "Want to come in for a cup of coffee?" I nodded and followed
him into the small brick building. He turned as I entered the door
and motioned to a metal folding chair in the corner. The other men
filed in and took what I figured were their customary seats. Three of
them instantly lit up cigarettes. The older man poured each of us a
cup of coffee in small white Styrofoam cups.

I nodded my thanks and took a sip of the lukewarm liquid.
The man pouring the coffee was clearly the eldest. The rest were
scattered in ages, probably from mid-thirties to fifties. All of
them had grizzled beards or mustaches and looked like men of

the sea. The youngest man spoke first. "Where did you come from?"

"Well, I've been paddling all summer. I started back in Duluth on June seventeenth." I watched his blue eyes, caught the look of surprise, waited for him to speak next.

"All alone?" he asked.

"No, my paddling partner is back a ways. We split up on the Keweenaw. I was starting to have wrist problems, so I paddled through the ship canal. He went around." I studied each of the men's faces. They were careful not to look directly at me. I felt like a kid invited into some special, secret fraternity. I was curious, but cautious.

"This here's the Ontonogan Marina office," said the older man. "We got a pretty nice deal here. Showers for members, rest rooms in the back." While he was talking, I was studying the Lake Superior navigation charts on the walls of this ten-foot-by-eleven-foot room. "I'm the harbormaster. Anything I can do for you?"

"Well, I'm going to need a place to camp tonight."

"Down the road a piece is a real nice RV park." I wondered if they realized I didn't have a car parked in the marina parking lot.

"How far down the road?"

"Well, maybe a mile or two, but you can paddle right there. It's on the river."

The youngest man, who was wearing a baseball cap and not smoking, said, "I'll drive you there so you can check it out."

"Thanks, that would be great. I'd need to see if there's a place to land my boat." I stayed awhile longer, listening to them talk about how fast this blow had come up, about their predictions for its duration. Then I excused myself and asked where the rest room was. It had been three hours since I'd left my campsite, and I was desperate to pee. They all nodded their heads as I left the room, and undoubtedly let loose with their assessment of me as soon as the screen door clicked shut.

When I came out of the rest room, the younger man motioned me to follow him to the parking lot. He climbed into a faded, lime-green Plymouth sedan with a lot of rust on it, then leaned across the seat and opened the door for me. "The women who run the campground are really nice. I think you'll like them," he said.

On the five-minute ride I learned that he was a sailor from Minneapolis who had taken the summer and fall off hoping to sail from Ontonogan to Florida through the Great Lakes. He parked by the side of the road while I got out and studied the steep banks of the river. I walked about fifty yards and found a place where the banks dropped into an area of marshy cattails. I made mental notes of the landmarks: a large cottonwood fallen into the river on the opposite bank; a dilapidated, once-red rowboat half filled with water on the edge of the cattails. Paddling up the brown, slow-moving river I would see little of homes or RV parks or even cars driving along. The ten-foot banks sheltered river-goers from the reality of being in a city. I climbed back in the car and said, "I think I'll talk to the owners after I get my boat here."

He drove me back to the marina and said, "I'd like to talk to you later, after you get set up. *Trish* is the name of my boat." I thanked him, climbed out, walked down to my boat, untied it, and climbed back in carefully.

I was still wearing my wet suit when I walked into the office of the RV park. A short, gray-haired woman was standing at the counter. She stared at me. I knew I was unusual-looking because of the wet suit, but she seemed to be looking beyond my external appearance. She broke the silence. "Did you just paddle in off the lake?" I nodded. "It must be awful out there. This blow is knocking branches off our trees."

She was studying me, but I was not uncomfortable. "There is something different about you," she said. "You're not afraid of dying, are you." I was startled, returned the fullness of her gaze.

"No, I'm not." My arms were resting on the glass countertop between us. She reached her left arm forward and rested the tip of it on my right forearm.

"I'm not either, and it has to do with this," she said, motioning with her head toward the arm, which was missing its hand. She proceeded to tell me the story of how she lost it in a farm accident twenty years ago, how she became aware on the operating table that she was leaving, was in white light, how she chose to come back. "Once you choose to be here, you've got a guardian angel. I can tell that about you. You've chosen."

Tears formed at the corners of my eyes, at the corners of her eyes. "I've got something I want to give you." She lifted her arm off mine, turned, and walked into the back room. When she returned, she laid a quarter-size cellophane package on the counter. "It's for you. Pick it up."

I picked it up, removed the paper, and let the tears fall down my cheeks as I gazed at an inch-high gold angel. "Wear it on your shoulder," she said. "I'm not one of them Bible carriers, but I think it's right helpful to remember the angels on our shoulders when we need 'em." I reached across the counter and hugged her.

I stayed in the campground for less than twenty-four hours, but was treated like family. The woman loaned me a bike so I could easily manage the two-mile trek downtown, called her good friend who managed the local café and asked her to "fill her up good." On my way into town I biked to the beach, dismounted, and stood with my hair blowing in the wind, gazing out across the sea of whitecaps. "Thank you, God. Thank you for my life," I said.

In the café I ordered a half-pounder on a homemade hoagie bun with mushrooms, tomatoes, onions, lettuce, and cheese. The seventy-five-year-old owner was too busy cooking to come out and join me in the booth, but she made me promise to come back for breakfast before I left so we could share a cup of coffee.

Riding the bike back the two miles to my tent, I stopped at the marina to see if I could find the boat *Trish*. The man was there, cleaning it. He was pleased and surprised to see me. "Come aboard," he said. I stepped from the dock onto the deck of his white sailboat. It wasn't new, but it was well cared for. "Can I get you something to eat?" he asked. "I just cooked up some fresh lake trout I caught yesterday."

"No, thanks, I ate my fill at the café."

"Well, how about a Coke or something?"

"If you have a bit of rum, I'd like that." He smiled, disappeared into the cabin, and returned with an old, corked bottle and two cheap glasses. He poured the drinks ceremoniously and offered a toast.

"To people with dreams," he said. "If you don't have a dream, you don't have anything." He proceeded to tell me that he was busy cleaning his boat so he could set sail as soon as this blow was over. He had started out en route to Florida a couple of weeks ago but had turned back in a storm, had gotten scared. "When I seen you come in today in that little boat in that big wind and heard you've been paddling around the lake all summer, well, I decided then and there I was going to head to Florida."

We sat and talked, sipping our drinks. The first conversation, of course, was about the weather and when it might change. As a sailor, he had a different perspective on the wind, but he said even *he* wouldn't be out today, unless he got caught by surprise. He gave me a tour of his boat, and then we shook hands, wishing each other well on our journeys.

Back in the campground, I busied myself using the Laundromat, repacking food supplies, preparing for an early start so I could be at the café by 6:30 A.M. At dusk the wind was still roaring through the pines above my tent, but I was optimistic that the lake would settle down enough for me to take off early in the morning.

I was tired, so I crawled into my tent about 9 P.M. hoping to write in my journal. I penned in the date, "August 10, 1992," but I was too tired to write and fell instantly to sleep.

Sometime in the middle of the night I awoke in a bright light. For an instant I couldn't remember where I was. There was no sound of the lake. Oh, yes, I was in the campground. But there shouldn't have been any lights. I had pitched my tent out in the pine field away from all the lights.

Suddenly, I became warm. My body relaxed. My eyes remained open, could see the bright white light everywhere around me. I actually had a hard time seeing the tent walls because it was so bright.

Almost before I had the thought, my mouth moved and said, "You're here, aren't you? I feel you in my body. You're here." I didn't need a response. I knew. My body had not felt like this since that morning after I had carried her down from the mountain.

After I carried Betty down from our hike to the Emerald Pools in Zion National Park, I drove us immediately to the motel. The ten steps from the car to the door of our room were a gigantic effort for her. She sat down as soon as she got to an armchair, and then looked to me for direction.

"I'll run some water for a hot bath. We've got to get you warmed up. I don't know if you'll feel like it, but I'll cook up some spaghetti." She nodded. I started the water. She was still sitting in the chair with her wool stocking cap and down jacket on. "Can I help you get undressed?" She nodded again. She held my arm as she walked naked from the chair into the bathroom. I turned off the water, tested the temperature in the tub, and put my arm around her waist to steady her while she lifted first one foot into the tub and then the other. Once she was safely seated, I asked if there was anything else I could get her. She shook her head.

I couldn't think anything while fixing the spaghetti. Anytime my mind tried to wander beyond "Chop peppers," "Stir pasta," "Simmer sauce," it froze. My mind would try to ask "What if . . . ? Is she . . . ? What can I . . . ?" but fear paralyzed me. When I heard her call "Ann," I literally ran into the bathroom.

"Could you add a little more hot water, please?" she asked. She looked so thin, so frail, so pale sitting there. I added some hot water, taking care to swirl it with my hands so it didn't collect in one spot and scald her.

"The spaghetti is almost ready."

"I'll be out pretty soon. I'm almost warm." I closed the door and lay down on the bed.

My mind had been released from its paralysis. It prayed, "God, please don't let her die tonight. You gave me the strength to carry her down from the mountain, now please don't let her die." After a while, she emerged from the bathroom dressed in flannel pajamas. I reached for her hand and we walked over to the table where I had lit two candles. She thanked me for the candlelight dinner, tried to eat, but was too exhausted. She mostly just moved the spaghetti around on her plate.

Finally she said, "I think I need to go to bed." She pushed her chair back from the table and walked to the bed. I pulled back the blankets, covered her up, kissed her on the forehead, and turned out the bedside lamp. "Sleep well, my friend."

I ate a little bit of spaghetti and all of my green salad, but my stomach was in knots. All I could think about was being in this tiny southern Utah town with no doctor for miles and Betty maybe dying from the shock of the afternoon. I just kept praying, "God, please don't let her die." It was only 7 P.M. by the time I finished the dishes, but I changed into my night-shirt and crawled into bed next to her anyway. I wanted to be close enough to hear whether or not she was breathing. I lay flat on my back, rigid, two feet from her.

She wasn't breathing very loudly. I didn't know if she was awake or asleep. "Betty?" I whispered. No answer. I lay like that all night —listening, making sure her breathing did not stop. Once or twice she rolled over, but she never said anything, never snored, just kept breathing slowly, steadily.

At dawn the desert mountain sun streamed into our motel room. As was her custom, Betty rose, washed her face, flossed her teeth. Then she shuffled over and sat on my side of the bed. Timidly she touched my face. I reached for her hand. Tears began to roll down my cheeks.

She looked puzzled. "Why are you crying?"

I smiled and reached for her other hand. "Because you're alive and I love you."

She stiffened. I traced the outlines of her fingers with mine, stroked her arms, slid over to make room for her. She remained sitting for a minute, then stretched her body out next to me.

Thousands of beams of light filtered through the half-open slits in the venetian blind. The beams converged and illuminated the entire bottom half of our bed. Betty's face glowed softly on the pillow next to mine.

I began to stroke her cheeks. She touched mine. Her touch was awk-ward and afraid, but tender. And then the tears began to fall from her eyes, down her cheeks. The first tears I had seen since this awful ordeal with liver cancer had begun five months ago. I rolled over on my side and caught a salty drop on my lips as I kissed her cheek. She turned to meet

me. Turned and looked at me, through me. In that moment of surrender,
anything became possible again. There was no disease here. No fear. Only
hope and light.

Ten days after our trip to Zion National Park, she died.

In my little tent, surrounded by that white light and those memories, I was oblivious to the passage of time. I remember looking
around at the tent and thinking, "Now it's beige in here. The tent
walls are beige, not white. How long was I in that white light?" There
was barely enough light to see, but I rolled over and looked at my
watch. Six A.M. I was supposed to be at the café in thirty minutes. I
felt chilled. The feeling of warmth and well-being had passed. I
pulled on my clothes, unzipped the tent, stood up into the cool
morning air, and said aloud, "God, I can't believe what happened."
Slowly I walked over to the bathhouse, testing my footing with each
step, reassuring myself that I was still a body.

No one was awake in the campground, adding further to the
feeling of otherworldliness. I went to the bathroom, doused my face
with cold water, and looked at myself in the mirror. A woman with
sun-bleached blond hair and tanned, freckled face stared back at
me. I noticed that even the tips of my eyelashes had been bleached
white. I looked strong, beautiful, normal. I did not look like a
woman recently returned from a startling paranormal experience.
Reassured, I walked out of the cement block building in search of
the single-speed, balloon-tire black bike, and pedaled the two miles
to the café.

Sometimes when we have been called into other realities, it is so
unnerving that we must immerse ourselves in normalcy and ponder
the immensity of the experience from a safe distance. I was glad to
be greeted by the clatter of cups and people's voices when I opened
the café door. The owner waved at me from the kitchen, walked out,
and motioned to a table near the window. She and I were as different
as two women could be. She was large. I was small. She was gray-
haired. I was blond. She wore a silk paisley dress. I wore my Lake
Superior T-shirt and purple pants. She had driven here. I had pedaled here. She had lived right here by the shore of the lake all of her

seventy-plus years and never been out on it. I had lived on its shore some fourteen years and was now paddling around it. We were different, yet similar in the independence of our spirits. I was comforted sitting across the table from this solid woman who my campground owner had said was a legend to many, including innumerable grandchildren. She was curious about me, wanted to hear some of my adventures. We did not judge each other, but rather learned from each other.

After a time, she motioned to one of the waitresses who was bringing fresh coffee to another table. "Are them pasties done yet?" Minutes later a foil package was placed in her hands. She transferred it to mine. "I'm famous for my pasties. People all over these parts have me make 'em for weddings, parties, whatever. Lots of meat, that's the secret. Lots of meat. This one here is real warm. Be just right for your lunch today." She patted my hands, then pushed herself away from the table. "Got to get to work, you know. Get fired for drinking too much coffee."

Four hours later I unwrapped the package, which I had insulated in my wool stocking cap. A strong odor of beef stew came drifting out from the opened aluminum foil. I was sitting on a driftwood log on a small sand beach just below Highway 64 outside of Silver City, after paddling through small waves for three hours. Everyone zooming by in cars above me on the road was oblivious to the presence of this lake woman with her treasure. The pasty was still warm! My mouth watered even before I took the first bite of crust. I was sure that no one who had ever tasted one of these pasties in all the years she'd been making them appreciated them as much as I did. I remembered her and the waking white light dream and shook my head in wonder at the miracles of my life.

Silver City, Michigan, is the gateway community to the Upper Peninsula's biggest tourist attraction, Porcupine Mountain State Park. The park's steep, heavily forested hills are mountainlike in their rugged lushness. They contain some of the farthest east pocket of large hemlock and beech trees and are as heavily used in the winter as in the summer because of the downhill and cross-country skiing.

Roads into the interior of the park are minimal. Access to its farthest reaches, including the rugged shoreline of Lake Superior, is mainly by hiking or skiing trails. I left Silver City about 1 P.M., the water still with a light chop, the sky remaining the color of an old garbage can.

I paddled onto the rocky shore near Buckshot Cabin in the state park in midafternoon. Paul's youngest daughter, Eva, and our dear friend Fran were standing on a rock waving to me. This was our final resupply, our last planned connection with family and friends until we finished. Paul arrived two hours after me — by land.

He had been buffeted by his own share of bad weather and was still two paddling-days behind me. However, he had met some people on a beach who agreed not only to store his boat but also to give him a sixty-mile ride so he could rendezvous with his wife, daughter, friend, and me. After hiking the three-mile trail into the cabin we had rented for this rendezvous, his first words to me were, "Okay, Ann, now even *I* believe in God!"

Paul's wife, Mary, daughter Eva, and seventy-four-year-old Fran had had to backpack everything in over that three-mile trail, but they fed us as if we were on a catering service delivery route. The cabin was just a ten-foot-by-ten-foot wooden shack, with bunk beds in it and a fire pit outside for cooking, but Fran and Mary prepared food that could have come from a chef's kitchen. The first night we had steak, potatoes, corn on the cob, wine, and Mary's famous blueberry cheesecake. The second night we devoured helpings of beef Stroganoff that were probably enough fuel for all the remaining days of the trip.

I remember the deep thinking I was doing about the white light in my tent. I was too stunned to write in my journal, certainly too skeptical to talk to anyone about it, though Fran in the wisdom of her years and the steadiness of her friendship would have been a wonderful person for me to talk to. I tried to initiate some mention of it when the two of us were collecting blueberries the first afternoon, but I couldn't find words that didn't seem strange to me. In retrospect, I know the sharing would have deepened our friendship, but in the moment I was afraid and unwilling to risk it. For me, who risked so much physically, learning to transfer that level of courage to emotional risks would be crucial to the adjustment that awaited me at journey's end.

The second night at Buckshot Cabin, we made a campfire on the rocky beach. It was August 13, the full moon, the time of falling stars. The moon made it hard to see the stars, so everyone retired early, but me. I sat next to the fire adding stick after stick of wood for a long time. About midnight the stars began to fall out of the sky in an astounding procession. One from the north. One toward the north. The next all the way across the sky. The next from the east. The next from the center. On and on they came. As I let the fire die, I could see them more and more clearly. One after the other. A procession of heavenly white lights.

The longer I watched, the more my body resonated with a feeling of connectedness to everything around me — the night sky, the stars, the silhouettes of boulders, the lapping of waves on the shore. This communion was the way I had felt "paddling like heaven" and singing Spirit Song in the big blow three days earlier. It was like the warm presence I'd felt from the angel visitation two nights earlier. It was like the moment I sat on the cobbles near the ancient stone altar, or the moment weeping on the island near Old Woman's Bay, or the morning making love to myself on Whitefish Bay.

It was as if my mind dropped down into my body, merging totally. There was no autonomic nervous system sending signals to a distant brain in the head, no thought about a time and place different from now. Just presence, awareness of deep integration, total oneness. When I can get to that place, reverence pervades all I do. Knowing how to help myself find and sustain that sense of reverence is the single most important gift I received from my trip around the lake. It was not a gift I had immediate understanding of, nor one I can always easily find. But it has become the guiding hand of my life.

Mary drove Paul to his boat so he could begin his long days of paddling to catch me in the Apostle Islands. I got an early start from the cabin and paddled along mostly undeveloped shoreline to a spot just past Little Girl Point, Wisconsin. It was so warm and calm all day that I took my wet suit off at noon and for the first time on the trip paddled only in a swimming suit and T-shirt, stopping often to swim, delighting that there were NO sand flies. Knowing that August 20 was our return-home deadline, that the weather was conducive to putting mileage behind me with an unfeathered paddle, that my wrists weren't hurting too much, I paddled until sunset — a distance of nearly thirty miles.

The weather-band radio predicted calm seas for another day, so I stopped on an itty-bitty pebble beach cut off from the main shore by house-size black boulders. I pitched my tent no more than ten feet from the water. My kayak rested next to it, tied to one of the big boulders. I stripped off my suit and T-shirt and dove into the clear water. Oooh, so beautiful, so cool. Too cool to swim, though. I quickly climbed out, and leaned against a dark boulder still warm from the day's heat. The water rolled down my skin and evaporated in the last heat of the summer day. I pulled out my journal and made this entry:

August 14, 8 P.M.

When the sky is this clear, the water this calm, paddling becomes a meditation into the deepest part of my soul. The question that emerges, that comes to my lips from these depths is: Was the white light a visitation from Betty's angel?

I stopped for a break on a sandy beach, still feeling bloated from the wonderful food at the cabin, so I didn't eat anything. Just changed out of my wet suit, swam, drank some water. Then pulled out my sacred pouch, prepared an altar on the bow of my boat, and asked the question out loud. Asked for a sign.

Almost immediately after I began paddling, a bald eagle started to lead me down the shore. Waiting until I got close, then flying to the next perch. Waiting, then flying. Waiting, then flying. It was unusual enough that I *could* take it as an affirmative response to my question, but I'm skeptical. I don't want to be skeptical. I want to know. I am going to pray for a dream tonight.

By the time I finished penning the journal entry, my skin was dry and had goose bumps on it. I pulled on a T-shirt and shorts and crawled into my tent. I'm not sure why, but there were no mosquitoes. I considered not erecting a tent at all, but worried about morning dew on my bag, so I put up the tent without the rain fly. Lying atop my sleeping bag on a mattress of fingernail-size pebbles, I could see the blurred images of stars through the mosquito netting in the top of the tent. Once or twice I saw a falling star, then I drifted off to sleep.

Again I awoke in the middle of the night surrounded by a bright light. Was it the nearly full moon? No, the light was inside the tent, not outside. I didn't dare move, just lay very still in my sleeping bag with my eyes wide open. Again words spilled out of my mouth almost before they were formulated in my brain. "Hello. Have you come to answer my question?" There was no sound; not even the lake, lying calmly just feet from my head, was speaking tonight. But there was light, and it was bright. I could see the moon through the netting on the tent, but this light was inside the tent and it was warm. Yes, that was it. I felt heat from this light. I waited. Slowly a flushed feeling came over my entire body. Then I knew. This was the same presence I'd felt in the tent after surviving the storm alone. I did have a guardian angel. "Thank you," I whispered.

I did not lie awake the remainder of the night, as I had after the previous visitation, did not rise at dawn feeling disbelief. Rather, I went back to sleep and rose with a new sense of purpose and readiness. I felt joy and skill in each stroke of the paddle that day, and I began looking forward to seeing Paul again. We had not spent any time alone together since beginning our solos on Point Abbaye ten days ago. We had shared some stories at the Porcupines, but always in the company of others. I had been very aware that this was his first time with Mary in many weeks and consciously gave them as much space as they wanted.

On August 16 we reunited at Big Bay State Park on Madeline Island in the Apostle Island National Lakeshore. Friends took the ferry out to the island to bring us supper. Since the weather was nice, we took turns taking them out in the boats before eating. By the time we finished, it was dark and we were exhausted. Our first real conference as a twosome came in the morning over breakfast and, appropriately, it was about the weather. "Scattered, severe thunderstorms," said our weather-bands. "Let's go ahead," said Paul, "but we'll paddle close together." I had forgotten how nice it was to have help making decisions, especially in the never-ending job of paying attention to the weather. We were a team again, but I did not yet know if we were still just an athletic adventure team or if our solo times had changed the ways we would be companions for each other.

As we crossed from Madeline Island to Hermit Island, the southwest wind picked up. The Apostle Islands are one of the busiest areas on the lake. The frequency of sand beaches and the sheltering effect of the twenty islands make this area a favorite with sailboaters, motorboaters, and kayakers. But on this day the wind was apparently intimidating, because we saw few boats until we got to Oak Island.

Approaching that island, we saw a thirty-six-foot voyageur canoe floating in the choppy water with over a dozen women standing knee-deep in the lake holding it in place. Several women were on the beach gathering up packs. We landed on a stretch of sand just beyond them, took out our lunches and radios, and sat down. "There is a severe thunderstorm warning issued for one P.M. for the Apostle Islands. Areas of high wind, hail, and heavy rain are likely . . . small craft advisory." We looked at the blackening skies to the west and then at each other.

"I think we should say something to those women," I said.

"Yeah, it's about time we played guardian angel for someone else," Paul answered. "But you should talk. I don't think they're going to take kindly to advice from a man."

We walked over to the simulated birch bark canoe. I asked one of the women who the leader was. She motioned with her head to the shore. A woman dressed in a plaid wool shirt and blue jeans walked toward us.

"Pardon me, but we just listened to our weather-band radios and there's a severe thunderstorm predicted to hit here in the next hour. You might want to wait awhile before taking off."

"Do you know how far it is over to Red Cliff?" she asked.

"Yeah, about four miles," answered Paul. "It's going to take you one to two hours to get there in these seas."

"Thanks. I'll talk to everyone and see what they decide." We waded back to our boats, pulled out our tents, and set them up. Two years ago in the Apostles Paul had gotten caught in a severe thunderstorm that produced a waterspout (tornado over water) and six- to eight-foot waves in a matter of minutes. He insisted that we take no chances. At this point in the trip we had a long-established routine of putting up shelter and holing up inside to wait out the worst weather.

As we were setting up our tents, we noticed that the women had lifted the boat out of the water and turned it on its side well beyond the surf's reach. All of us sat scattered along the beach watching the purple-black cloud with its lightning flashes move toward us. I took a moment and penned a letter to my family, knowing I could give it to a ranger at Little Sand Bay to mail.

August 17, 1992
My dear family,

I hope this gets to you before I do. Please read this all together. I am eager and ready to come home, but it occurs to me that we should all think about what that means.

You have each grown and changed, and I have grown and changed. We have some reacquainting to do. Each of you has had a different summer than normal because of my trip. You may feel some anger about that. It's okay. I do want you to know that I understand you've made sacrifices for me and I DEEPLY appreciate the privilege of this trip. Thank you.

Let us try to come together, as much as possible, in a spirit of celebration. Depending on when I get in and what your schedules are, I'm going to take us all out to eat.

I am ready to come back and work to keep our family strong. Ready to do my work out in the world. I am stronger physically, mentally, emotionally, and spiritually than I've ever been in my life.

Keep me in your safety prayers for yet a few more days — I'm sure the lake is not done with us yet. I love you and look forward to seeing you soon.

Mom/Ann

Halfway through writing the letter, rain spits drove me into the tent, but they didn't last long. By the time I reemerged twenty minutes later, the women had launched their boat and were paddling across the bay with a white flag flying in the bow and eight coordinated paddles stroking on each side. Paul and I loaded up our kayaks and took off in the opposite direction of the voyageurs.

That night he and I were sitting at a picnic table at Little Sand Bay Campground watching the galloping thunderstorms around us, drinking hot chocolate. We were feeling lucky that none of the storms had hit us directly.

"How was it for you on your solo?" I asked.

"Unlike anything I've ever known," he replied.

"Yeah, me too."

"You heard me talk some about the long paddles into the night when we were together at the Porkies, about crashing on the beach in my sleeping bag, but that was just the half of it." He set his cup of hot chocolate down, leaned forward on the elbows of his old green down jacket and confided, "Ann, I heard the lake sing. A wonderful, high, haunting song. I heard it and couldn't believe it, stumbled out of my tent on the end of the Keweenaw in this huge storm, and stood on the beach. There was nobody there except the lake, and she sang to me!" Tears came into his eyes, then he reached for his cup and took a sip. I gave him a few minutes to be lost in the memory and recompose himself before sharing my news.

"Paul, Betty came to me." I recited the whole story about the light in the tent, showed him the pin on my shoulder. He reached across the table and held my hand. We said nothing for a long time.

I broke the silence. "We are coming back united. It's really important we're not coming back separately. For as different as our journeys have been, we are both profoundly changed. We are going to need each other."

Sandpipers scurried on the beach below us, busybody little birds poking at the sand with their beaks, taking tiny steps, always moving. Sparrows flocked in the bushes around us. Loons were gathering in a large raft just off shore. Fall was arriving on the big lake. The birds were switching from summer picnickers to fall foragers, making serious preparation for the long migration. Paul and I were also making a switch. No longer fledglings or even inexperienced travelers, we, too, were preparing for the important journey ahead . . . and what awaited us at home. Were we ready? Were they ready?

13

The Herons

When we can hold council with fellow creatures of all species,
then we are beginning to understand the presence of sacred in our lives.
But the most challenging creature to hold council with is our own kind.

W E EMERGED in predawn light from our tents at Little Sand
Bay to a stiff, cool breeze. I stood and let the wind stroke my face,
peering at the opposite shore, and said aloud, "Sometime today I
will be able to see Minnesota again. We are nearly home, God. Having come so far, please let us arrive safely."

Paul and I were quiet, efficient in our well-established morning
routine. Take down the tents; pour hot water from our thermoses
into a bowl of dried oats, raisins, and brown sugar; eat; pack the
boats; change into wet suits; set off paddling. There were times on
the coldest parts of the trip that the ritual took nearly two hours.
This morning it took scarcely an hour. Sixty-seven miles and the
routine of whatever camp details were necessary was all that stood
between us and home.

My wrists felt strong, directing the paddle blades in and out of
the cool, choppy water. Strong and pain-free. Though I was experiencing swelling, discoloration, and tenderness at the end of each
day, I was confident that I would be able to finish the trip. All I
was thinking about in the invigorating coolness was that distant
shore. Despite my reservations and anxiety, the word "home" defi-
nitely conjured up images of rest, security, and familiarity. One
part of me wanted to be with these images. Another part of

me was equally determined not to return home to business as usual.

I remember as a child sitting in the back of our wood-paneled Ford station wagon and peering for hours at the western horizon. I could not wait to glimpse the snowcapped tops of the mountains we were going to visit. Once we drove past Fort Morgan, Colorado, on our annual summer pilgrimage from Minnesota to our grandparents' houses in Denver, there was a chance to see those mountains that held the promise of adventure I couldn't quite find in the creeks and woodlots back home.

I thought about those summer trips as I leaned forward in my kayak to get even closer to the blue-gray horizon in front of me. My mother and father had given their four daughters a great gift in those annual excursions. I didn't know what memories they held for my sisters, but for me they were about "coming home" to expansiveness and wildness. They were a glimpse beyond the small world of a midwestern farm town where girls grew up, got married, had a family and maybe a part-time job. They stirred my desire for something different, something beyond the horizon of what I knew.

There. There it was! Yes! My eyes were discerning the gentle blue silhouettes of Minnesota's hilly north shore. I let out a "YAHOO!" into the wind and paddled faster. Paul was some distance ahead of me, nearing the Squaw Bay sea caves. I switched my sight to him, but kept glancing to the right, looking at that shore left behind so long ago.

When I was a child, the distant vista had held a promise of adventure and grandeur. Now as a woman having found my greatest adventure, I didn't know what that distant vista promised. I had mailed my letter to Dave and the children to prepare them for this change and transition, but I didn't know how to prepare myself. The opposite shore grew more and more clear on the late-summer lake. Familiar. Mysterious. Home. Not home.

Paddling around the sea caves was challenging enough that my focus shifted from thinking about the end of the trip to paying attention to where I placed each blade of my paddle. The steady two- to three-foot waves ricocheted off the cliffs, creating a several-hundred-yard-wide area of confused water.

Paul and I had paddled to the sea caves many times. We had brought friends and even our children to make the mile-and-a-half journey from the parking spot in the Apostles to this stretch of caves and cliffs. As we paddled safely past the last set of caves, I spotted a half dozen sea kayaks on a tour-guided outing heading toward us from that parking spot. The caves would not be safe places for them to explore today, but I remembered one day when the sea caves had been magical.

I had just met Christina. She was a teacher of journal writing with a flair for adventure. She told me that her students wanted to take their journals outdoors and write, but that she didn't have the skills to know how to do much outdoors with them. She suggested that we team-teach seminars for women that combined introspective writing and outdoor exploration. The timing was perfect for me. My children were getting old enough that they weren't always interested in coming to family workshops. I was looking for another direction to grow professionally. The spring before I'd left on this trip, Christina and I had taught several such workshops, and had several more lined up for the coming fall.

It was almost one year to the day since I had brought her to paddle to the sea caves. She had never been in a kayak before, but unlike today, the weather was flat calm. She listened to my instruction. I helped her into spray skirt and boat. She nodded her readiness. I pushed her boat off the sandy shore.

She laughed in almost instant delight. "I love it!" she shouted. "This is how I've always wanted to be on the water!" Her body was at home. Her face a broad smile, she propelled the boat forward as if she'd paddled for years.

When we rounded the corner of the first red sandstone cliff and glimpsed the deep cavern in front of us, she gasped. Iridescent green moss was dripping from the top of the fifty-foot cliff, finding its way down cracks and onto ledges, luring our eyes into the dark shadows of the smooth, red rock carved by the master hand of the lake.

We paddled forward in tandem. Slowly. Two worshippers entering an ancient temple. It was so dim, we could scarcely see the walls. Certainly not the altar. Could not see, but heard the sounds! Groans and moans of water drumming itself against rock. Water moving deeper and deeper into unknown chambers.

There was a bump against my boat. I pulled Christina's boat even with mine. We held them side by side. Silent, as the chorus continued its concert. Silent, as our eyes slowly adjusted to swallow nests and ferns and mosses adorning the temple walls. Silent before this ancient spectacle.

Each cave that we entered, each arch we paddled under, bestowed its own blessing. In some caves we had to lie prone against the front decks of our kayaks, pushing the boats forward by paddling with our hands to reach the inner chambers. In others, rounded rock arches led from one opening to the next.

In one recess, the top of a seventy-five-foot sandstone cliff stood adjacent to the top of another cliff. Between them spanned a ten-foot-long stone bridge. Beneath the bridge, blackness plunged into the crack in the earth. Passageway into the unknown. We entered side by side, but soon the way grew too narrow. We proceeded one boat behind the other. The walls kept closing in on us. The passageway grew so narrow that we didn't have room to dip our paddles. "Are you comfortable continuing?" I asked as I turned to look behind me in the dim light. My friend nodded.

We used our hands to guide us along the rocks until we could go no farther, and still the blackness continued. We were squeezed between cliffs, tiny explorers at the edge of forbidden territory. I searched for a way to share the racing pulse of my heart.

The water lifted us in rhythmic undulations. "Boom," rumbled a wave from somewhere in the darkness. A deep, unearthly, almost inaudible sound. "Boom," another echoed in response. The liturgy of this place spoke to us from a place beyond words, a place in deep resonance with our cellular memories.

We backed out of the crack, then turned and pointed our boats toward the open lake. I wanted to keep going, to keep exploring. But I knew it was late in the day, and remembered that this was my friend's first paddle.

"Shall we return?" I asked. She nodded, and stroked over next to me on the nearly flat-calm water. She rafted up with my boat and embraced me in silent benediction. We had reawakened our most ancient connection

to the earth. This awakening was the covenant between us, the basis for
what we would do with our teaching.

By the time Paul and I paddled into the tiny Wisconsin town of
Cornucopia, it was close to noon. "Care to join a gentleman for
lunch?" he asked. I grinned and did a curtsy with my spray skirt. We
pulled our boats safely up on the sand shore, stashed our gear inside, and walked through the beach grass into town and into the
first café.

"Treat's on me," said Paul. At this point in the trip, we were tired
of our food rotations. It was now warm enough that our cheese was
going moldy in three days, so that made one less form of variety.
However, we were still paddling ten and eleven hours a day, so we
needed to stay interested in eating. Stopping at cafés in small towns
had become an important ritual.

It was 11 A.M., so no one but us and the waitress was in the dimly
lit restaurant. We spread our gear bags and jackets out on the third
and fourth chair around our small table. I ordered a Reuben on dark
rye, a large order of fries, and a Mountain Dew. Paul ordered a hot
roast beef sandwich and a cup of coffee.

After a few bites, he broke into our comfortable silence. "Ann,
I'm really thinking a lot about returning home. I still feel bad about
Mary taking that trip." I was surprised at his directness. Last night
my quiet friend, who mostly paddled for hours in silence, had
shared his profound experience of hearing the lake sing. Today he
was again speaking to me from the heart. I recognized his moment
of truth and the invitation to council.

Our waitress set the food before us. I wanted to have a candle
burning, or a sage bowl, or even the lake's presence, before I responded to him. Now that I was back in a place of strength I was
much more conscious about how I was communicating. No longer
the needy woman, I was aware of mutuality in my conversations
with Paul, and the way I best knew how to ensure mutuality of
connection was to sit in council together — to converse and ask
Mystery or God or Spirit to be the guiding presence in the sharing.

All Paul and I had for a centerpiece was a cheap glass with a blue plastic flower, an unused ashtray, and a container of sugar packets. To remind myself that this was a conversation that I wanted to bring full presence to, I slipped the leather thong, which held a gray, circular rock, over my head and laid it on the table between us. It was a gift from Fran on the first day of the trip, a symbol of her determined faith that I would indeed complete the circle all the way around the lake. Paul smiled when I set it down.

"I'm worried about going home, too," I admitted. "I wrote Dave and the children a letter asking them to think with me about this transition back into whole family. But I'm scared. I don't know if they'll get what I'm asking. I look at that Minnesota shore where we are aiming and I think, 'I am coming home a different person. How am I going to fit back in? Do I even want to fit back in?' "

He took a sip of coffee, set the white ceramic cup back onto the saucer, and looked into my eyes. Searching. After a time, his eyes shifted to the plastic flower and he said, "I hear you. What are we going to do?"

I finished chewing a large bite of my sandwich, set the remainder back on the plain white plate and said, "Ask for help. Ask for guidance from the lake these last few days. Keep talking to each other."

He looked at me and nodded. We didn't say anything else for the remainder of our lunch, just chewed in thoughtful silence, much as we paddled in thoughtful silence. By the time we left the restaurant and returned to the beach, the wind had died down and the air was warmer. "Do you feel comfortable just meeting in Port Wing this evening?" he asked.

"You bet," I said. "I need the time and space to think, too." We stood side by side looking at his map. It was about fifteen miles to Port Wing. I reached forward and put my hand over his heart. "Blessings, friend. Safe journey." He smiled.

"I'm going to sit here and write in my journal for a while," he said. "See you at supper."

At first I paddled far away from the hilly, aspen-and-birch-forested shore, making a long crossing from Roman Point to Bark Point, starting the southwesterly trek to Port Wing and avoiding going close to the shore near Herbster, Wisconsin, where I could see homes and boats and cars. I stayed a distance away from the shore until my mind stopped running its video screen of busy thoughts: "Those mountains you used to look to in the west, those are your home, you belong in the west. . . . It will be so good to take Brian and Sally to the beach, to play together before they start school. . . . I wonder if any of my fall workshops have filled. . . . Dave will probably be so relieved to have me back taking care of the kids that he'll disappear even further into his work. . . ."

All summer my mind had played this game on long paddles when the lake wasn't demanding much attention. The game would go on for hours: run out all of the thoughts of my life until only silence remained, until the only thought possible was of the moment and all that was around me. This time that moment came on a remote, steep stretch of shoreline between Herbster and Port Wing. It came when a bald eagle flew in front of me and landed on a large dead tree on the shore. I paddled in closer for a look. The eagle flew off. At the same moment, a weasel darted out from behind a log near shore, looked in surprise at me, and disappeared into the brush. I pulled my boat up on the beach, dove in for a quick cooldown, and pulled out my journal.

August 18, 4 P.M.

Something is happening these last days of the trip that I do not understand. I just saw a weasel. Not so unusual, perhaps. But I've been seeing lots of animals lately: deer, fox, beaver, otters. The curious thing is that I never see them when I'm lost in my thoughts. I only see them when I'm really paying attention. And I've been seeing them before they notice me.

The other thing that's happening for me is seeing shapes along the edges of cliffs or rocks that often look like faces. When I see one, I get a very real feeling, a stirring inside, kind of like I'm receiving a message from it. Last night when I was leaning up against the big birch tree by the shore in the campground, I felt it supporting me.

Not just as in a backrest, but as another living being inviting me to
lean the weight of my burdens against it.

I reread what I'd written. My first thoughts were, "It's your imagination. You've been out in the wilderness too long." But the infiltra-
tion of doubt could not penetrate the innermost fibers of my new
belief. They were strong, tightly woven. I sat on the log a long time,
amazed at myself. Eventually I got back in my boat and paddled on
toward the hazy horizon of the unknown.

Paul caught up to me a couple of miles shy of Port Wing. I was
tired and ready to stop, but not depleted, not counting the minutes
until it was time to quit. After two months on the water, ten hours
and thirty miles of paddling did not leave me with the feelings of
total vulnerability and near-collapse that I had experienced each
night on the north shore. And, of course, temperatures and weather
had gotten much kinder.

We pulled our boats up onto a sandy beach in view of the tiny
town just as the orange-red sun was sinking into a silvery-orange
sea. It was still warm, so we both swam and washed before putting
up our tents. By the time we were eating our dinner of homemade
pizza, it was nearly dark. The campfire, the first stars, the beauty of
twilight set the stage for talking in council in a way that the restaurant at noon did not.

We were sitting across the fire from each other, each nestled in
our own space on the sand. Each with plates of partially eaten pizza.
There was a speech I'd been formulating in my mind all afternoon. I
was nervous about delivering it. The longer I waited, the more nervous I got. Finally, I broke the silence.

"Paul, there are some things I want to say before the close of the
trip." My voice sounded so formal to me. I didn't *want* this to be a
speech. It felt so hard to talk with Paul about my feelings. How
could this still be? I pushed forward with my words, like a paddler
approaching confused waters for the first time.

"I am honored to have taken this trip with you." He was looking
right at me now. "Your skill, your integrity, your spirit are more

amazing to me than ever." Then I paused to gather strength for the most important thought: "I want you to know I consider you the brother I never had." My voice cracked and I could not finish speaking. He got up from his place across the fire, came and sat next to me, reaching for my hand.

"Thank you, I'm deeply honored. You are also the sister I never had. And you know what else? You're also the finest paddler I know!" He gave my hand a little squeeze and then raised it in triumph, and we both grinned.

We could see the lights of Port Wing down the beach. We could see the lights of Two Harbors, Minnesota, winking across the lake. Slowly, surely, we were leaving the wilderness behind, moving out of our respective immersion in deep solitude into community with each other. I went to bed early. Paul stayed up a long time, adding sticks to the fire.

Dawn was bitter cold. There was a heavy dew on everything and a low cloud of fog over the water. We did not see frost, but my weather-band radio reported it at several nearby communities. It had been nearly a month since we had experienced temperatures in the low thirties. I had forgotten how painful and uncomfortable those temperatures were. My fingers burned from the effort of taking down the wet tent and rolling it up. I had to keep blowing on them between tasks. My feet hurt when I stuck them into the water to push my boat away from the shore. We were returning just in time. Fall was beginning. I didn't have it in me anymore to live outdoors in brutal conditions.

Yesterday after eating lunch in the café, we had decided to call home and give people an arrival time to encourage some kind of reception: 10 A.M., August 20, at the S curve on Park Point. We planned to camp close by the night before, so we could arrive strong and rested. That was our plan; we could only hope the lake would cooperate.

So, on this August 19 morning in the bare, cold light of dawn, we set another thirty-mile goal for ourselves. We began paddling in tandem, spent some time photographing an eagle, talked a lot about plans for writing up the trip. Confident of our timing, even for such a long day, we enjoyed several exploratory stops along the shore. But by the time we got to the Brule River, we were both feeling the need for solo. I knew I'd never make it the remaining twenty miles to Wisconsin Point if I didn't start moving steadily. Paul wanted to stop and write in his journal.

We were like the tortoise and the hare, he and I. The entire trip I just kept plodding along, slowly but surely getting to my goals. His ability to paddle faster gave him more freedom to be serendipitous about stopping. Since early on in the trip when I spoke to him about how discouraging it was to be behind, he had compensated for my slower speed by often lagging behind himself so he could do more looking around. The difference between the classic tortoise and hare and us was that there was no one way to win this race. We each took separate journeys, the journeys we needed to take, and we both completed our journeys.

Almost immediately upon leaving Paul, I began again to spot animals along the shoreline. First I saw a medium-size black bear ambling along the brushy hillside not a hundred yards from my kayak. It seemed oblivious to my presence. Then I saw a fox trotting down the beach a similar distance ahead of me. After a time, it turned in to the brush and disappeared. I don't think it ever saw me. The most stunning interaction I had, though, was with an otter.

We had seen otters all along the south shore. In one place in Michigan, I even watched five of these wonderfully playful creatures swimming together. But this otter came looking for me. I was paddling along slowly on the flat calm of this warm summer day. I had shed my wet suit when Paul and I stopped at the Brule River and was stopping every hour just to dive in and cool off. About ten minutes after one such swim, I spotted a large otter swimming from the bank directly toward my boat.

Its movement was so purposeful, so directed, that I quit stroking. The otter kept moving, in a direct course toward me. The perfect V of the wake created by its body pointed straight at the bow of my boat. I actually felt a little nervous because the otter was a large adult, was swimming fast, and was behaving unusually. Yet I dared not move.

It swam within five feet of the front of my boat, turned, and swam along my lake side not more than ten feet away. It was looking not at me but straight ahead. When it got to the rear of the boat, it turned again and came along the shore side of my boat and began to slow down. I could see its black eyes. Its feet and tail were clearly visible under the water. Exquisite! Huge! A miniature brown kayak. It came to a complete stop when it drew even with the bow of the boat. I could have touched it with my paddle blade. My heart was pounding wildly. The otter turned and stared at me.

It was not a long look. For a brief second we locked gazes, and then it dove underneath my kayak. "My God," I said aloud. The otter didn't come back up. I turned in my boat and looked all around. After what seemed a long time, I finally saw it surface half-way back to shore. It just kept swimming, then crawled up out of the water and disappeared into the brush.

The whole time it was swimming away I kept whispering, "Come back. Come back. There is something I want to tell you." But the moment the last bit of its body movement blended into the brush, I knew there was no need for words. The communication had been complete. My communion with the lake, my belonging in the scheme of life along the shore, had sent forth an invitation. The otter, being the nearest creature tuned in to that universal unspoken language, had come forth in response and literally surrounded me in an accepting embrace.

When two creatures meet as naturally as lake lapping against shore, or river flowing into sea, there is a melding, a magic that transcends the everyday. I felt myself drawn forward into under-standing Mystery and Higher Purpose. I felt myself anointed and belonging. I didn't know what was about to happen to me in the human community toward which I resolutely aimed, but now I knew I had a community that had claimed me. She-Who-Was-Afraid had been changed by this journey, had become Sister-To-Otter. Had become Woman-At-Home-In-The-Wild.

I had no words for this experience, just flooding recognition. Aha. Awe. And then, in silence, I let this opening sift its way into my being — changing, changing, changing the very chemistry of my existence.

I stared for a long time at the spot where the otter had disappeared. Eventually I returned my hands to the sleek shaft of paddle resting in my lap. Moving my fingers up and down along the smooth, black surface, I remembered the first time I had picked up a kayak paddle — it was almost exactly five years ago to this day on an inland lake in this same state of Wisconsin. I dipped one blade in the water. *Grace* responded immediately, gliding forward on the smooth glass surface. I dipped in the other blade and noticed the beautiful trail of bubbles and swirling green water that followed the blue wand along its course. In and out of the water moved the paddle blades. Smooth, strong strokes. Sleek, purposeful movement. Quick, sure response from my boat.

I thought about the hundreds of hours that my arms had created this amazing dance between paddle and boat and water, this rhythm that was about movement and purpose. It had been a long time since I had stopped to admire this particular beauty. And now on this day before the trip was to end I once again knew the absolute joy of being water's creature.

When I began to see the silhouettes of Duluth's skyline in the hazy distance, my euphoria disappeared. Lethargy settled in like a giant hand pushing against every stroke of the paddle blade. It was so hot that even dipping a bandanna into the water and tying it around my forehead provided only temporary relief. My weather-band radio said it was eighty-five degrees Fahrenheit. At first I allowed myself to stop every hour for a swim. Then I started stopping every thirty minutes. Finally I realized I didn't *want* to get to Wisconsin Point.

I pulled my boat up on a sandy beach, plunked my swimsuited self down in the warm, shallow water, and stared at my home city. The image of Paul and me paddling off in gray, rolling surf nine weeks ago kept replaying in my mind. I remembered the hope, the excitement, our belief that the storm was just a passing cold spell before summer began. Then came the unrelenting wet and cold and big seas. I remembered our innocence of what would be demanded day after day, the slow, creeping presence of fog and doubt, my painful movement through doubt to this place of strength and knowing. Here I was. And now in completion of one journey, I was about to set out on another — returning to the life I'd left behind at summer's beginning.

I sat. One woman with skin now darker than the sand, with eyelashes and hair bleached ash blond, with body taut with muscle carrying not an ounce of fat, with a soul raw and open . . . and a heart afraid. What would I do back in that city? How will my children receive me? Dave? My friends? I imagined the little house on the hill where we lived, the small, square, familiar rooms. The space crowded with children's toys, newspapers, and magazines, piles of details waiting for me to pick up life as usual. I could already hear my neighbors asking, "Did you have a nice trip?" What would I say?

I stood up and waded into the water, dove head first, and swam out from shore feeling the strength of my arms, the skill of my strokes. The coolness of Her, the bigness of Her purged the thoughts, brought me back into this moment. My last moments alone. I swam slowly back to the beach, emerged into the heat, walked over to my boat, opened the front hatch, and pulled out my sacred pouch.

I cupped my hand and used it as a shovel. Scooped out a hole about the size of a softball in the wet sand. Reached into the small bag of Betty's ashes and laid a few bone chips in the small depression. "Thank you for safe passage, my friend. Please stay with me. I'm going to need you." Then I covered over the bone fragments and dust with wet sand, patted the spot, and rose to finish the day's paddle.

Paul didn't arrive until sundown. I knew from the slow way he got out of his boat that he, too, was battling ambivalence. We embraced. He said nothing, just shook his head.

"I've got some hot water on if you care for soup or something."

"Naw, I'm not hungry. I'll get my stuff set up, then join you." By the time he was organized, the first stars were beginning to appear. It was cool enough to need pants and a jacket, but there were no mosquitoes. Our families could drive to this spot, but I was glad no one knew where we were. I wasn't ready yet.

"Long paddle, huh?" I said to Paul as he sat down next to me.

"I didn't think I'd ever get here. I didn't *want* to ever get here."

"It was the same for me. Know what saved me?"

"No."

"Betty. She just kicked me in the butt and said, 'Hey, you can't quit now. The first woman to paddle around Lake Superior doesn't quit ten miles from the end.' "

He laughed. A little twinkle came back into his solemn eyes. "That damn Betty — where is she when I need a good kick?"

I made Paul a cup of hot chocolate. We sat staring at the lake for a long time. He broke the silence. "So, how do you think we did it?"

"What do you mean?"

"I mean how did two people who nobody recognizes as world-class kayakers ever paddle around this whole lake?"

"Determination, Paul. Just sheer determination."

"Bullheadedness, you mean."

"No, it was more than that. Absolute determination to put our whole hearts into this journey. And a lot of grace."

"No kidding. We are damn lucky to be alive." He stood up and walked over to his stash of gear bags and returned carrying a small plastic bottle. "Fran gave me the rest of the Kahlua before I left the Porcupines," he said.

He held the bottle up, said, "To a damn good trip and a damn fine friend," took a sip, and handed it to me.

I took my swig, then held up the bottle. "For courage to deal with all that lies ahead." I took another drink and handed the bottle back to him.

"Amen," he said, and finished the last. And that was the ceremony of our closure, all we knew to do, the last council time we would be able to carve out of the tumult of our lives for weeks.

My last journal entry reads:

August 20, 5 A.M., Wisconsin Point

Alone in my tent. I have been awake an hour already. What used to be dawn is still dark at this fading end of summer. I write with a flashlight, but the eastern horizon is beginning to color.

I am glad we chose to arrive home in this way. To come in strong, rested. To invite a reception.

Paul just came over to my tent! He said, "We are so wise to come back this way. I even thought about starting this way — camping on the beach, listening to the waves, going when we were ready."

"But we didn't yet belong to the lake, Paul. We didn't know how to listen."

"Yeah, we almost came back that way — rushing into the arms of chaos."

"But we didn't, we've learned."

At exactly 10 A.M. on August 20, sixty-five days and twelve hundred miles after we started, Paul and I returned to Duluth. Two boats paddling in perfect synchronicity on flat, calm seas, twenty-six people waiting in welcome.

Our children ran out into the water to hug us. Brian, Sally, and my nieces and nephew draped me in a garland of balloons. Paul insisted that I land first, since I had taken off first. Everyone clapped as I threw my paddle on the shore and stepped out of *Grace*. I walked straight over to hug Dave. Then Paul landed. We clapped and cheered. Everyone hugged everyone. Then Fran, being the elder of our group, gathered us in a circle on the sand.

One by one we shared prayers, gifts, and stories as we passed a talking stick and small pouch of tobacco around the circle. People spoke of how our journey had changed their own lives. One woman said, "I heard the weather was really tough, but as long as you kept going, I knew I could keep going. It was a tough summer for me, too." We all stood with arms around one another. Tall bodies next to short ones. Gray heads next to blond and dark ones. Bare feet next to hiking boots. In the safety of the circle I had no thoughts beyond this moment, no wondering about who in this circle would be part of my new life and community. Just total presence in the final moment of the outer journey.

Slowly the circle disbanded in groups of twos and threes. A friend came up, touched my arm, and motioned toward the lake.

Twelve great blue herons were flying in to land. Magnificent large birds of ancient heritage. One by one they slowed, flapped in place for a minute, then delicately settled their long, spindly legs in the shallow water where we had just landed.

Except during nesting season, herons are usually solitary birds. I had never seen twelve of them gathered on the shore at one time. I looked in awe at these elegant blue-gray messengers standing against the purple morning sky. I was grateful they had come to join our circle, felt them as a final benediction from She-Who-Is-The-Biggest.

Epilogue

To discover one's courage is the first step.
To implement it is a much bigger step.

March 20, 1994

IT IS THE SPRING EQUINOX. Day of equal light and dark. Day of leaving behind the darkness, of returning to the time of greater lightness. I am standing on the Washington shores of the Pacific Ocean. Behind me lies the more than two thousand miles of frozen lakes, prairies, forests, and mountains I have driven through to begin my new life out here on the edge.

Christina and the puppy are farther up the shore, small silhouettes in sunshine and surf. Her new purple wind suit keeps her warm in the coolness of the shore, the sun just turning toward spring. We have made it through a long Minnesota winter, over the high snow-covered passes to open water and sunshine and new lives. At first we ran across wet sand, laughing and chasing Willow, the Welsh corgi. Then we paused and prayed thanksgiving. That is when Mystery compelled me to release her. I returned to the car for a small package.

Now back at the great water's edge, I am purposefully standing close enough to let the surging tongues of surf lick at the toes of my jogging shoes. I survey the rolling green waters stretching out before me in sun and scattered, fast-moving low clouds. BOOM . . . BOOM . . . BOOM . . . Each beat of the surf, each roll of its waves, sets a cadence, alerts me to Spirit Song. I hold the small cloth pouch with Betty's few remaining ashes tightly in my hand and let the rhythm of the surf reverberate through my body. BOOM . . . BOOM . . . BOOM . . .

I begin with the song that so often leads me into Spirit Song. By the time I've sung three phrases, I become ocean — she imbues me with Her power, Her song. The words now come as my own lyrical prayers. I sing to my friend four years gone, who has so deeply companioned me on this journey into new life. I sing to my friend just yards away, who is as determined as I to claim her power in this new land. I sing to Brian and Sally, who will follow us in two weeks.

When Spirit Song ends, I notice that my feet are under water. The tide has come in to carry away that which is hers. I lift the cloth bag up in the air in front of me, kiss it gently, untie it, and slowly turn it upside down. Betty's remaining ashes scatter across the water's surface in a fine white line. The leading edge of a wave comes in and moves the ashes in around my feet in final salute. Then the wave recedes, carrying its precious cargo out to sea.

Tomorrow there will be a moving truck to meet. Each of us will face the long task of creating our respective homes, setting up offices for our new business, and discovering where everything is located. But today is not about making plans or meeting schedules. Today is a time for good-byes, a time for moving from the season of darkness into the season of light.

There was great darkness I had to pass through upon my return from the lake. I had so totally left my life that I did not know how to find my way back in. Indeed, I was a misfit even at the most basic physical level. My sense of hearing had become so keen that we had to have the phone ringer set to mute for weeks. My sense of smell was so acute that I couldn't walk down the street without smelling neighbors' back-yard garbage cans. And I had virtually no ability to engage in small talk. The inevitable question, "Did you have a nice trip?" left me dumbfounded, unable to speak.

I had gotten as close to becoming a woman of primitive culture as a white, North American, middle-class woman could become in the twentieth century. Off the lake and away from the literal battle for survival, the metaphoric cycle of storms, big seas, fog, confused water began. It was not until I landed on the western shore of my new life eighteen months later that the inner journey begun June 17, 1992, could find resolution.

August 20, 1994

It is exactly two years since I paddled off Lake Superior. Again I am by the shore of big water — the biggest of all waters, the Pacific Ocean.

An hour earlier Brian, Sally, and I stood knee-deep at the frothing edge of the surf when my fourteen-year-old son said, "Let's go out deeper." He and Sally, now eleven, had on life jackets. I had on a wet suit. The Pacific is cold, but the waves enticed us with their power. Slowly, first thigh-deep, then waist-deep, we waded, until Sally was on tiptoes.

"I'll stay in the middle. As soon as the next wave hits, swim fast," I said. "We'll get beyond the surf zone and be able to bob around out in the ocean free as corks."

"Are you sure, Mom? I don't like being out over my head," Brian worried.

"I'm sure. How you doing, Sal?" I asked.

"Good, Mom. I'm ready."

"Okay, let this one go, then swim as fast as you can." The wave towered over our heads, broke about ten feet beyond us, came foaming forward. "Swim!" I yelled, and all three of us stroked like miniature kayaks through the froth, past the line of breaking waves, and into the rolling clutches of the open ocean.

Sea creatures. We were seals; we were dolphins; we were tiny beings on a sea with no end. We couldn't see the shore most of the time because the wave troughs were so deep, but we were together out here on the biggest ocean and we were fine.

"Mom, this is so cool," said Sally.

Not to be outdone, but obviously not as comfortable as his sister, Brian asked, "Do we get to bodysurf back in?"

"Not without practice," I replied. "We'll just sneak back in between waves like we came out. If we try surfing in and really catch one, we could get smashed into the sand pretty hard." We floated on our backs. We watched gulls fly overhead. We delighted in swimming up the undulating walls of waves until, finally, the coolness of the water eclipsed the euphoria and we swam in.

I have always connected most deeply with my children when we're sharing time outdoors. It was true when they were toddlers. It is true now when they are adolescents. It is as if there is no filter between me and the larger helping hand of the universe — we are working in tandem to love these children.

All that was an hour ago; now Brian and Sally, who have long outgrown sandboxes, are busy creating a sand castle on the beach next to me. I leave them to their creation, wrap myself in a towel to ward off some of the chill remaining from our swim, and pull out a pen and pad of paper to write to Paul. It has been a month since he and I were together.

I had returned to Duluth to lead a women's sea kayaking trip on the big lake. Paul and I were together for the first time since he had helped me load the final boxes onto the moving truck. We had scheduled an afternoon picnic on the sandy beach of Park Point. The weather was dicey, a mixture of sun and galloping thunderstorms. We carried lunches, water bottles, and rain gear.

We stopped often to skip rocks, exchange stories, and embrace each other in friendly hugs. I was eager to hear of the changes in his life. He was eager to hear of mine. The farther away from our parked car we got, the more threatening the clouds became. Suddenly, the wind started to blow strongly and the waves kicked up. We stopped, looked at each other, and burst out laughing. The routine of putting on rain jackets and venturing farther into the unknown was a familiar, comfortable, part of the bond between us.

We walked on through wind and rain to the very end of Park Point, out on the breakwater wall that separates Wisconsin Point from Park Point. By the time we'd walked to the end of the breakwater, the rain had stopped and we could see the spot where we had made our final campsite of the trip.

"So, are you really planning to paddle around Superior again?" I asked.

My brother-friend, with his handsome blue eyes and curly hair, grinned. "I know you always tell people at the slide talks that you don't have any more long trips planned, that you went in search of the rest of your life and found it, but it's not the same for me. I probably will go around the lake again, and I dream about taking a whole year off to paddle somewhere."

"Are you coming out to kayak with me next spring during whale migration?"

"You bet, and maybe I'll even get that custom kayak I've been searching for."

We walked in silence for a while back along the breakwater toward the parked car. I was thinking about what he had said about taking more long trips. I knew the desire for the long, challenging, physically grueling trip was gone from me.

For one thing, my body can't take it anymore. It took nearly half a year for my wrists to heal, and even now I still eat left-handed just to give my right hand some relief. After two years, my weight is mostly back, but the sudden blood sugar drops I experience are probably the result of a pancreas severely stressed by hard exercise and inadequate sustenance. And I can tell that the trip aged my body several years. I recover more slowly from strenuous bouts of soccer with the children, or long bicycle rides, or hard games of racquetball, than I did before.

I became an athlete in part to battle the limitations placed on girls and women in my generation and in part to condition my body so my scoliosis wouldn't limit me to a life of inactivity. In the grueling circumnavigation of Lake Superior, I finally pursued a sport to its ultimate, and in my mind permanently laid to rest any claims that women were somehow inferior. This sense of inferiority is not a solitary battle — every female faces some form of it. The struggle to claim ourselves as the authority in our own lives, while living in a culture where we are conditioned to give men our authority, is basic to our freedom. Circling the lake was my path to freedom.

Paul was right — I did find the rest of my life out on Lake Superior. That life includes Dave as the father of Brian and Sally, but not as my partner. We've moved out of conflict as spouses and into friendship, freeing each other to become more fully ourselves. And that life, of course, includes Brian and Sally, themselves.

They have now created an entire sand city next to me on the beach — a city way beyond their imaginings from sandbox years, replete with *three-foot moat, four-foot watchtowers, and miniature houses. They are dreaming and building, and so am I.*

The physicality that has been my lifelong pursuit has brought me to a greater understanding of why I've trained and pushed and risked so deeply with my body: This is how I learn. From the body. Through the body. My passion for the long race has become integrated with my passion for finding my self in nature, because the natural world is the wellspring from which I draw sustenance. The natural world is where and how I connect to God-Goddess-Spirit-Mystery.

With Christina, I've formed PeerSpirit — a partnership dedicated to bringing into the culture the sense of spiritual center and personal empowerment I found on the lake. We do this by teaching council skills in small groups, organizations, businesses, civic and religious settings. We form a circle around the belief that by rotating leadership, sharing responsibility, and attending to Spirit, people may realign with their own dreams, social awareness, and spiritual values.

I have moved from circumnavigation to the circle. From solitary determination to win against all odds and the forces of nature, to companioned vision and work to hold heartspace, to re-create community, to find the courage to respond to the pressing needs of the earth, its people and culture.

Here on the edge of the continent, day by day I rise up to implement the courage I learned from She-Who-Is-The-Biggest.

I turn my head now, once again to pounding surf, once again to a body of water I cannot see across. I am humble, respectful, grateful to be alive.

Acknowledgments

THIS BOOK BEGAN with a dream: to embark on a sea kayaking trip around Lake Superior that would challenge me to claim my greatest life strengths. Innumerable people were helpful in the realization of that dream.

First, I thank Paul Treuer, who companioned me on the journey. I could not have endured the physical challenges, nor the emotional/spiritual stripping down, without his steady friendship and extraordinary paddling/navigating skills. Before the trip, I counted him among my closest friends. Since the trip, I claim him as brother-friend. Paul also read and critiqued the entire manuscript and lent valuable insight to its development.

David Schimpf, friend and former husband, supported me during the trip financially, as primary parent, and as principal resupply person. His attention to detail and duty are among the many things I will always respect about him.

I pay special tribute to Fran Skinner — friend, mentor, woman of great heart. Every day we were on the trip, she walked from her home to the shore of the great lake and held us in prayer space. Twice she was part of the resupply crew. More times than that, she managed to get homemade bread to us. Fran died eighteen months after our trip ended. Duluth lost a giant of a woman, who for three-quarters of a century showed all of us how to live with dignity and honesty of purpose.

Numerous people answered our call to join us somewhere around the lake. To each of them a thank-you for their presence, which was deeply felt and appreciated. In addition to our families — David, Brian, and Sally Schimpf; Mary, Ramona, Galen, and Eva Treuer — the following people came and let the spirit of the big lake touch them: Nancy Nelson; Zoe Treuer; Annette and Bianca Rose Smith; Bob McFarland; Jim and Linda Belote; Mary Duff; Anna Lujan; Jacksun Sneve; Annie Roe; Ely Salyards; Peter Harris; Carrie and Ben Anderson; Gayle Held; Doris Park; Steven Maxim; Betsy and Jim Haggerty; MaryBeth Nevers; Jon, Josef, and Alayna Tofte; Sue Betz; Connie and Larry Julien; David Hieb; Mary Sue Taalerud; Bob Stachowiak; Dave Kleive; Lisa, Gilah, and Sarah Messerer; Candy and Erin Geary; Lance Rhicard and the twins; Sue and Jay Woltersdorff; Erik Ringerud; Joe, Lyn, Forest, and Dawn Passineau; Judy Gibbs; Martha Hotchkiss; Kathy, Joel, Anna, and Molly Harrington; Marina Lachecki; Kathy and Dave Allen.

The extension of that trip beyond physical endeavor into written word has been another deeply companioned journey. Janelle Brown, longtime friend, fellow journalist, and companion in adventure, was a steady hand in early editing drafts.

To sister writers in my Split Rock Writers group, a special thank-you for two years of support as I matured into being able to write this book: Evelyn Anderson, Sister Mary Luke Baldwin, Sandy McCartney Ehlers, Floralyn Flory, Ann Lonstein, Jan Nelson, Pat O'Kane, Sister Miriam Ross, Katy Madden, Genie Smith, Karen Verburg, Lois Wiederrecht Finke, and Maryann Weidt. Special thanks also to Mara Hart of Duluth.

My friend David Kyle believed strongly enough in the early drafts to encourage me to seek a wider audience. Meredith Bernstein, agent and woman of vision, embraced the story and helped pave its way into print. And thank you to Elizabeth Cavanaugh, Meredith's able assistant and the book's first reader in New York. Don and Nancy Tubesing, friends and publishers of my first book, released me with deep blessings to editor Jennifer Josephy and the quality crew at Little, Brown.

Whether pondering the correct tenses of verbs, the nuances of phrases, the choice of subtitles, or the design of covers, Jennifer was always prompt, thoughtful, and helpful. Thank you, Jennifer, for companionship and teaching on my first solo journey through the world of book publication.

To Barbara Borden and Naomi Newman, dear friends, thank you for being a bridge to my future.

To my children, Brian and Sally Schimpf, deep thanks for following Mom on all her adventures.

Finally, I thank Christina Baldwin for accompanying me the whole way — mantling for the journey, phone conversations from remote outposts that kept me from the edge of despair, editing and reading sessions, visioning of new life. In the middle of my life it is a great joy to find myself so deeply partnered in life purpose.

About the Author

ANN LINNEA is an eco-feminist with fifteen years' teaching experience in the field of the sacred and nature. She is coauthor of an award-winning book on environmental education for children, *Teaching Kids to Love the Earth* (Pfeifer-Hamilton, 1991). Her Sense of Wonder workshops for families, children, and teachers reached wide areas of the Midwest in the 1980s and early 1990s.

Linnea holds a B.S. in biology from Iowa State University and a master's degree in education from the University of Idaho and now lives on an island in Puget Sound near Seattle, where she has cofounded PeerSpirit™ with Christina Baldwin.

PeerSpirit offers classes, seminars, books, and consultations to people ready for spirit-based change in their lives. This business seeks to extend the work of council and circle to women and men, both outdoors and indoors, through four internationally known seminars: Women and the Planet, Calling for Change, Circle Leadership Training, and Tenfold.™

For more information about these seminars or to share comments on *Deep Water Passage,* contact Ann at: PeerSpirit, PO Box 550, Langley, WA 98260, USA.